Revision Guide

Cambridge
International AS and A Level

Business Studies

Sandie Harrison and David Milner

Hodder Education, an Hachette UK company, 338 Euston Road, London NW1 3BH

Orders
Bookpoint Ltd, 130 Milton Park, Abingdon, Oxfordshire OX14 4SB
tel: 01235 827827
fax: 01235 400401
e-mail: education@bookpoint.co.uk
Lines are open 9.00 a.m.–5.00 p.m., Monday to Saturday, with a 24-hour message answering service. You can also order through the Hodder Education website: www.hoddereducation.co.uk

© Sandie Harrison and David Milner 2013
ISBN 978-1-4441-9203-2

First printed 2013
Impression number 5 4 3 2 1
Year 2018 2017 2016 2015 2014 2013

All rights reserved; no part of this publication may be reproduced, stored in a retrieval system, or transmitted, in any form or by any means, electronic, mechanical, photocopying, recording or otherwise without either the prior written permission of Hodder Education or a licence permitting restricted copying in the United Kingdom issued by the Copyright Licensing Agency Ltd, Saffron House, 6–10 Kirby Street, London EC1N 8TS.

Cover photo reproduced by permission of Kalafoto/Fotolia

Typeset by Datapage (India) Pvt. Ltd.
Printed in Spain

This text has not been through the Cambridge endorsement process.

Hachette UK's policy is to use papers that are natural, renewable and recyclable products and made from wood grown in sustainable forests. The logging and manufacturing processes are expected to conform to the environmental regulations of the country of origin.

P2268

Get the most from this book

Everyone has to decide his or her own revision strategy, but it is essential to review your work, learn it and test your understanding. This Revision Guide will help you to do that in a planned way, topic by topic. Use this book as the cornerstone of your revision and don't hesitate to write in it — personalise your notes and check your progress by ticking off each section as you revise.

☑ Tick to track your progress

Use the revision planner on pages 4 and 5 to plan your revision, topic by topic. Tick each box when you have:
- revised and understood a topic
- tested yourself
- practised the exam-style questions

You can also keep track of your revision by ticking off each topic heading in the book. You may find it helpful to add your own notes as you work through each topic.

Features to help you succeed

Expert tips
Throughout the book there are tips from the experts on how to maximise your chances.

Questions and answers
Use the exam-style questions and answers to consolidate your revision and practise your exam skills.

Definitions and key words
Clear, concise definitions of essential key terms are provided on the page where they appear.

Key terms from the syllabus are highlighted in bold for you throughout the book.

Now test yourself
These short, knowledge-based questions provide the first step in testing your learning. Answers are at the back of the book.

Revision activities
The activities will help you to understand each topic in an interactive way.

My revision planner

AS topics

		Revised	Tested	Exam ready
1	**Business and its environment**			
7	Enterprise	☐	☐	☐
11	Business structure	☐	☐	☐
14	Size of business	☐	☐	☐
17	Business objectives	☐	☐	☐
21	Stakeholders in a business	☐	☐	☐
2	**People in organisations**			
25	Management and leadership	☐	☐	☐
29	Motivation	☐	☐	☐
34	Human resource management	☐	☐	☐
3	**Marketing**			
42	What is marketing?	☐	☐	☐
50	Market research	☐	☐	☐
55	The marketing mix	☐	☐	☐
4	**Operations and project management**			
65	The nature of operations	☐	☐	☐
69	Operations planning	☐	☐	☐
74	Inventory management	☐	☐	☐
5	**Finance and accounting**			
78	The need for business finance	☐	☐	☐
80	Sources of finance	☐	☐	☐
85	Forecasting cash flows and managing working capital	☐	☐	☐
90	Costs	☐	☐	☐
94	Accounting fundamentals	☐	☐	☐
101	**AS questions and answers**			

A level topics

		Revised	Tested	Exam ready
6	**Business and its environment**			
107	Business structure	☐	☐	☐
110	Size of business	☐	☐	☐
112	External influences on business activity	☐	☐	☐
7	**People in organisations**			
125	Human resource management	☐	☐	☐
130	Organisation structure	☐	☐	☐
137	Business communication	☐	☐	☐
8	**Marketing**			
142	Marketing planning	☐	☐	☐
148	Globalisation and international marketing	☐	☐	☐
9	**Operations and project management**			
152	Operations planning	☐	☐	☐
153	Capacity utilisation	☐	☐	☐
155	Lean production and quality management	☐	☐	☐
159	Project management	☐	☐	☐
10	**Finance and accounting**			
163	Costs	☐	☐	☐
166	Budgets	☐	☐	☐
169	Contents of published accounts	☐	☐	☐
172	Analysis of published accounts	☐	☐	☐
177	Investment appraisal	☐	☐	☐
11	**Strategic management** *NEW*			
183	What is strategic management?	☐	☐	☐
185	Strategic analysis	☐	☐	☐
191	Strategic choice	☐	☐	☐
195	Strategic implementation	☐	☐	☐
201	**A level questions and answers**			

207 **Now test yourself answers**

My revision planner 5

Countdown to my exams

6–8 weeks to go

- Start by looking at the syllabus — make sure you know exactly what material you need to revise and the style of the examination. Use the revision planner on pages 4 and 5 to familiarise yourself with the topics.
- Organise your notes, making sure you have covered everything on the syllabus. The revision planner will help you to group your notes into topics.
- Work out a realistic revision plan that will allow you time for relaxation. Set aside days and times for all the subjects that you need to study, and stick to your timetable.
- Set yourself sensible targets. Break your revision down into focused sessions of around 40 minutes, divided by breaks. This Revision Guide organises the basic facts into short, memorable sections to make revising easier.

Revised ☐

4–6 weeks to go

- Read through the relevant sections of this book and refer to the expert tips and key terms. Tick off the topics as you feel confident about them. Highlight those topics you find difficult and look at them again in detail.
- Test your understanding of each topic by working through the 'Now test yourself' questions in the book. Look up the answers at the back of the book.
- Make a note of any problem areas as you revise, and ask your teacher to go over these in class.
- Look at past papers. They are one of the best ways to revise and practise your exam skills. Write or prepare planned answers to the exam-style questions provided in this book. Check your answers with your teacher.
- Use the revision activities to try different revision methods. For example, you can make notes using mind maps, spider diagrams or flash cards.
- Track your progress using the revision planner and give yourself a reward when you have achieved your target.

Revised ☐

1 week to go

- Try to fit in at least one more timed practice of an entire past paper and seek feedback from your teacher, comparing your work closely with the mark scheme.
- Check the revision planner to make sure you haven't missed out any topics. Brush up on any areas of difficulty by talking them over with a friend or getting help from your teacher.
- Attend any revision classes put on by your teacher. Remember, he or she is an expert at preparing people for examinations.

Revised ☐

The day before the examination

- Flick through this Revision Guide for useful reminders, for example the expert tips and key terms.
- Check the time and place of your examination.
- Make sure you have everything you need — extra pens and pencils, tissues, a watch, bottled water, sweets.
- Allow some time to relax and have an early night to ensure you are fresh and alert for the examination.

Revised ☐

My exams

Paper 1
Date: ....
Time: ....
Location: ....

Paper 2
Date: ....
Time: ....
Location: ....

Paper 3
Date: ....
Time: ....
Location: ....

1 Business and its environment

Enterprise

Enterprise is the qualities and skills needed to start up and create a new business venture. It involves understanding the nature of business activity and the conditions required for business success.

The nature of business activity

Revised

Purpose of business activity

Business activity can be looked at in two ways:

1. **The transformation of inputs into outputs.** The **inputs** are resources: the **factors of production** (land, labour, capital and enterprise). These incur financial costs: rent, wages, interest on loans and payments to business owners. The **outputs** are physical products or services represented by sales revenue or profits.
2. **The use of resources to supply goods and services to meet the needs and wants of consumers and society.** These may be private needs from individuals and households, or social needs like medical services, transport and education.

In doing these activities, jobs and incomes are created, goods and services are produced and the lives of individuals and society are improved. Enterprise involves the process of taking decisions about the best way for a new business to transform inputs and meet the needs of individuals and society. Taking these decisions always includes elements of risk, and enterprise deals with assessing these in relation to possible rewards.

> **Factors of production:** these are the following resources used to produce goods and services:
> - Land, including buildings, minerals, oil and forests.
> - Labour — work done either manually or mentally in managing and decision making.
> - Capital — machinery and equipment, including intellectual capital such as education and qualifications.
> - Enterprise — the qualities and skills needed to start up and create a new business venture.

The concept of adding value

When transformation of inputs to outputs takes place to produce goods and services it occurs in a number of stages. Each stage is more valuable than the one before as work will have been done on the inputs (economic added value). This value will also be the added value that consumers place on a finished product (marketing added value). The example opposite shows how value is added at each stage of production in car manufacturing.

Example

Car production

Each stage of production shown below adds value by transforming inputs into an output.

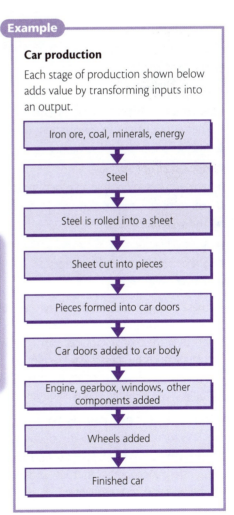

Enterprise 7

The nature of economic activity, the problem of choice and opportunity cost

Economic activity means taking decisions about the transformation of inputs to outputs and always involves choices. This is because resources are always limited in relation to needs and wants. Individuals, businesses and society generally always want more than they can afford so choices must be made.

Opportunity cost is the real cost of making a decision about using resources. The real cost of something is what is given up when you choose it.

> **Opportunity cost:** the next best alternative given up when a choice is made.

Table 1 Opportunity cost examples

Individual examples	Opportunity cost
Studying A levels	Not taking a job
Taking a holiday by the sea	Not visiting mountains
Buying a shirt	Not buying some shoes
Business examples	**Opportunity cost**
Buying a new computer network	Not buying new lorries
Spending on research and development	Not increasing advertising
Hiring some workers	Not being able to lower price
Society examples	**Opportunity cost**
More hospitals	Fewer soldiers and weapons
Powerful cars	Safer roads
Lower taxes	Less government spending on education

> **Revision activities**
> 1. Draw up a list of five different businesses. Briefly explain how each business adds value.
> 2. Using the same businesses draw up a list of decisions each business might have to make and show the possible opportunity cost of making each decision.

> **Now test yourself**
> 1. Define 'added value'.
> 2. Define 'opportunity cost'.
>
> **Answers on p.207**
>
> Tested

Businesses need to be aware of the opportunity cost of any action before they make final decisions.

Business environment is dynamic

Businesses operate in an environment that includes:
- the actions of other businesses
- the labour market
- government economic and social policies
- consumer tastes and demand
- the legal framework
- political factors
- social and demographic factors
- changing technology

All these change over time. Some changes may take place slowly, such as an ageing population, increasing incomes or consumers wanting increasingly better-quality products. Some change is quick, such as a new competition law or a competitor decreasing price. Businesses have to monitor their environments and be ready, able and willing to change what they are doing in order to adapt to changing markets. Carrying on in the same way is an option that often leads to failure.

What a business needs to succeed

The keys to business success are effectiveness in the following areas:
- **Enterprise** — the ability to see possible opportunities in the market for transforming inputs to outputs and gaining a reward that takes into account the risks and choices involved.
- **Organisation** — the ability to choose the appropriate resources and combine them together profitably to produce products at a price the consumer is willing to pay.
- **Financial monitoring** — keeping track of the flows of money in the organisation so that decisions on resources can be made knowing the real opportunity cost.

- **Human resource management (HRM)** — so that the right number of appropriately skilled and trained people are hired.
- **Marketing** — so that products meet the consumers' needs in terms of design, price, availability, information and value.
- **Objectives** — so that appropriate organisation structure and strategy can be used.
- **Coordination** — so that all the functional areas (finance, marketing, operations, HRM) work together to achieve corporate objectives.

> **Revision activity**
>
> A friend visits and tells you about a new idea she has for a business selling toy animals made of plastic. Draw up a list of ideas that might help her business to succeed.

Why many businesses fail early on

As many as 60% of businesses fail in the first 2 years. Common reasons include:
- lack of well-researched objectives and business plan
- too little cash (cannot afford appropriate resources), or too much cash (spent on wasteful resources)
- too much borrowing, leading to high interest payments
- cash-flow difficulties (spending at the wrong time or not getting payments quickly enough)
- unexpected growth too soon, which stretches resources
- unplanned-for competition and lack of market knowledge and research
- poor marketing, i.e. too much, too little or not appropriate
- poor initial location decision or credit arrangements
- lack of experience and underestimation of time and money pressure
- not enough passion, commitment or risk assessment

The role of the entrepreneur

An **entrepreneur** is a person willing to take a risk and start a new business by bringing together all the resources necessary for success. This may be done by:
- producing and selling a new product
- building an existing business in a different way
- extending an existing brand into different markets

To avoid the reasons why a new business might fail it is essential to have particular skills and abilities.

> **Entrepreneur:** a person willing to take a risk and start a new business by bringing together all the resources necessary for success

Qualities an entrepreneur is likely to need for success
- Determination, drive and energy.
- Passion, initiative and self-confidence.
- Good leadership — being able to persuade and involve others.
- Good network-forming skills.
- Low fear of failure.
- Good assessor of risk and moderate risk taker.
- Clear goal- and vision-setting.
- Good organisation.
- The ability to determine and focus on market needs and wants.

The role of business enterprise

Business enterprise is essential for starting and then making a business grow. If there is no vision and organising mechanisms, a business will drift and increasingly poor decisions will be taken. Workers will become demotivated, efficiency falls and costs rise, sales become harder to achieve and cash flow becomes less manageable.

New businesses are usually small. Typically small businesses supply 40–70% of the jobs in a country and 20–30% of the wealth created. Many countries

> **Revision activity**
>
> You are trying to interest the government in starting a new college to encourage enterprise and entrepreneurs. Prepare notes for a government minister that include two reasons why this is important for your country/region together with an explanation of the sort of students that you would hope the college would attract.

Enterprise

therefore encourage new businesses by tax incentives, providing infrastructure and advice and low cost start-up finance or development loans.

Enterprise in the form of new businesses generates:
- new ideas, new products and new ways of working
- the seeds for future growth into large businesses
- competition that ensures markets are efficient and existing firms are not complacent
- employment opportunities and training

> **Now test yourself**
>
> 3 Identify three characteristics of a successful entrepreneur.
> 4 Identify three changes that could occur in the business environment.
>
> **Answers on p.207**
>
> Tested

Social enterprise

Revised

Business enterprise measures risks and rewards. Private enterprise focuses on financial reward. Social enterprise focuses on improving society.

The range and aims of social enterprise

A **social enterprise** is a business that trades for a social or environmental purpose and uses its profit for this, rather than distributing it to the owners. Social enterprises:
- are set up to make a difference to society with a clear social/environmental mission
- gain income from selling goods and services, not from donations
- reinvest profits for their social purpose/impact
- operate in a range of sizes and structures

> **Social enterprise:** a business that trades for a social or environmental purpose and uses its profit for this, rather than distributing it to the owners.

Examples might include:
- providing employment for drug addicts and recovering addicts
- increasing employment for women
- improving the local environment by clearing litter, and landscaping
- recycling furniture to low income households or making new products from old ones
- providing IT resources to charities and low income households
- providing coffee producers with a fair income and market outlets

Social enterprises have to have a business structure that is different from the normal partnership or joint stock companies because social objectives, the requirement to reinvest the profits and the need to pass on any assets to similar enterprises, have to be written in. Examples include cooperatives, community enterprises and not-for-profit companies. They are found in many countries, often working with development agencies or charities.

Triple bottom line

The bottom line of many businesses is to achieve targets related to profit. Social enterprises use targets in relation to all these areas:
- **Economic or financial performance** — costs, revenue, surplus.
- **Social impact** — related to their core objectives.
- **Environmental sustainability** — relating to their effect on the environment in the long term.

> **Now test yourself**
>
> 5 Give three examples of social enterprise.
> 6 Briefly explain the meaning of triple bottom line.
> 7 Identify three differences between a profit-making business and a social enterprise.
>
> **Answers on p.207**
>
> Tested

Business structure

Businesses have to have a legally recognised formal structure. There are various possibilities linked to business size, finance requirements and the type of product and market.

Economic sectors

Primary, secondary and tertiary sectors

Economic activity can be divided into three sectors, each one with industries of a particular type. Businesses generally operate in one of the following three sectors:

- **Primary sector businesses** are those that deal with the extraction of natural resources so they include farming, forestry, fishing, oil, gas, quarrying and mining. These industries form the first stage in the chain of production.
- **Secondary sector businesses** are those that manufacture products or process raw materials. They turn raw materials and components made from raw materials from the primary sector into semi-finished or finished goods. Examples include manufacture of cars, furniture, buildings and processed food.
- **Tertiary sector businesses** are those that provide a service. No physical product is provided. Examples include banking, insurance, education and travel services.

As economies develop they tend to move from being focused on employment and output in the primary sector to the manufacturing sector then the tertiary sector.

> **Primary sector businesses** deal with extracting natural resources, e.g. farming, forestry, fishing, oil, gas, quarrying and mining.
>
> **Secondary sector businesses** manufacture products or process raw materials, e.g. to produce cars, furniture, buildings, processed food.
>
> **Tertiary sector businesses** provide a service, e.g. banking, insurance, education, travel.

Public and private sectors

Economic activity is carried out by **private sector** businesses that are owned by individuals or **public sector** businesses that are owned and run by the state (local or central government).

Private and public sector businesses often have different objectives, e.g. public sector businesses do not have the objective of maximising profit. They also have different legal structures and financial arrangements.

> **Private sector:** contains businesses that are owned and run by individuals.
>
> **Public sector:** contains businesses that are owned by the state (local or central government).

Now test yourself

8 State two examples of businesses from each of the primary and tertiary sectors.
9 State two examples of businesses from each of the public and private sectors.
10 State two ways a public sector business might differ from a business in the private sector.

Answers on p.207

Private sector legal structures for a business

The factors that influence the choice of a particular legal structure include size, owners' responsibility, financial arrangements, the level of owners' risk and possible sources of finance. The ability to raise finance is a crucial factor. A small firm with one owner will find it harder to raise finance than a large business with a record of sound borrowing. A key factor is the ability of the business to become a complete legal entity, separate from the owners.

The importance of limited liability

Limited liability means that the responsibility of the owner of a business for business debts is limited only to the specific amount invested in the business, and does not include all their other assets. This means that an owner cannot lose more than the money invested in the business and is therefore encouraged to invest. It enables shares to be issued and large amounts of money to be raised. It occurs because the business is registered as a separate legal entity, capable of suing and being sued in a court. This also means that possible lenders to the business are more likely to lend, knowing their loan is not dependent on individual persons.

Unlimited liability means that the responsibility of the owner for business debt is not limited to the amount invested so business debts might have to be paid from not just the assets of the business but all the assets of the owner.

Main features of private sector legal structures

Sole trader

A **sole trader** is an individual who owns and runs a business, taking final decisions. A few sole traders are large businesses with many employees, many others have a small number of employees or none. The owner has unlimited liability and few administrative or legal requirements. The business is not a separate legal entity so finishes if the owner dies. Typical examples are small retailers and personal services.

Advantages of being a sole trader
- Cheap, quick and easy to set up.
- Owner controls business and has confidentiality.
- Flexible.

Disadvantages of being a sole trader
- Unlimited liability — might lose house to pay business debts.
- Difficult to raise finance from loans.
- Demands owner be skilled at all aspects of business operation.
- Difficult for owner to be absent from business — no sick leave.

Partnership

A **partnership** is when two or more people own and run a business together. Many countries have a maximum number of partners allowed. There is no requirement for formal documents or agreements, but these are common and set out how much each partner has contributed, what responsibilities they have in running the business and how the partnership may be ended. Partnerships generally have unlimited liability and are not legal entities so individual partners have legal responsibility. Some countries allow some partnerships to have limited liability and be a separate legal entity. In this case, there will be formal procedures to go through. Common examples are in the professions, e.g. medicine, law and architects.

Advantages of a partnership
- Easy and cheap to set up.
- More capital raising ability as more than one person and extra partners can be recruited.
- Possibility of 'sleeping partners' to raise finance.
- Shared responsibility, workload and stress.
- Wider range of skills.

> **Limited liability:** the financial liability of the owners of a business is limited to the amount they have invested.

> **Now test yourself**
> 11 Define limited liability.
> 12 Briefly explain one reason why limited liability is so important when a business has to raise large sums of money through a bank loan.
>
> Answers on p.207
>
> Tested

> **Sole trader:** a business owned and run by one person responsible for decisions and taking all the profit.

> **Partnership:** a business owned and run jointly by a number of partners who share the profit.

Disadvantages of a partnership
- Unlimited liability restricts ability to raise capital and partners may be forced to use personal assets to pay business debts.
- Slower decision making and less control for individuals.
- Possible arguments about work arrangements and share of profits.
- Partnership finishes if one partner leaves so no continuity.

Limited companies
Private or public limited companies share the following features:
- **Incorporation** — the company is a separate legal entity from the owners and can sue and be sued.
- Ownership is through share issue and can be sold.
- The company continues when shareholders change.
- Limited liability of owners.
- Management is by a **board of directors** elected by the shareholders.
- Setting up requires formal registration, regular filing of accounts and reports open to the public.
- Limited liability and share issue enable large amounts of capital to be raised.

This means that limited companies are more expensive to set up but have access to greater sources of capital, are seen as more secure and continue until wound up or taken over. Generally, private limited companies are smaller than public limited companies.

> **Incorporation:** occurs when a business is set up as a limited company, meaning it is a separate legal entity and its owners have limited liability.
>
> **Board of directors:** elected by the shareholders of a company to take decisions about running and managing the business.

Private limited company
- Often relatively small family owned businesses.
- Relatively cheap to set up.
- Shares can only be traded privately, not advertised for sale.
- Not all accounts and reports are open to the public.
- Cannot be taken over without agreement of shareholders.

Public limited company (plc)
- Usually large businesses.
- Shares issued for sale publicly to anyone via a stock exchange.
- Expensive to set up.
- Accounts, reports and AGM open to anyone.
- Easier to take over as shares available in open market.
- Huge amounts of capital can be raised via share issue.
- Complex to run, directors separate from shareholders so directors might seek different objectives from shareholders.

> **Now test yourself**
>
> 13 Identify three differences between a private and a public limited company.
>
> Answer on p.207
>
> Tested

> **Expert tip**
>
> Identify the exact structure of a business when you consider the above issues. Remember that a company is a specific business structure: not all businesses are companies.

Franchises
A **franchise** is a smaller business that uses the advantages of a large well-known brand in return for payment. The franchisor often supplies a name, logo, generic marketing and lays down conditions for the product. The franchisee supplies the premises, equipment and staff. Typical examples are McDonald's, The Body Shop, Holiday Inn.

The franchisee gets:
- access to a successful marketing model and product, but this may be restrictive
- low cost starting up but weak negotiating position for further supplies
- cheap resources due to access to economies of scale but could have franchise withdrawn if conditions are not met

> **Franchise:** a smaller business that uses the marketing advantages of a large well-known brand in return for payment.

The franchisor gets:
- guaranteed regular income, assuming the success of franchises
- access to local knowledge, but brand name could be damaged if a franchise is poorly run
- control over the final product or service, but high cost of monitoring and coordination

Cooperatives

A **cooperative** is a business that is owned and run by its members. Cooperatives may be consumer-based, with members being customers, or produce-based or worker-based with members being workers. Members own and run the business and share in the profits.

An example of a small-scale cooperative may be several people who decide to buy their weekly food together or several people who set up a shop and work in it.

Cooperatives enable their members to:
- achieve economies of scale to lower costs or prices
- control their own business activities
- gain greater power in markets, e.g. farmers wanting control over planting or selling

It is difficult for a cooperative to become a large business but there are examples in many countries. Raising finance on a large scale is not easy and taking decisions can be complex as all the members are entitled to have a say. Cooperatives are often set up as social enterprises.

Other structures

There are other models for business structure. In the private sector these are often social enterprises and take the form of community enterprises, or not-for-profit companies. In the public sector these may be public corporations or chartered businesses set up by government.

Problems resulting from changing from one legal structure to another

A common progression as a business grows is from sole trader to partnership to private limited company to public limited company. Any change from one legal structure to another involves a change of ownership and management. Sole traders are the only form of structure that can be dissolved without going through administrative and regulatory requirements. These will cost time and money to fulfil. Setting up a new structure will also cost time and money to complete the regulatory requirements.

For businesses with multiple owners, these owners must agree to dissolve the business and set one up with a new structure, and getting this agreement can be difficult. It can also be difficult to find new owners or shareholders for a different structure.

> **Cooperative:** a business that is owned and run by its members.

> **Revision activities**
>
> 1 Draw up a table showing the advantages and disadvantages of the following types of legal structure:
>   - private limited company
>   - public limited company
>   - franchise
>   - cooperative
> 2 Giving reasons, recommend an appropriate legal structure for the following:
>   - A large transnational corporation setting up a new steel plant in another country.
>   - Five neighbours who embroider shirts and dresses for sale.
>   - A group that wishes to set up a wind farm to supply electricity to a village.
>   - A restaurant owner who wants to expand by taking over two other restaurants and a vegetable supplier.
>   - A newly qualified hairdresser.
>   - Six engineers who want to go into business designing bridges.

Size of business

Measurements of business size

Revised

Different methods of measuring the size of a business

Methods of measuring business size are shown in Figure 1.

Figure 1 Measures of business size

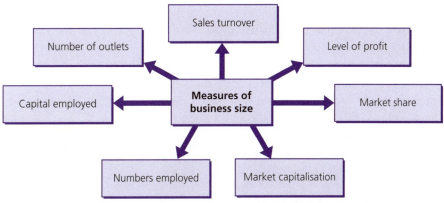

Difficulties of using these methods
The various methods are not a definitive measure of the size of a business for the following reasons:
- A business using a highly mechanised process will employ fewer workers than a business using labour intensive methods.
- A high value of capital employed might reflect the fact that very expensive equipment is essential for the business to function.
- A business could have a large market share but the market itself might be very small.
- The current market value of a business might be due to a sudden surge or decline in its share value, e.g. some of the dot.com companies.
- Sales turnover can be high due to the sale of only a few but very high value items such as highly specialised computer control mechanisms, e.g. parts being used on space exploration missions.
- A large business might produce a very small profit if market conditions are difficult.

Revision activity
Make a list of three small businesses and three large businesses. Identify the factors that allow you to judge the size of each particular business. Write out your reasons for each judgement.

Now test yourself
14 Identify two methods of measuring the size of a business.
15 Explain two problems that might occur when measuring the size of a business.

Answers on p.207

Significance of small businesses

Advantages and disadvantages of being a small business
Advantages
- Small businesses are often able to respond quickly to market changes because they do not always have highly specialised equipment that is specific to a small range of products.
- It is often the small businesses that are providing a personal and/or specialised service to customers, e.g. hairdressers and local independent shops. They know their customers personally and are able to help and advise them on an individual basis.
- The owner(s) of a small business might be able to retain more power and control over the business than if it grew larger and involved more people in management and/or ownership of the business.
- Employees in a small business might all be known to the owner, leading to a better working relationship that can in turn lead to more loyalty from the employees.

Disadvantages
- Small businesses sometimes find it difficult to obtain bank loans because they have fewer assets to offer as collateral. This can lead to a lack of finance for growth or development of the business.
- A smaller number of employees might mean that the business lacks the opportunity to employ a range of specialist workers.

- A combination of a lack of finance and specialist knowledge could mean that a small business might not have the opportunity to undertake market research and therefore might be unable to maximise its presence in the market. Opportunities might be missed.
- Due to not enjoying economies of scale, the cost of goods and materials might be higher than those paid by larger businesses. This could mean that a small business must charge a higher price and therefore could struggle to remain competitive with larger businesses.
- The business might have to specialise in one product or a small range of products. This could leave it exposed to larger businesses, who can offer more variety.

Strengths and weaknesses of family businesses

Strengths
- The family business is more likely to have members that will be loyal to each other and therefore to the business.
- The family bonds should lead to a stronger working relationship.
- The family employees will all know how to approach one another when discussion is needed.

Weaknesses
- Family feuds might affect the working relationship.
- Family members who are not performing well at work might resent any discipline from another family member. Alternatively there could be a hesitancy to discipline another member of the family. This can cause resentment from other non-family employees.
- Family members are likely to be in the managerial roles and this can prevent the introduction of employees from outside the business who might have expertise that could prove very beneficial to the business.
- The emotional involvement of family members might make some decisions difficult. For example, if one family employee is worthy of promotion another relative might resent this.

Now test yourself
16 Give one advantage and one disadvantage of being a small business.
17 Explain one weakness of family businesses.

Answers on p.207
Tested

The importance of small businesses in the economy
- Small businesses act as suppliers to large businesses.
- Collectively small businesses provide a large number of jobs in an economy.
- Today's small businesses might be the big businesses of the future.

The role of small businesses in some industries
- Small businesses are often a crucial part of the supply chain, e.g. small manufacturers supplying various car parts to a large car manufacturer.
- In some industries small businesses might provide some specialist services for the larger business, e.g. IT updates and servicing or conflict resolution in the case of industrial unrest.
- Recruitment of staff is often undertaken by small businesses working to meet the needs of the large businesses in many industry situations.

Now test yourself
18 Explain one reason why a government might encourage the start-up of small businesses.

Answer on p.207
Tested

Internal growth
Revised

Internal growth means that the business will increase its scale of operation by producing and selling more, by opening new outlets or factories and by employing more workers. Internal growth is often a slower means of growth than external growth but it avoids some of the problems associated with external growth.

Why a business might want to grow internally

- To gain the benefits of economies of scale.
- To increase potential for sales and hopefully profit.
- To become a more influential business in the market and therefore perhaps have more power over the price of the goods/services sold.
- To gain more bargaining power with its suppliers.
- To gain a larger market share and therefore more influence in the market.
- By becoming larger a business might be less vulnerable to takeover by a larger business.
- Internal growth is usually a gradual process and allows management changes to take place at a more leisurely pace.
- Because of the slower rate of growth, internal growth can help a business to avoid the dangers of overtrading.

How a business might grow internally

- The business might actively seek more orders for its products/services.
- More equipment and/or premises might be purchased.
- Finance might be obtained to allow additional premises and equipment to be purchased.
- When more orders and additional production capacity have been secured, the business can increase its scale of production.
- A business might diversify into other products/services as a means of growth allowing it to appeal to a larger range of customers.

> **Now test yourself**
> 19 Explain why a business might want to grow internally.
> **Answer on p.207**
> Tested

Business objectives

Business objectives in the private and public sectors

Revised

Business objectives are goals or targets that a business will work towards. The objectives will determine all activities that the various sections of the business undertake.

> **Business objectives:** goals or targets that a business will work towards.

The nature and importance of business objectives at corporate, departmental and individual levels

All objectives and targets must be SMART:

- **S**pecific in what they want to achieve.
- **M**easurable so that progress or ultimate achievement can be assessed.
- **A**ttainable/agreed so that everyone involved will feel capable of reaching the goal and, hopefully, will be motivated to achieve that aim.
- **R**ealistic because setting unrealistic objectives can demotivate a workforce. It might be that it is the timeframe that must be realistic; some goals will take longer than others. For example, it is likely to take longer to grow a business by 100% than to increase sales by 10%.
- **T**ime-specific — without this element the objective would lack an essential element against which the business success would be assessed. For example, an objective to increase market share by 10% would be meaningless if it was not to be achieved within a stated time, e.g. 3 years.

> **Now test yourself**
> 20 What does the acronym SMART stand for?
> **Answer on p.207**
> Tested

Typical business objectives

Typical business objectives may be:

- profit related; either to maximise profits or to be profit satisficing
- growth of the business
- to increase market share

- to increase sales revenue
- survival

The nature of objectives set can be influenced by:
- **The size of the business.**
- **The business culture.** Some businesses are risk-takers while others are more cautious.
- **The current economic environment.** Is the economy buoyant or is it in recession?
- **How long the business has been in existence.** New businesses might not have the financial resources to support some objectives. In the early stages of a business its only aim in the short term might be to survive. Once established, its focus might change to increasing sales or market share.
- **Whether the business is in the private or the public sector.** An organisation in the public sector might aim simply to provide more people with better products/services. This is unlikely to be an aim of a profit-seeking business in the private sector.

Objectives can be set at a corporate level, e.g. to increase market share by 10% in 5 years; at a departmental level, e.g. the production department might aim to increase output by at least 10% through increases in efficiency, and an individual might be set short-term targets, e.g. to increase productivity by 10% and achieve zero defects.

Objectives are important to businesses because:
- they provide a focus and a framework for business activity
- they ensure that all departments or divisions within a business are working towards the same ultimate goal

> **Now test yourself**
> 21 Identify two business objectives.
> 22 Identify two factors that can influence business objectives.
>
> **Answers on p.207**
> Tested

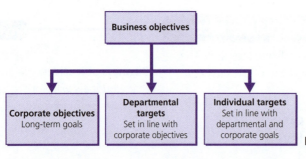

Figure 2 Business objectives

Corporate responsibility as a business objective

Corporate responsibility, also known as **corporate social responsibility**, is increasingly important to businesses because customers are becoming more aware of how businesses behave. Buying decisions can be influenced by the level of corporate responsibility demonstrated by a business.

> **Corporate social responsibility:** the action, legally required or voluntary, needed for an organisation to act responsibly to all its stakeholders.

Businesses can benefit if they can be seen to be behaving in a socially responsible manner, e.g. that they are aware of and working to avoid causing any environmental damage. Also many businesses strive to behave in an ethical manner. For example, a business selling face creams will ensure that the product has not been tested on animals and a business manufacturing car batteries will aim to ensure that it does not cause any pollution or environmental damage. Social responsibility is demonstrated by a business that considers the local community and tries to minimise the impact on local people by aiming to limit the amount of noise and traffic caused by business activities.

Businesses can use a high level of corporate responsibility as a marketing tool. A failure to demonstrate corporate responsibility can lead to adverse publicity that can severely damage the reputation of the business.

> **Now test yourself**
> 23 Briefly explain what is meant by 'corporate social responsibility'.
>
> **Answer on p.207**
> Tested

Relationship between mission statement, objectives, strategy and tactics

A **mission statement** is a public statement of the overall intent of an organisation and is often displayed in a public area of the business. For example, a school or college might have as its mission statement 'To educate the next generation to be highly skilled and meaningful contributors to society'. The objectives or long-term goals would be set to achieve that mission. One objective might be to increase the number of A-level passes by 20% over the next 2 years. A **strategy** would then be devised to help to achieve this. This might involve a change in teaching methods, which might also create the need for more training for the teachers. Alternatively, it could mean that more up-to-date facilities would have to be acquired and this could mean some financial decisions would have to be taken.

The **tactics** involved could be to increase the rate at which students learn. This could be achieved by extending the number of teaching hours or by setting more home study, which students could be encouraged to undertake by the setting of individual objectives.

The same approach is used in business. The corporate objectives are set, then the ways in which the objectives are to be achieved are decided followed by the setting of departmental and/or individual targets that will all contribute to the achievement of the overall objective.

> **Mission statement:** sets out an organisation's purpose, identity, values and main business aims.
>
> **Strategy:** an overall plan designed to achieve objectives.
>
> **Tactics:** the methods a business uses to carry out a strategy.

Objectives and business decisions

Revised

The different stages of business decision making and the role of objectives

The stages in the decision-making process include:
1. Identify the problem or the goal to be achieved.
2. Collect relevant data.
3. Analyse and evaluate the data in the context of the identified goal/problem.
4. Discuss the advantages and disadvantages of strategies that could be used to achieve the goal.
5. Implement the chosen strategy.
6. Review the effectiveness of the strategy and possibly refine or change the approach used.

Decisions made in a business will be made with the corporate objectives in mind. All decisions must contribute to the achievement of the overall business objective. For example, businesses must decide what resources are needed and where.

How objectives might change over time

- Business circumstances change and so does the economic environment in which businesses operate. This can cause a business to change its corporate objective of increasing market share to focusing on survival in the short term.
- A new competitor might arrive in the industry or the existing competitors might begin to be more aggressive. A business might change its objective from increasing market share by 10% to merely maintaining market share in the face of the increased competition.

Translation of objectives into targets and budgets

Business objectives are usually achieved in stages. These stages are the basis of shorter-term targets that must be achieved if the business objective is to be reached. The targets can be departmental or set for an individual employee.

The business objective will have an overall budget, which will then be divided into smaller budgets that are allocated to each department or division. The size of the budget will be determined by the requirements placed on each department. If a department is expected to increase its output and/or its contribution to the overall business objective, then it is likely that the budget for that department will be increased.

The communication of objectives and their likely impact on the workforce

Objectives are usually communicated to the workforce through the agreed channels of communication within a business. This might be through line managers or via a staff meeting at which all staff are informed of the key aim(s) of the business.

- A workforce is likely to be informed about objectives when those objectives will have an impact either on the way in which they work or on the output they will be expected to produce.
- The objectives might be motivating to the workforce by making them aware of their contribution to the overall aims of the business.
- Being aware of business objectives might give the employees a feeling of team spirit as they will all be working to achieve the same overall goal for the business.
- There could be a demotivating effect on the workforce if the declared aim of the business involves an increase in the use of machinery that could lead to some of the workforce being made redundant.

How ethics may influence business objectives and activities

Ethics are not limited to matters of legality but can be a moral guide to how a business might conduct itself. Ethics can influence business objectives because consumers are becoming increasingly aware of when a business is thought to have behaved in an unethical or immoral way.

> **Ethics:** a moral guide to business behaviour. Ethics consider what is morally acceptable behaviour rather than what is legal.

Ethics might influence a business objective or activities in the following ways:

- A business seeking to increase its profits might lower its labour costs by employing child labour. As customers could view this as unethical it might deter them from purchasing the product(s).
- Using non-polluting methods of production could be much more expensive than a method that causes substantial pollution. A profit-maximising business might be tempted to use the cheaper option but this would not be ethical.
- Some businesses choose to locate in countries where the laws restricting business activities are very limited or weak. Some might argue that such a move makes good business sense whilst others might argue that it is immoral/unethical because the move was made purely in order to exploit the weaker laws of that country.
- The testing of products on animals is seen as morally unacceptable by some customers. However, a business might be trying to confirm the safety of their products before selling them. Is such a business unethical?

> **Expert tip**
>
> When answering a question about ethics do not restrict your answer to discussing pollution. Ethical and environmental issues are connected but can require some different content from you in your answers.

> **Revision activity**
>
> Consider any business that you are familiar with and the extent to which it can be seen to be behaving in an ethical manner. Make a list of the factors that might determine whether or not it is an ethical business.

In order for a business to succeed, it must have customers. If modern businesses are judged to be unethical it is likely that they will lose customers. Increased press coverage and the increased use of the internet means that customers are much better informed about the behaviour of businesses now than ever before.

> **Now test yourself**
>
> 24 Briefly explain how ethics might influence the customers of a business.
>
> **Answer on p.207**
>
> Tested

Stakeholders in a business

A **stakeholder** is any individual or group of individuals who have an interest in the activities of a business. These may be internal or external.

Groups involved in business activity

Revised

Stakeholders include:
- employees
- shareholders
- customers
- local community
- lenders of finance, e.g. banks
- suppliers
- the government

> **Stakeholder:** an individual or a group of individuals who have an interest in the activities of a business.

Roles, rights and responsibilities of the stakeholders

Revised

- **Employees** use their skills and expertise to work in the business and to help the business to achieve its stated aims. They expect to be paid fairly and on time and to be treated in a way that complies with employment law. Employees have a responsibility to the business to work efficiently and not to breach their contract with the business.
- **Shareholders** provide permanent finance for the business in return for a share in the ownership of the business. They expect to receive dividends on the shares they hold if the business makes a profit. The shareholders are expected to use their voting power to appoint the best people to the board of directors and to ensure that the business follows ethical policies.
- **Customers** justify the existence of a business; without customers there is no reason for the business to exist. Customers can expect to receive a product in good condition and that is safe to use. In return customers are expected to pay on time for goods and services received and not to make any false claims against the business. For example, customers should not claim that they had been injured as a result of using a product if that claim was untrue.
- The **local community** allows the business activity to take place and possibly supports the business by providing local goods and services to the main business. The local community will expect a business to carry out its activities in such a way that it is not harmful to the local inhabitants, e.g. noise or water pollution.
- **Lenders**, e.g. banks, provide finance for the business and have a right to expect that repayments will be made by the business in accordance with the lending agreement. The banks will be expected to make funds available to a business once an agreement has been reached. The banks might also be expected to allow only reasonable loan agreements to be made. If a bank lends more than a business can afford to repay, this can result in severe financial difficulty for the business and might result in its closure.
- **Suppliers** are the providers of goods and services required by businesses. They expect to be paid for all goods and services provided and within an agreed time limit. Suppliers are expected to supply goods and services of

a required standard or to a standard agreed between the supplier and the purchasing business.
- **Governments** create the legal framework in which businesses operate. They also manage the economy of the country and so can influence the economic environment in which a business operates. Governments expect any business operating in their country to abide by the laws affecting business activity and employment laws.

> **Now test yourself**
>
> 25 Identify two stakeholders in a business and briefly explain what they would expect to gain from the business activities.
>
> **Answer on p.207**

Impact of business decisions/actions on stakeholders

- **Employees** — a business might decide to switch from labour-intensive production to capital-intensive methods. Employees might resist this change due to some workers fearing that their work will be done by a machine and that they will lose their jobs. Other workers might see this as an opportunity to be trained to use the new equipment and therefore to gain new skills and experience.
- **Shareholders** — an announcement of a large investment in a research and development programme might be received with mixed feelings by shareholders. Some shareholders will see profit being put into the new project rather than being given to them as dividends. Others might take a longer-term view and feel that reduced dividends in the short term could result in even larger profit and dividends in the future if the project is successful.
- **Customers** — the launch of a new product gives customers more choice. However, if the new product replaces an existing one, some customers might be unhappy if they preferred the original product.
- **Local community** — if a large business announces that it intends to relocate to another part of the country, the local community is likely to feel betrayed. Local employment is likely to suffer and the local support businesses will probably lose the business of the larger business. Alternatively, the expansion of a business can put a lot more strain on the local infrastructure and can negatively impact on the lives of the community around the business.
- **Lenders** — the ability of a business to repay loans can be jeopardised if the business decides that it wants to pursue rapid growth. The result might be that if the business grows too fast, it becomes financially unstable. A business might decide to move some of its resources from credit control to what it sees as more profitable activities. This could result in the debts of some customers remaining unpaid and therefore the cash flow of the business could be negatively affected.
- **Suppliers** — a relocation decision might cause suppliers to lose orders, which could in turn mean that they will require fewer workers. The size of the suppliers' businesses might have been in response to the orders placed by the relocating business, and to lose a significant number of orders might cause substantial hardship.
- **Government** — the growth of a business can lead to an increase in the number of people being employed. This helps the government because one of the aims of government is to reduce unemployment. In addition, when a business has growth as an objective there is the hope that this will result in the business becoming more profitable, which means the government should receive more tax revenue from the business.

> **Expert tip**
>
> Remember that some stakeholders are internal, e.g. employees, managers and directors, and some are external, e.g. the government, nearby residents and suppliers, and that all of them might be affected by business operations.

> **Now test yourself**
>
> 26 Briefly explain how stakeholders of a business might be affected by a decision to close a local branch of the business.
>
> **Answer on p.207**

Why a business needs to be accountable to its stakeholders

Businesses must meet the needs of their stakeholders if they want to continue to have their support.

- **Employees** will seek employment elsewhere if they are not treated fairly and lawfully. This could cause frequent recruitment and selection to take place, which adds to the costs of the business.
- **Shareholders** might sell their shares and purchase shares in other businesses. This might result in competitor businesses being strengthened as they receive additional funds from the issue of new shares.
- **Customers** might cease to purchase products or services from the business if their expectations are not met. Competitors might benefit as customers switch to their products.
- The **local community** might be less tolerant towards the business activities if they think that a business is not considering the impact of its actions on the local inhabitants. For example, if a business does not take care to prevent water pollution, the local community might object strongly to any proposal from the business to increase its scale of activity.
- **Lenders** might refuse further loans or, in the case of an overdraft, might demand that any money owed is repaid immediately. Many businesses need a source of loan funds in order to be able to achieve their objectives.
- **Suppliers** might be more willing to supply goods at short notice if the business has treated them well by giving them regular orders and by paying them on time.
- **Governments** might restrict the activities of a business that has not complied with the legal framework of the country. For example, a business could face large fines if it constantly breaches employment legislation and fails to treat employees according to the laws in force. Businesses that do not comply with legislation are not likely to be considered for government loans and/or grants.

> **Now test yourself**
>
> 27 Briefly explain why businesses need to satisfy their stakeholders.
>
> **Answer on p.207**

How conflict might arise from stakeholders having different aims

Stakeholders might have different expectations of a business. For example:

- Customers want good-quality products at low prices, but if the highest possible profit is to be gained then higher prices might have to be charged. Higher profits will be desired by shareholders because high profit can mean higher dividends being paid to them.
- Shareholders want the business to have large profits but this might be in conflict with the employees who want to be paid higher wages. Higher wages will increase costs but reduce profit.
- The government usually aims to have lower unemployment and will therefore be in conflict with a business that wants to increase its use of machinery and reduce the number of people employed. However, a change in production methods might make the business more profitable and therefore liable to pay more tax to the government.
- If suppliers charge higher prices for their goods, a business will have increased costs, so reducing profits and dividends paid to shareholders.

> **Revision activity**
>
> Make a list of stakeholders in a business and write alongside each one some of the possible causes of conflict between different stakeholder groups.

How changing business objectives might affect its stakeholders

Revised

A change in business objectives can impact on stakeholders, either positively or negatively.

From profit maximisation to increasing market share
The aim of profit maximisation would satisfy the needs of shareholders to receive dividends paid out of profit. On the other hand, a change in objectives to increase market share of the business might result in a reduction in profit due to more money being spent on building an image or perhaps a unique selling point (USP) that might allow a business to gain a stronger position in the market.

From survival to growth
In the early stages of a new business survival might be its only goal. However, as a business becomes more established it might change its aim to that of business growth. This can give some security to the employees and might ultimately produce a larger profit that can be paid to shareholders in the form of dividends. The change of objective might also be beneficial to suppliers because they might expect an increase in the size of orders received as the business achieves its goal of growth.

> **Revision activity**
>
> Make notes on other possible changes in business objectives and which stakeholders might be affected. Note whether the impact is likely to be positive or negative.

2 People in organisations

Management and leadership

It is not always easy to distinguish between a **leader** and a **manager**.

- A leader might be able to inspire people to goals that they would not have thought possible, but the leader might rely on a good manager to organise the day-to-day activities that make the achievement of those goals possible.
- A leader might have a vision of where the business could be at some time in the future. Once that overall strategic aim has been determined, the managers of the business make the tactical decisions (short-term strategies) designed to move the business in the desired direction.
- The leader might be the originator of overall business objectives but managers will implement decisions on a day-to-day basis in order to make the 'vision' of the leader a reality.
- Managers will use the resources of the business as efficiently and effectively as possible in order to achieve the leader's goal.
- Good leaders are sometimes also good managers but not necessarily. Some good managers do not have the personal characteristics of a good leader but they can manage resources effectively and efficiently. Similarly, a good leader might be able to inspire their managers and workforce and might also be able to develop excellent long-term goals for the business, but they might be less able to implement decisions and manage resources on a day-to-day basis.

> **Leader:** someone who can inspire and drive other people to achieve a goal or target.
>
> **Manager:** someone who can control and direct within a business. A manager can develop and implement tactical decisions to enable a business to achieve the overall corporate objectives.

Management and managers

Revised

The functions of management

Fayol

The functions of management as described by Henry Fayol are:

- **Planning** — to outline tactical strategies and to set and implement short-term objectives.
- **Organising** — allocating resources as efficiently as possible. Make sure that the business has the resources that it needs, at the right time and in the right place.
- **Commanding** — give clear direction to ensure that workers know what is expected of them.
- **Coordinating** — prevent duplication of effort and ensure that all departments within a business are working to achieve stated objectives within an agreed timescale.
- **Controlling and monitoring** — check progress towards agreed targets. This could require a reassessment of the resources being used and perhaps a change to motivational techniques being applied.

Mintzberg

Mintzberg identified three distinct roles of management: the interpersonal role, the informational role and the decision role.

> **Revision activities**
>
> 1 Write down an example of actions that might be taken by a manager/owner when undertaking each of the functions outlined by Fayol.
> 2 Make brief notes about why it might be seen as essential to be constantly 'controlling and monitoring' in a food processing factory.

> **Now test yourself**
>
> 1 Explain three of the functions of management.
>
> **Answer on p.207**
>
> Tested

Table 1 Mintzberg's management functions

Interpersonal role involves:	Informational role involves:	Decisional role includes the role of:
• Being a figurehead — people expect managers to guide, lead and inspire them. • Being a leader — make it clear to everyone what is expected of them. • Liaison — ensure that effective communication can occur within the business and with outside agencies.	• Being a monitor of information — decide which information is important (both internal and external information). • Disseminating information — make sure that relevant information is passed to the appropriate people in a suitable way. • Being a spokesperson — passing relevant information to the appropriate agency, for example, when dealing with local authorities or trade unions.	• Entrepreneur — change managing. Introducing new ideas. Encouraging and managing innovation. • Disturbance handler — resolving any actual or potential disagreements within the business or with outside agencies. • Resource allocator — ensuring efficient and effective allocation of all resources (finance, people and/or equipment). • Negotiator — in disputes between departments or individual workers or with other businesses or customers. Negotiate with trade unions.

Revision activity

Write down an action that a manager might take when performing each of the management functions/roles identified by Mintzberg. For example, a business might wish to expand the size of its factory and so managers would need to communicate with the local planning authority to gain the relevant permission.

Expert tip

Be prepared to relate any management functions to a specific business context, e.g. to a retail or a manufacturing situation.

Leadership

The purpose of leadership

Leaders are those individuals that drive and inspire the people around them towards a specific objective. They inspire others to trust them and to support them in their pursuit of targets or goals.

Leadership roles within a business

Within a business the leaders might be the directors, managers, supervisors or worker representatives, each of them interacting with the people around them as described above by Fayol and Mintzberg.

The success of any business can depend on the ability of the leaders within it to communicate with and to drive their teams to work as a cohesive unit towards achieving the overall business objectives. This is true whether a leader is guiding 100 people or 10.

Expert tip

Strong leaders are not always good leaders or good for a business. They might have the charisma to get the workforce to believe in them and to follow them by working towards a particular goal but that goal may be not be sensible nor achievable. Leaders sometimes need to listen to others.

Now test yourself

2 Explain two of the characteristics of a successful leader.

Answer on p.208

Table 2 The qualities of a good leader

Quality	Definition
Self-confidence and self-belief	Leaders need to believe in their ability to make the right decision and to drive a business in the right direction.
Intelligence	They must have sufficient intelligence to be able to determine when their ideas are realistic and achievable. They must also have some idea how their goals might be achieved.
Creativity	They might need to be able to find new solutions to old problems and be able to create innovative ways of improving and presenting an existing product. They need to be able to set their business apart from others in the same industry by devising something to make it different.
Charisma	They need to be able to inspire the workforce and to make them want to follow the leader because they believe in the leader and what he or she believes the business can achieve.
Multi-skilled	Leaders need to know and understand the tasks within a business. Some leaders cannot perform all of the tasks but they need to be able to hire the people who can.

Choice of leadership style

Revised

Leadership styles

The chosen style of leadership can influence the efficiency of a business and the level of motivation of the workforce. Different styles of leadership can be appropriate for different business situations. For example, an authoritarian style is appropriate in an emergency situation when decisions need to be made quickly. Tables 3 to 5 outline the characteristics plus advantages and disadvantages of the **autocratic**, **democratic** and **laissez-faire** styles of leadership.

Table 3 Autocratic leadership

Characteristic	Advantages	Disadvantages
One-way communication	Time is not taken waiting for feedback to information or instruction given to employees.	Workers might not feel valued or trusted. Often only given information essential to their work. Some employees would enjoy feeling more involved and knowing the overall direction of the business.
Close supervision	Workers are told what to do and are supervised to make sure that the job is completed as expected.	Workers do not 'think for themselves' as they are always told what to do. Can stifle their potential creativity.
No feedback from employees	No time is spent seeking the views of employees.	Perhaps the employees can contribute ideas that are better than those of the leader.
Leader makes all decisions	Quick decisions can be made.	Involvement in decision-making can be motivating and can provide some job satisfaction.

Table 4 Democratic leadership

Characteristic	Advantages	Disadvantages
Two-way communication	Workers get feedback and leaders will also hear what the employees believe about some decisions or information.	Sometimes a quick decision is needed and there is not the time to consult the employees.
Participation of employees in decision-making	Can be very motivating as the employees will feel valued and trusted.	Some employees might feel that it is not their job to be making decisions. Some issues cannot be discussed with employees, e.g. proposed takeover plans of another business.
Feedback taken from employees	Better ideas can sometimes come from the employees.	Getting feedback can be time-consuming.
More general information is given to employees about the business, i.e. its long-term goals	Higher levels of involvement due to understanding what the business is aiming to achieve.	Employees might not like or agree with the long-term aims of the business. This might affect their motivation or the labour turnover.

Table 5 Laissez-faire leadership

Characteristic	Advantages	Disadvantages
Laid-back, hands-off approach by management	Workers feel trusted and therefore this approach can be a positive influence on motivation. Workers do not need constant supervision.	Workers might retain too much control over how work is to be done.
Employees work within parameters laid down by management; workers are not free to do as they please	It allows employees to have some flexibility about how their work is carried out and the structure of their working day.	Lazy managers can use this leadership style as a means of avoiding making decisions about work-related issues.
Workers are free to make their own decisions about how they work	Employees are likely to increase their self-discipline and to work as a team to achieve the desired outcome.	Managers might become remote from some decisions and become out of touch.
High level of trust given to employees	Time is saved because employees can take decisions.	Wrong choices in terms of organisation policy may be made.
Typically used with highly skilled and motivated employees such as in design or research businesses	Employees motivated because they can achieve personal goals.	Employees may pursue their own objectives using organisation resources.

Douglas McGregor: Theory X and Y

The way that managers view their workers' attitudes to their work can determine or influence how managers treat those workers. McGregor divided workers into Theory X and Theory Y workers.

A manager who sees his or her employees as Theory X workers is likely to believe the workers to have a negative attitude to their work and might choose to use an autocratic leadership style to manage them. A manager who believes his or her workers to be Theory Y workers might place more trust in them and adopt a democratic style of leadership (see Table 6).

Table 6 McGregor's Theory X and Y

Theory X	Theory Y
• Such workers need to be given clear instructions of what to do and require close and constant supervision. • They will avoid taking on any responsibility if at all possible. • They do not particularly enjoy their work and will avoid doing anything more than the minimum required of them.	• Such workers enjoy their work and are likely to enjoy some involvement in decision-making. • They are not afraid of responsibility and will accept it in the hope that their efforts will be recognised. • Workers might be creative and be willing to offer ideas to the business.

Now test yourself

3 Identify two benefits to a business of adopting a democratic leadership style.
4 Explain two disadvantages of using a democratic leadership style.
5 Explain two advantages of using an autocratic leadership style.
6 Explain two characteristics of workers being managed using a laissez-faire leadership style.

Answers on p.208

Expert tip

Read questions such as those opposite carefully. Make sure that you write about the advantages and/or the disadvantages as required by the question. It is not unusual for students to write about advantages when the question required discussion of disadvantages.

Expert tip

Paternalistic leadership/management style is not currently assessed on the CIE syllabus.

Emotional intelligence (EQ)

Goleman's four competencies of emotional intelligence

Goleman's theory is based on a need for managers to know and understand their own feelings and those of their employees. Managers need to be aware of what motivates them and what are their hopes and aspirations. If managers understand this about themselves then they might be able to understand the emotions of their employees.

Emotional intelligence: the ability to recognise and understand your own feelings and those of others.

Goleman's theory is based around four key 'domains': self-awareness, self-management, social awareness and social skills.

- **Self-awareness.** Managers must be able to recognise and understand their own emotions if they are to understand those of others. They need to understand how they feel, when and why.
- **Self-management.** They need to be self-motivated and to appreciate how their behaviour can affect the feelings and performance of their employees. They need to be able to control their emotions and the way in which they treat their employees so that their employees are not negatively affected. An obviously angry or fearful manager is likely to convey those feelings to his or her employees. Keeping extreme emotions under control can be a positive influence on employees. Managers should be aware of what motivates them

and so appreciate that their employees might share those same motivation needs.

- **Social awareness.** Managers need to understand the emotions of their workers and be sensitive to their different needs. They must be aware of the aims and ambitions of their workers because these will affect their attitude to their work. This can also apply to customers.
- **Social skills.** Managers who are aware of the emotions of others are more likely to be able to manage those people effectively because they will realise that they perhaps need to adapt their approach to some employees. Understanding the cause of certain emotions, e.g. disappointment, can enable managers to deal with situations more sympathetically and effectively.

> **Now test yourself**
> 7 State the four key competencies of Goleman's emotional intelligence theory.
> 8 Explain one advantage to managers of understanding the emotions of their employees.
>
> **Answers on p.208**
> Tested

Motivation

Motivation as a tool of management and leadership

Revised

Motivated workers are likely to feel more involved in the workplace and can also feel as though they are an important and valued part of that business rather than 'just an employee'.

The need to motivate employees

Employers and managers spend a lot of time and money trying to ensure that their employees are as motivated as possible. Motivated employees are more likely to work as hard as possible to help the business to achieve its stated aims and objectives. These might include:

- **An increase in productivity**. Motivated workers will work harder and produce more output during each work period.
- **Improved levels of customer service** possibly leading to:
  - The ability to differentiate one business from another. This is particularly so in retail businesses but also applies to manufacturing businesses. All businesses have customers whether they are purchasing a product or receiving a service.
  - An increase in returning customers.
- **Better quality goods**.
- **Fewer mistakes** due to employees being eager to do the best possible job for their employer or manager.
- **A possible decrease in production costs** due to lower levels of faulty goods being produced and therefore less wastage of materials.
- **Reduced labour turnover**. Motivated employees are less likely to look for work elsewhere because they are happy and satisfied in their current post. This can also be described as an increase in the loyalty of employees. This can have the benefit of reducing the recruitment and selection costs caused by the need to replace employees when they leave.
- **Lower levels of absenteeism**. Employees are less likely to be absent from work if they are happy and satisfied at work.

> **Motivation:** a desire to do something; a desire to work willingly towards a stated aim or goal.
>
> **Productivity:** output per person per time period (per hour or per shift worked).

> **Now test yourself**
> 9 Define 'motivation'.
>
> **Answer on p.208**
> Tested

> **Expert tip**
> Make sure that you discuss motivation issues in the context of the given situation. If the business is a retailer, avoid discussing points in a manufacturing context.

Human needs

Revised

A simple explanation of human need

You need to understand the **human needs** that can be satisfied in the workplace and the ways in which this might be achieved.

> **Human need:** the wants or desires of people whether at work or in their life in general.

Common needs

These include the need to:
- be able to enjoy the basic requirements for life, i.e. food, clothes and shelter
- be part of a social group
- have the respect of the people around you
- feel useful and valued at work and in life in general
- have the potential to improve yourself and also your standard of living

How human needs may or may not be satisfied at work

You need to be able to discuss how and to what extent human needs might be met by employers/managers. For example, a person might feel more valued and important at work if they are given some extra responsibility as this shows that they are trusted by their employer.

> **Revision activity**
>
> 1. Take each of the common needs mentioned opposite and suggest ways in which a business might meet that need in the workplace using the examples opposite as a guide.
> 2. Now take this one step further. Try to think of any possible problems or disadvantages that a business might experience when trying to satisfy the human needs of employees. For example, when giving extra responsibility to one employee this might upset other workers who might feel that they should have been given more responsibility too.

Motivation theories

The specified motivation theorists are:
- **Abraham Maslow** — the hierarchy of needs.
- **Frederick Taylor** — the notion of 'economic man'.
- **Elton Mayo** — the Hawthorne experiment.
- **Frederick Hertzberg** — the two-factor theory.
- **Douglas McClelland** — achievement, authority and affiliation.
- **Victor Vroom** — the expectancy theory.

You must be able to explain the content of the theories of each of the theorists above and be able to apply their ideas to an actual business situation. You should also be aware of any possible key differences or similarities between the ideas of each of these theorists.

> **Expert tip**
>
> A comparison of the ideas of various theorists can be a useful analytical approach to use when answering examination questions.

The ideas of motivation theorists

Abraham Maslow

Maslow's theory is based on successive human needs. He arranged these needs in the form of a pyramid with their order indicating the priority that they would take in the eyes of most employees (Figure 1). He identified a range of needs that he believed applied to employees. The basic needs must be satisfied first, then a series of needs arranged in a hierarchy. Satisfying these in turn can be used to motivate employees.

> **Now test yourself**
>
> 10 Explain the difference between 'social' and 'esteem' needs on Maslow's hierarchy of needs.
>
> **Answer on p.208**

Figure 1 Maslow's hierarchy of needs

Key points
- The needs at the bottom of the pyramid need to be satisfied first.
- Once a need has been met that need will no longer motivate.
- Needs are likely to change throughout a working life.
- People want different things out of life, and therefore each employee is likely to be motivated by wanting to satisfy different needs.

What implications does this have for employers and managers?
- Managers might need to change the ways in which they try to motivate workers.
- Workers are unlikely to all be motivated to satisfy the same need at the same time. This implies that there might be a need for managers to employ a different method of motivation for each employee.
- Managers also need to recognise that what might motivate workers is likely to be different at various times in their working life.

Frederick Taylor

The basis of Taylor's theory was that employees will give a fair day's work for a fair day's pay and that they are motivated by financial incentives. Put simply — find the best way of completing a task, train employees to employ the best method and pay them according to their output, i.e. **piece work**.

Taylor's theory assumed that people work harder in order to earn more money. Such ideas of motivation were believed to be more appropriate in a manufacturing environment where an actual measurable product was made. However, some people may strive for promotion in order to earn more money whilst at the same time they might be gaining greater job satisfaction and could be meeting their 'security needs' as identified by Maslow. Equally, whilst promotion might yield a higher rate of pay, it might also serve to satisfy the esteem needs of the employee due to being deemed suitable for a more responsible position. Success might earn the respect of his or her employees and co-workers.

As incomes rise people change their lifestyles as they aim to buy a bigger house, a better car and perhaps go on more holidays. This can then lead them to wanting to earn still more money to afford an even better lifestyle. Perhaps then, Taylor's ideas are still relevant for the increasing service sector of today.

Elton Mayo

Mayo's ideas developed out of the 'Hawthorne' experiment at the General Electric Company in Chicago. Mayo believed that the motivation levels of employees could be influenced by changes in their working conditions. However, he found that even when changes were made to the physical environment the level of output remained constant. This led him to conclude that employees were reacting to the attention being paid to them rather than to any changes in their working environment. They felt important to be part of the experiment and had also developed a team spirit that had a positive effect on their output.

Frederick Herzberg

Herzberg is known for his 'two-factor theory', the two factors being hygiene factors and motivators (see Figure 2 overleaf). He believed that hygiene factors do not motivate but that they prevent dissatisfaction, whereas the motivating factors can actually inspire people to work harder and better.

Revision activity

Draw up a table of how an owner/manager might ensure that the hygiene factors and motivators identified in Figure 2 overleaf can be satisfied.

Expert tip

You need to be able to discuss how employers/managers might meet the needs of their employees. For example, the basic needs of food, clothing and shelter can be met by earning a wage that is sufficient to purchase them.

Revision activity

For each of the 'needs' identified on Maslow's hierarchy suggest possible ways in which employers might try to meet them.

Piece work: workers are paid a stated amount for each unit produced.

Now test yourself

11 Explain what is mean by the term 'piece work'.
12 Explain how piece work might motivate employees.

Answers on p.208

Tested

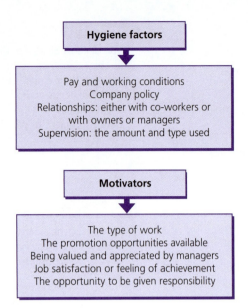

Figure 2 Herzberg's two-factor theory

> **Now test yourself**
>
> 13 Identify and explain the difference between the two factors of Herzberg's two-factor theory.
>
> **Answer on p.208**
>
> Tested

Douglas McClelland

McClelland's theory is based on the idea that employees need to feel a sense of **achievement**, **authority** and **affiliation**.

- **Achievement** is wanting to meet targets and goals that have been set either by the individual or by the business.
- **Authority** for employees is the need for power or influence over other employees or having some power over the way in which they undertake their work.
- **Affiliation** is seen as being the need of most employees to work in a 'friendly' environment and to be liked and included in formal and informal groups.

> **Now test yourself**
>
> 14 Explain the three key elements in the theory of Douglas McClelland.
>
> **Answer on p.208**
>
> Tested

Victor Vroom

Vroom's thesis was that employees would be prepared to work hard if they received suitable reward — hence the name of his **expectancy theory**. The three key factors in this theory are **valance**, **expectancy** and **instrumentality**.

Table 7 Vroom's factors

Valance	Expectancy	Instrumentality
Relates to how much employees feel the need for reward.	The extent to which employees believe that a better performance can be achieved if they increase their efforts.	The level of belief by employees that if their efforts are increased and their performance improves they will be rewarded appropriately.

Certain conditions are required in order for Vroom's theory to be used effectively:

- The employees must be capable of increasing or improving their performance. They might lack the required skills or they might already be working as hard as they possibly can.
- It must be possible to assess the performance of the workers in order that any increase in effort and performance can be rewarded.
- The rewards offered must be such that the employees want to obtain them.
- Finally, it is essential that the rewards offered are actually given when performance improves as expected. A failure to deliver expected rewards will undermine the motivational benefits of this approach.

> **Expert tip**
>
> If a question asks you to discuss motivation theory but does not specify which theorist(s), do not attempt to write about all of them. Select one or perhaps two that relate best to a situation that might be given in the question.

> **Now test yourself**
>
> 15 Explain why an effective appraisal system is essential if Vroom's motivation theory is to be successful.
>
> **Answer on p.208**
>
> Tested

Motivation methods in practice: financial and non-financial

Revised

Different payment methods

- **Piece work** — employees will strive to produce more units in order to receive more pay.
- **Commission** — paid to sales staff to encourage higher sales, usually giving a stated amount or percentage of the sale price for each sale made.
- **Bonuses** — often paid for hitting targets for levels of output or for meeting completion dates.
- **Salaries** — monthly payments for work done can give employees a feeling of security about their level of earnings.
- **Performance-related pay** — payments made for meeting or exceeding expected performance.
- **Profit-related pay** and **share ownership schemes** — both of these are based on unifying the aims of the business with those of the employees. If the business is profitable, the employees receive a share of the profit or receive shares in the business as a reward for their efforts.
- **Fringe benefits** such as the use of a company car. This reduces the costs to the employee of running a car.

> **Piece work:** where payment is made to workers based on the number of units produced, i.e. payment per unit produced.
>
> **Commission:** a payment made according to the number of sales achieved. This is usually a percentage of the selling price of a product.
>
> **Salary:** a monthly payment made to employees as a reward for their work. It is usually a fixed and agreed amount.
>
> **Performance-related pay:** a payment made to employees, usually half-yearly or annually, that rewards them for achieving or exceeding expectations in their performance at work.

Different types of non-financial motivators

These can be used as well as or instead of financial motivators.

- **Training** — induction training or in-service training that might be on-the-job or off-the-job.
- **Promotion opportunities** — the possibility of future promotion can encourage employees to work with more effort in order to be noticed and hopefully rewarded.
- **Staff development** — opportunities to obtain new skills and experience that can improve job satisfaction and can also increase the status of the employee as well as improving their chance of promotion in the future.
- **Status** — this appeals to the 'esteem needs' of employees and can be achieved by giving an employee a job title, e.g. team leader. This can also be achieved by giving an employee more responsibility. This is not a promotion but gives the employee a feeling of higher status and importance.
- **Job re-design** — restructuring a job or changing some of the tasks involved. This can include job rotation where a team of workers periodically change the task they perform within the group. This can help to prevent boredom and can include job enlargement (job widening) where an employee is given other, different tasks to complete.
- **Job enrichment** — an employee is given a wider range of tasks that are more complex and therefore more challenging (job deepening). Being asked to perform tasks requiring higher-level skills is likely to raise an employee's sense of importance.
- **Teamworking** — encouraging groups of employees to work together towards a common goal, e.g. cell production and quality circles.
- **Empowerment** — allowing employees to make some of the decisions regarding their tasks, e.g. let them decide how a particular task should be carried out or who, within a group, will carry out which task. 'Empowered' teams are also expected to solve any problems that they encounter by discussing the issue within the group and agreeing on an appropriate solution.

> **Expert tip**
>
> A possible analytical approach might be to consider the relative costs of various incentives. The financial incentives might be too costly for a business particularly if it is experiencing a downturn in demand or if the economy is in recession.

> **Expert tip**
>
> Frequently candidates write about all the incentives that they can remember. Make sure that you only write about incentives that are relevant to the question and the context given.

> **Revision activity**
>
> Draw up two tables, one for financial motivators and one for non-financial motivators. Using one column for each type of motivator write in as many work situations as you can think of where each motivator might be appropriate. For example, teamworking might be effective in a production facility or in a retail store where different departments can work together as one team.

- **Participation** — involvement in decision-making, e.g. by inviting some employees to management meetings or through the use of regular departmental meetings and works councils.
- **Perks**, e.g. giving some extra days holiday to employees, improving the canteen facilities or by offering them subsidised meals.

Ways in which employees can participate in the management and control of business activity

These are outlined under 'participation' above and can also include worker directors. Whether using financial or non-financial motivators, it is important that the method used is appropriate to the employee and to the type of work being undertaken.

> **Now test yourself**
>
> 16 Explain two financial motivators that might be used by a retail business.
> 17 Explain two non-financial motivators that might be used by a manufacturer of plastic buckets.
>
> **Answers on p.208**
>
> Tested

Human resource management

Purpose and roles of human resource management

Revised

Human resource management (HRM) aims to ensure that a business has the appropriate number of employees with the appropriate skills at the time and place that they are required.

The role of HRM in meeting organisation objectives
- Recruit and select new staff when additional personnel are required.
- Induction: arrange for new staff to be familiarised with the organisation, structure, policies and working practices.
- Organise any necessary training. This might be for new or existing personnel who might need to acquire new skills or improve existing ones.
- Record key performance indicators and conduct staff appraisal.
- Advise management and employees on issues such as staff training and development needs and opportunities, promotion routes, employment contracts and redundancy issues.
- Disciplinary and grievance procedures — provide advice to employees and managers.
- Monitor staff morale and welfare.
- Negotiate with employees, management and trade unions.
- **Workforce planning** — anticipate the future labour requirements, comparing those needs with the current workforce and making plans to correct any imbalance so that the business will have the correct number of employees when required and with the appropriate skills.
- Dismiss staff when necessary.
- Administer a redundancy procedure if required.
- Ensure that employment legislation is complied with and deal with issues arising if the legislation is breached.

> **Workforce planning:** anticipating and acquiring the number of employees with the knowledge and skills that will be required by the business in the future compared to those currently employed.

> **Now test yourself**
>
> 18 Explain three of the functions that would be undertaken by a human resource management department.
>
> **Answer on p.208**
>
> Tested

Recruitment and selection

Revised

Labour turnover

The rate of **labour turnover** within a business will determine the amount of recruitment and selection that will need to be undertaken.

The possible causes of a high rate of labour turnover include:
- employees leave to work for another business
- employees retire

> **Labour turnover:** the number of people leaving a business in a specified time period as a percentage of the average number of employees. It is calculated by:
>
> $$\frac{\text{number of employees leaving in a year}}{\text{average number of employees}} \times 100$$

- dismissal
- redundancy

Methods of recruitment and selection

A business might need to recruit workers for the following reasons:
- growth of the business
- workers have left to work elsewhere
- the business has relocated or is now operating in an additional location
- changes in the business's activities mean that the business labour requirements have changed either in numbers or with regard to the knowledge and skills required

Recruitment

Internal and external recruitment

Internal recruitment is filling a vacant post with a person already working within the business.

Table 8 Advantages and disadvantages of internal recruitment

Advantages	Disadvantages
The business already knows the candidate.	There might be a better candidate externally.
Saves time and advertising costs.	Prevents new ideas being brought in from outside of the business.
Faster: the selection process is likely to be much shorter due to so much already being known about the candidate.	It can be difficult for someone to have to supervise their former colleagues.
Motivating: employees see that their efforts might be rewarded by internal promotion.	It can be demotivating for unsuccessful internal applicants.

External recruitment means appointing someone from outside of the business, i.e. someone who is not currently working for the business.

Table 9 Advantages and disadvantages of external recruitment

Advantages	Disadvantages
The business can gain from new ideas being brought in and can possibly benefit from knowledge and skills acquired in other businesses.	Can be more expensive and time consuming.
Avoids the potential for line management problems that can occur when recruiting internally.	An unsuccessful internal candidate might be demotivated and might look for work elsewhere.
	The new appointee will not be familiar with the internal structure and systems of the business; an internal appointment would already have that knowledge.

Revision activities

1. Draw up a list of reasons why a retail business might benefit from using internal recruitment to fill a shop manager's post.
2. Draw up a list of reasons (for and against) a business in a high technology industry sector using external recruitment to fill a vacancy for someone to join its research and development team.

Now test yourself

19 Explain two reasons why a business might prefer to recruit internally.
20 Distinguish between internal and external recruitment.

Answers on p.208

Job descriptions, person specifications, job advertisements

Revised

Once it has been decided that there is actually a post that must be filled, the HRM department will find out exactly what tasks and responsibilities will be involved in the job. A job description and a person specification/profile will be written.

Purposes of job descriptions
A **job description** includes details such as the tasks and responsibilities that the successful candidate would be expected to undertake. It can also include the pay for the job and any holiday entitlements. It also usually explains who a person would report to and who they will be responsible for.

Purposes of person specifications
A **person specification** describes the qualities, skills and qualifications that applicants should have if they are to be considered for the advertised post. Some aspects might be declared as essential and others as desirable.

Purposes of job advertisements
A **job advertisement** must be written so that only suitable applicants are attracted to apply. There should be sufficient detail to attract appropriate candidates and to deter those who do not have the relevant qualities, skills, qualifications or experience.

> **Job description:** outlines the tasks and responsibilities of a particular job. It also outlines who reports to the person and who they report to.
>
> **Person specification:** details the personal qualities, experience and qualifications required to fill a vacant post. Essential and desirable requirements are likely to be stated.
>
> **Job advertisement:** a notice placed in appropriate places, e.g. newspapers and notice boards, designed to encourage suitable applicants to apply for a vacant post. Job advertisements should give sufficient information to attract suitable candidates and to deter unsuitable ones.

Details required in a job advertisement
These include:
- job title
- where the job is (some larger companies might have several branches)
- essential skills, qualifications and personal qualities (and sometimes desirable ones)
- brief details of what the job involves
- the pay and conditions package
- how to apply, i.e. by letter, by telephone or online, application form or curriculum vitae
- who to address the application to, e.g. the HR manager or to a recruitment agency

When drawing up a job advertisement the business must comply with all relevant employment legislation and should ensure that the advertisement does not imply any disadvantage to any applicants because of their religion, gender, any disability or their sexual orientation.

Methods of reaching potential applicants
- **Recruitment agencies** including online agencies.
- **Head-hunting** — poaching experienced people away from other businesses.
- **Government funded careers/job centres** — many countries have a network of offices to support job searches.
- **Internet sites** — this might be through the business's own website or others specialising in job searches.
- **Personal contacts** — the people already in the business might know of suitable friends and/or family.

> **Now test yourself**
>
> 21 Explain the difference between a job specification and a person specification.
> 22 Describe two methods of advertising that a business might use to attract applicants to a vacant post.
> 23 Identify three methods of reaching potential applicants for a job.
>
> Answers on p.208
>
> Tested

> **Expert tip**
>
> When answering questions on HRM make sure that you do not confuse the recruitment process with the selection process.

Selection

Once a business has received applications for the vacant post it must decide if any of the applicants are suitable to be offered the post. After any unsuitable applicants have been rejected the process of selecting the most suitable applicant begins. This might be achieved by:

- **Interviewing all suitable applicants.** Interviews can be formal or informal. Questions can be asked by both the interviewer(s) and the applicant and the body language of the applicant can be assessed, unless a telephone interview is used. However, some people perform well in interviews and can mislead the interviewers about their ability to perform the task in question. Effective interviewing is not easy and the success of interviews depends on the skill of the interviewer(s). Interviewing can also be very time-consuming.
- **Aptitude tests** — short tests designed to test the suitability of the applicant to the actual tasks to be performed.
- **Psychometric tests** to assess, for example, how an applicant might react to a highly stressful situation or whether he or she is likely to be an effective member of a team.
- **Demonstrations or presentations** given by the applicant. For example, a person applying for a supervisory post might be asked to take part in a role play to show how he or she might deal with a difficult situation or conduct a staff meeting.

> **Now test yourself**
> 24 Explain two methods of selection giving examples of how each of them might be used.
> **Answer on p.208**
> Tested

Employment contracts

Revised

In many countries the law requires that a new employee, or one that has had a change of position within a business, must be given an **employment contract**.

> **Employment contract:** a legally binding document outlining the terms and conditions of employment such as pay, holidays, tasks and responsibilities.

The main features of a contract of employment

- Details of the job including the job title and the main tasks and responsibilities involved.
- The agreed working hours — hours per week or month or perhaps annualised hours.
- How long the contract will be valid for if it is a short-term contract.
- Details of pay and how payment will be calculated and paid, e.g. weekly or monthly.
- Holiday entitlement.
- Details of how the contract can be ended, e.g. the notice required to terminate the contract by either the employer or the employee.

The benefits of an employment contract

The contract ensures that the employer and employee are both clear about the terms and conditions that have been agreed. In the case of a dispute arising this can be resolved by checking the details of the employment contract.

Reasons for terminating an employment contract

- Agreed changes in the contract of employment as a result of negotiation or promotion.
- Resignation of the employee.
- Breach of the terms of the contract by either the employee or the employer.
- A short-term contract might have reached the end of the time period agreed.

> **Now test yourself**
> 25 State two features of an employment contract.
> **Answer on p.208**
> Tested

Human resource management

Disciplinary procedures

Revised ☐

The importance of disciplinary procedures
- To avoid claims of wrongful or **unfair dismissal**. If an employee is dismissed without appropriate procedures being followed they might argue that they should not have been dismissed.
- To inform employees of the process that they and the employer must follow in the case of any failure to comply with rules and systems in place.
- To comply with employment legislation. If details of the disciplinary procedures are outlined in the contract of employment and are not then followed when disciplinary action is taken, the employee can deem that the employer is in breach of contract. This can result in the employer having to pay compensation to the employee who was a victim of unfair dismissal.

> **Unfair dismissal:** when the employment of a worker is terminated without just cause.

The information an employee needs to know
- What rules and regulations they must follow.
- Who they report to in the case of disciplinary action being taken or who they should appeal to if a decision is taken that they do not agree with.
- What steps will be followed during the procedure and as a result of disciplinary action being taken, e.g. the number of verbal and written warnings that will be given before dismissal becomes a possibility.
- What kind of behaviour can result in immediate dismissal.

Behaviour that might lead to disciplinary action being taken
- **Persistent lateness or absenteeism.** The need for punctuality and regular attendance at work is often an implied contract term and although not stated explicitly can be the subject of disciplinary action.
- **A persistent failure to meet targets for work completed.** This could be interpreted as an inability to complete the work required in a particular job. Perhaps the employee is not capable of working faster or more accurately. Further training may be needed in some cases rather than disciplinary action.
- **Unacceptable behaviour.** This can include acting in a way that might cause damage to property or injury to fellow workers or acting in a way that humiliates another worker.
- **Theft of goods or property from the business.**

Grievance procedures
- These are sometimes caused by disciplinary action being taken against an employee. A grievance can be pursued either informally or formally through the official channels available within the business.
- Employers must make the details available to employees. This might be via an employee handbook or they can be included in the contract of employment. Employers are required to ensure that employees know of the existence of such procedures and where details of them can be found.
- Employees feeling that they have a valid grievance are often advised to speak to the person or persons involved on an informal basis first. Sometimes the reason for the grievance might be seen to be unreasonable once a thorough explanation of any action has been given to the employee.
- A formal procedure is likely to involve a meeting between the employee and the manager or other involved parties to determine the facts of the grievance. Issues can often be resolved at this stage by each party recognising the facts and reaching some form of compromise.

- If an initial meeting cannot resolve the issue, the manager(s) must investigate the problem and make a decision about any action that might need to be taken.
- Employees should be made aware of how they can appeal if they do not agree with the decision made.
- The rules affecting grievance procedures can vary from one country to another.

Redundancy and dismissal

Revised

Difference between redundancy and dismissal

Redundancy is when the business no longer requires a particular job to be done. It is important to remember that it is the job that is no longer needed not the person doing the job.

Dismissal is when the employment contract of a worker is terminated by the employer.

> **Redundancy:** when a business no longer requires a particular job to be done, which means that the worker doing that job is no longer required by the business.
>
> **Dismissal:** when the employment contract of a worker is terminated by the employer.

Reasons for dismissal

These include:
- failing to work to a required standard
- persistent absenteeism if absence was unauthorised
- persistent late arrival for work
- using violent or threatening behaviour
- being dishonest during the recruitment and selection process
- damaging the goods or the property of the business
- stealing goods or property from the business

The last four reasons in this list would justify instant dismissal without the payment of any monies in lieu of notice being given.

> **Now test yourself**
>
> 26 Briefly explain the difference between redundancy and dismissal.
>
> **Answer on p.208**
>
> Tested

Staff morale and welfare

Revised

The human resource management department aims to ensure high levels of staff morale and welfare. Low levels of staff morale and welfare can result in a poorer standard of work and can also cause an increase in absenteeism and labour turnover as well as poor punctuality. The welfare of workers is also important because if, for example, an employee is experiencing problems in their private life this can negatively affect their ability to work well.

The relationship between HRM and staff morale and welfare

The HRM department should do the following:
- Ensure that health and safety legislation is followed. The department should also deal with any problems that arise if there is a breach of health and safety laws.
- Offer help and guidance to employees who are being affected by problems outside work such as housing or personal issues, e.g. a serious illness in the family.
- Encourage and monitor the provision of some level of health care within the business.
- Monitor the levels of motivation in the business and encourage appropriate action when necessary.

> **Expert tip**
>
> For the purpose of analysis, staff morale and welfare can often be developed in the context of motivation. But do not write all you know about motivation — keep the focus on the precise question set — HRM in this case.

Staff training

The purpose of staff training and development

Training and development takes place in order to ensure that employees have the required knowledge and skills to perform their tasks to the best of their ability. Training needs can arise for a variety of reasons:

- When a person is newly appointed to work for a business they will need to be made familiar with the structure and systems in the business.
- When an employee takes on a new role if the business diversifies either into new products or into totally new business activities. For example, a food manufacturing business might begin to produce cooking utensils and therefore existing staff might need to acquire new skills and knowledge.
- If an employee is under-performing and it is believed that additional training might resolve the problem.
- The promotion of an employee to a more senior post. It could be that the employee will need to acquire some supervisory skills and to understand some management issues that he or she did not have to deal with in the previous post.

> **Expert tip**
>
> When writing about training, make sure that you are answering in context and that the training you suggest is relevant to the situation given in the case study or question. Do not write all you know about training if the question is about a specific type of training in a particular business situation.

Types of training

Training can take various forms:

- **Induction training** — given to new employees to help them to familiarise themselves with all aspects of the business and their role in it.
- **On-the-job training** — carried out at the place of work and involves learning by watching an experienced worker or by being given instructions about how to perform the required tasks.
- **Off-the-job training** — carried out away from the place of work, for example, at a local training centre or college.

Table 10 Training methods: advantages and disadvantages

Type of training	Advantages	Disadvantages
On-the-job	• Training will be directly relevant to the work to be done and to the business. • It can be motivating for the worker chosen to train the new worker. • Employees are contributing to production while training. • Generally cheaper than off-the-job training.	• The 'trainer' is being drawn away from his or her own work, resulting in lower output. • The trainee learns how to perform specific tasks but may lack any understanding of what else the business does. • Costly production errors can be made during training.
Off-the-job	• Employees are not taken away from their work to train new people. • Trainers are likely to be more experienced in teaching. • Employees might acquire a broader skills and knowledge base than on on-the-job training.	• The employees are not producing anything for the business while away being trained. • Not all of the skills and knowledge might be relevant to the business. • It can be expensive.

A disadvantage of any type of training is that more highly trained employees become more attractive to other employers, so they are more likely to leave. In addition, the employees might judge themselves to be worthy of a higher level of pay.

An advantage is the increased level of motivation that employees might feel because they are likely to feel more valued and important if their employer is willing to spend money on training them. They might also feel more able to apply for higher level posts and therefore feel more fulfilled in their working life.

Now test yourself — Tested

27 Briefly explain two benefits to a business of training its employees.
28 Distinguish between on-the-job training and off-the-job training.

Answers on p.208–9

3 Marketing

What is marketing?

The role of marketing and its relationship with other business activities

Revised

Marketing is the process of identifying, anticipating and satisfying customer requirements profitably. To market a product a business must:
- Find out through market research what customers want and how much they are prepared to pay.
- Use this information to produce appropriate products at a cost that will make the selling price acceptable to consumers and enable the business to make a profit.
- Communicate information about the product, its price and how to buy it to potential customers through a range of marketing activities in such a way that they decide to make a purchase.
- Ensure that the marketing functional area works together with other areas including production, human resources, finance and operations planning to make sure that the 4Ps — **p**roduct, **p**rice, **p**romotion and **p**lace — are right.

> **Marketing:** the process of identifying, anticipating and satisfying customer requirements profitably.

Example

Disposable barbecues will be made of inexpensive materials, sold at a low price in many shops, garages and holiday destinations and be promoted with in-store signs and posters.

> **Expert tip**
>
> Marketing integrates a range of ideas; it is not just about advertising and promotion and is integrated with other functional areas, e.g. production, finance and HRM.

Marketing objectives and corporate objectives

Corporate objectives are the goals or targets the whole business is trying to achieve. These provide a framework for all activities and set the purpose for all employees. The marketing objectives should be related to these and help to achieve them. In 2011, Unilever set an objective of doubling the size of the business while reducing the environmental footprint. This involves marketing objectives of selling increasingly environmentally friendly products and packaging, using promotion and advertising to encourage consumers to buy more environmentally friendly products, sourcing sustainably, not increasing prices and increasing the number of places Unilever products are available in.

Marketing objectives may relate to sales revenue, sales volume, customer awareness, changes in product ranges, market share, brand loyalty, repeat purchases, new markets, customer satisfaction and new products.

> **Expert tip**
>
> Remember that marketing objectives should be SMART — **S**pecific, **M**easurable, **A**ttainable/agreed, **R**ealistic, and in a **T**imeframe.

Now test yourself *Tested*

1. State a possible business objective and identify two appropriate marketing objectives.
2. For both of these marketing objectives identify an appropriate objective for each of the four P elements — product, price, promotion and place.

Answers on p.209

Supply and demand

Revised

Businesses sell their products in markets. A **market** is a place or system that enables producers of a good or service to meet potential buyers and exchange these products for money. Producers supply goods or services, customers demand goods or services.

> **Market:** a place or system that enables producers of a good or service to meet potential buyers and exchange these products for money.

Factors influencing supply

Supply is the quantity of goods or services being made available for sale at a particular price and time. Supply depends on how much profit businesses think can be made, so the main factors influencing supply are:

- **Price** — if the price of a good rises, a greater quantity will be supplied to the market (greater profits act as an incentive) and vice versa.
- **Costs** — if the cost of producing a good rises, a smaller quantity will be supplied to the market (less profits act as a disincentive) and vice versa.

As an example, the price of oil is rising, so many companies are exploring increasing oil production by fracking (using high pressure water to force oil from oil shale deposits). The cost of producing batteries and charging systems for electric cars is falling and the supply of these is increasing.

> **Supply:** the supply of a good is the quantity of goods or services being made available for sale at a particular price and time.

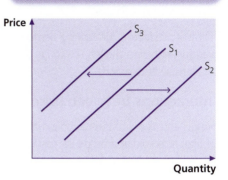

Figure 1 Supply curve shifts

The cost of a product is influenced by:

- the costs of production (labour, materials, fuel and rent)
- advances in technology resulting in lower costs, e.g. IT systems reduce administration costs
- taxes, which increase costs, e.g. increasing taxes on tobacco products, and subsidies, which decrease costs
- government regulations, e.g. health and safety requirements

The supply curve in Figure 1 shows the effects of these influences on supply. It plots the quantity of a good supplied against the price of the good. The curve slopes upward left to right (S_1) showing that as the price increases so does the quantity supplied.

If any of these four influences change, the supply curve will move its position. A fall in costs will move the supply curve to the right (an increase in supply) S_1 to S_2, and a rise in costs will move the supply curve to the left (a decrease in supply) S_1 to S_3.

> **Expert tip**
>
> Make sure that you consider changes in the factors influencing supply or demand one at a time. Each change has its own effect.

> **Now test yourself**
>
> 3 Identify two factors that might influence the supply of breakfast cereals.
> 4 What effect do the following have on the supply curve for taxi services?
>   (a) the price of taxi rides
>   (b) the introduction of very cheap electric cars
>
> **Answers on p.209**
>
> Tested

Factors influencing demand

Demand is the quantity of a good or service that customers are willing and able to buy at a particular price and time. Price is a key determinant of demand, as generally the cheaper a product is the more people will wish to buy it and vice versa because:

- with their income they can afford to increase their purchases
- it becomes relatively cheaper compared to other goods

Examples are foreign holidays and electric cars.

Other factors that influence demand are:

- **The price of related goods**, e.g. as computer prices have fallen, the sales of printers have risen (negative relationship), or as price of milk rises, sales of soya substitute milk also rise (positive relationship).
- **Income** — a person with increasing income will usually buy more of a product, e.g. foreign holidays, coffee or restaurant meals. But for some products demand falls as income rises, e.g. margarine, low-quality shoes.

> **Demand:** the quantity of a good or service which customers are willing and able to buy at a particular price and time.

- **Fashion and attitudes** — these are influenced by the media, government actions and advertising, e.g. smoking is decreasing as increased regulation and advertisements stress its harmful effects. Conversely, advertising and promotion are used to shift the demand curve to the right to increase demand for many products.
- **Seasonal factors**, e.g. ice cream is demanded more in summer, while the demand for Christmas decorations increases in November and December.
- **Demographic factors** — age and gender distribution affect demand, as different groups demand different products.

> **Now test yourself**
>
> 5. Identify three factors that influence the demand for fashionable boots.
> 6. What effect do the following have on the demand curve for taxi services?
>   (a) price of taxi rides
>   (b) train fares are reduced by a large amount
>
> **Answers on p.209**
>
> Tested

In Figure 2, the demand curve shows the effects of these influences on demand. It plots the quantity of a good demanded against the price of the good. The curve slopes downwards left to right (D_1) showing that as the price increases the quantity demanded falls.

If any of the factors influencing demand change, the demand curve will move its position, either to the left (D_1 to D_3, a fall in demand) or to the right (D_1 to D_2, an increase in demand).

Interactions between price, supply and demand

Supply and demand interact in a market to produce an equilibrium quantity bought and sold at a particular market price. Unless there are changes to the factors influencing supply and demand, the quantity and price will remain the same. Any changes will alter the quantity and price. This means that businesses must pay attention to market conditions and be ready to respond to changes in costs, competitor's actions, government policies and changes in society. They may wish to be proactive and try to change the demand or supply curves by investing in lower-cost equipment or increasing spending on advertising and promotion.

In Figure 3, at point A, S_1 and D_1 cross, giving a quantity bought and sold of q_1 at a price p_1. Then a factor influencing demand changes and demand increases, shifting the demand curve to D_2, crossing the supply curve at B, giving a new quantity and price of q_2 and p_2. Finally, a factor influencing supply changes and the supply curve shifts to S_2, crossing the demand curve at C, giving a final quantity and price of q_3 and p_3.

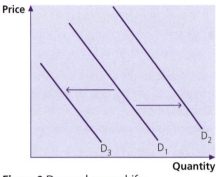

Figure 2 Demand curve shifts

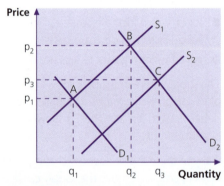

Figure 3 The operation of supply and demand curves

> **Revision activity**
>
> 1. Consider Figure 3 above showing the operation of supply and demand curves in the car market.
>   (a) Suggest two possible reasons for the shift of demand from D_1 to D_2.
>   (b) Suggest two possible reasons for the shift of supply from S_1 to S_2.
> 2. Choose a product you are familiar with. Outline the main factors that determine its demand.
> 3. Eazicut is a hairdressing shop, with separate facilities for males and females. It offers low price services and for 10 years has worked at nearly full capacity with a profit margin of 17%. This year customer numbers and revenue have fallen. The landlord has increased the rent and the semi-skilled workforce has succeeded in gaining a significant pay rise. Profits have started to fall. Two new hairdressing shops have opened and they both offer other services including manicure, head massages and henna tattoos. Family incomes in the town have risen and a fast main road to a city 25km away has been open for 6 months. The owner of Eazicut is seriously worried. She is considering the following options:
>   - an advertising campaign
>   - better equipment to reduce the time taken for each customer
>
>   (a) Explain two supply factors that might have contributed to Eazicut's falling profits.
>   (b) Explain two demand factors that might have contributed to Eazicut's falling profits.
>   (c) Using supply and demand diagrams, show how each of the owner's two options will increase the number of customers.

> **Expert tip**
> Supply and demand diagrams may be drawn with no numerical axes but make sure you clearly label the axes, the supply and demand curves, the equilibrium prices and quantities.

> **Now test yourself**
> 7 Define the following terms:
>   (a) supply
>   (b) demand
>   (c) market price
>
> Answers on p.209
>
> Tested

Features of markets

Revised

A market brings buyers and sellers of a product together. However, it is not always easy to decide exactly how a product may be defined. For example, there is a market for footwear. Within this market there are submarkets for various types of shoes and boots. Very few people would think the market for ladies' fashion shoes is the same market as for work boots or golfing shoes. A business must be able to define its market for its own products in order to make sure that they are appealing to the correct type of customer when the business carries out marketing activities and takes account of its competitors. Businesses have a choice; their products can be either product- or market-orientated:

- **Product-orientated.** This means producing a product and then trying to sell it. This will involve a focus on research and development.
- **Market-orientated.** This means finding out the needs of the market and then producing a product to meet those needs, whatever they are. This will involve a focus on market research.

> **Now test yourself**
> 8 Is a company supplying steel toe safety boots in the building/construction industry or in the 'what to wear on your feet' market?
> 9 Suggest one way your answer to the above question might affect the way the business carries out its marketing.
>
> Answers on p.209
>
> Tested

Consumer/producer markets

Defining the buyer in a market is very important because this will determine how to market a product. The seller must try and meet the needs of the buyer. Many products are designed to be sold to consumers. Consumers are the end-users and buy goods such as shoes, cell phones, fizzy drinks, furniture and household items. They typically buy from a store or increasingly online and are looking for products that make them feel good. Other products are bought by producers who will use them in production. These include goods like tractors, office equipment, lathes and other machinery. Producers are looking for technical performance, efficiency and low cost. They will often buy from sales staff, from dedicated wholesale stores or direct from the seller.

Selling in a **consumer market** involves marketing to many people who the seller does not know and arranging suitable distribution channels. Selling in a **producer market** involves marketing to a smaller number of buyers, many of whom can be approached directly and are less influenced by advertising and more by specification and price.

> **Consumer market:** a market where the main customers are individuals or households.
>
> **Producer market:** a market where the main customers are other businesses.

> **Now test yourself**
> Tested
>
> 10 Consider the following products. For each, decide whether it is a consumer or a producer product.
>   (a) shrink wrapping machine
>   (b) evening dress
>   (c) bubble gum
>   (d) large computer system
>   (e) spreadsheet
>   (f) saloon car
>
> Answers on p.209

> **Expert tip**
> When answering a marketing question make sure you identify the type of market the product is being sold in before considering marketing methods.

Location

A market may be found in a national, regional or international setting. Each has customers with different needs and businesses must be aware of this. Some markets are extremely local with buyers looking for sellers who are nearby. Services such as small shops, restaurants and garages are often located close to where customers might be. Businesses in local markets are finding that the internet means that consumers far away may be able to buy online, and the increase in the size of businesses means many local services are now provided by large national firms.

National, regional and international markets

- **National markets** — many countries have consumers with national characteristics and needs. A country forms a distinct unit that makes it a target for marketing to. National transport systems, laws and behaviour mean that businesses that are large enough to market to the whole country can use mass media to do so.
- **Regional markets** — these are the next step up geographically. A regional market may cover a set of countries that have something in common, e.g. belonging to a free trade area like ASEAN, a political group like the EU or being close together geographically or culturally like the Middle East countries. Selling to a region means that the products offered across the region must be similar and marketed in similar ways.
- **International markets** — many consumers across the world have the same needs. Globalisation has meant that products that appeal to human needs are now marketed across the world. Soft drinks, coffee, fashion wear and cars are now globally marketed, with the same techniques possibly adjusted for small differences between countries and regions. This means that the global message must be the same in every place a product is sold.

> **Now test yourself**
>
> 11 Assign these products to one of the following types of market — local, national, regional or international.
> (a) jeans
> (b) painter/decorator
> (c) chocolate bar
> (d) golf club
> (e) oil drilling equipment
> (f) sports car
> (g) cigarettes
>
> Answers on p.209
>
> Tested

Market size, market share and market growth

- **Market size** is the total sales by all the businesses supplying that market. It is usually expressed in sales revenue that will equal total consumer spending on all products in that market. Sometimes sales volume is used as a measure of size. This could be total tonnes, litres or unit numbers. Market size measures how large a market is.
- **Market growth** is the percentage or absolute increase in the size of a market. This is a measure of how fast the market is growing.
- **Market share** is the percentage of the total market held by a business or product. Usually this is measured by value.

$$\text{market share} = \frac{\text{sales value or volume of business}}{\text{total market sales value or volume}} \times 100$$

> **Market size:** the total sales revenue or volume in the market.
>
> **Market growth:** the absolute or percentage increase in the size of a market.
>
> **Market share:** the percentage of the total market held by a business or product.

Problems associated with measuring market share and growth

- It may be difficult to define a market accurately.
- Data will never be totally up to date and are difficult to obtain.
- Products may change rapidly.

Implications of changes in market growth and market share

Understanding **market growth** is important because:

- the faster a market grows the more attractive it is to firms who might decide to enter it
- firms in a growing market are likely to see sales rise with the market growth
- firms in a growing market are likely to face more competition
- a declining market may mean falling sales and more competition

> **Expert tip**
>
> Make sure that you do not confuse the growth of a market (changes in market size) with changes in market share (changes in % of sales held by one firm).

Understanding **market share** is important because:
- it enables a business to compare performance with competitors and its own targets
- a high market share generally means a business has been successful in meeting customer needs and gaining some control over the market
- a high market share may mean either competition is likely or that any competition has been minimised
- a low market share may indicate a new product or that a product is near the end of its life, or possibly a market with a large number of businesses

Market share data must be analysed carefully in order to decide which explanation fits. This understanding will enable a business to make decisions about its marketing activities.

Revision activity

Computer tablets: Worldwide sales quarter 2, 2011–12, 000s units

Seller	Market sales 2011	Market share (%) 2011	Market sales 2012	Market share (%) 2012	Company growth (%) 2011–12
Apple	9,248	62	17,042	68	84
Samsung	1,099	?	2,391	?	118
Amazon	0	–	1,252	5	–
ASUS	397	3	855	?	116
Acer	629	?	385	2	–39
Others	3,668	24	3,067	?	–16
Total	15,042		24,994		?

Source: www.idc.com

1. Outline reasons why this data may not be accurate.
2. Calculate the following:
   (a) the missing market shares
   (b) total market growth, absolutely and as a percentage
3. To what extent is the worldwide tablet market growing?
4. Explain which company would be most pleased with these figures.
5. Explain which company would be least pleased with these figures.
6. Discuss whether the tablet market is becoming more competitive.
7. Choose two of the five named companies. Using the data, suggest possible objectives for each of them in the next year.

Now test yourself

12 Define the following terms:
   (a) market share
   (b) market growth
   (c) consumer market
   (d) national market

Answers on p.209

Tested

Industrial and consumer markets

Revised

Many products and services are sold to meet consumer needs. Consumers sometimes buy direct from a producer (restaurant meals, craft fairs) and often from a distributor, i.e. from a shop or market stall. It is difficult for a producer to communicate to all consumers who may buy on the basis of emotion or envy and be heavily influenced by fashion or advertising.

Producers are looking for different products, often components or machinery, and will buy in an industrial market, often referred to as business-to-business or B2B markets. Buyers are seeking performance, efficiency and low cost as they will use the products in their business to produce finished goods for sale. Suppliers will only need to find ways to market to appropriate businesses rather than engage in mass marketing.

> **Now test yourself** — Tested
>
> 13 Decide whether these products are sold in consumer or industrial markets:
>   (a) cough sweets
>   (b) 30 tonne lorry
>   (c) Wellington boots
>   (d) pocket radios
>   (e) brakes for cars
> 14 Identify one difference in the way a product may be marketed to a consumer market compared to a producer market.
>
> **Answers on p.209**

Product differentiation and unique selling point (USP)

Product differentiation is the degree to which customers perceive a product or brand to be different from the competition. It enables a business to build value and customer loyalty.

USP is the one particular factor that makes a product different. Consumers then feel that only this product meets their needs and will often be willing to pay a premium price.

Product differentiation or a USP can be achieved through:
- advertising, marketing or price
- individual design or performance
- packaging and branding
- distribution methods

Product differentiation: the degree to which customers perceive a product or brand to be different from the competition.

Unique selling point (USP): the one particular factor that makes a product different.

Expert tip
Be prepared to illustrate your answers with an example you have researched or know about.

> **Now test yourself** — Tested
>
> 15 Define USP.
> 16 State two ways a business may create a USP.
>
> **Answers on p.209**

Niche versus mass marketing — Revised

Niche marketing is when a business satisfies the needs of a small segment of a larger market. It is vital to identify the particular needs of this segment before marketing the product. Niche markets often:
- are concerned with specialist products
- enable the first company to enter to build a dominant position
- allow businesses to charge a premium price and are thus very profitable
- are relatively small with restricted growth potential and little opportunity for reducing average production costs
- become competitive as businesses are attracted to high profit margins

Mass marketing is selling to the whole of a market. This means a business must be able to supply large quantities of a product that appeals to all the market. Mass marketing businesses often:
- supply large quantities at low prices
- create a brand that customers can easily identify

Niche marketing: when a business satisfies the needs of a small segment of a larger market.

Mass marketing: selling to the whole of a market.

- need to spend large amounts on advertising
- need mass distribution channels
- operate in competitive markets
- try and build up a USP

Segmentation methods

Revised

Niche marketing is a particular form of segmentation. **Segmentation** is the process of identifying particular groups in a market that have similar needs and wants. It requires market research to establish the segments. These groups are likely to have the same characteristics meaning that:

- marketing can be aimed specifically at these groups and not at people unlikely to buy
- the product can be differentiated to appeal to the segment
- other niches may be found that have little or no competition

Important segmentation methods

Demographics
- **Age:** different ages tend to have different needs, e.g. most mobility scooters are used by older people; younger people have particular needs for entertainment.
- **Gender:** cosmetics are primarily used by women.
- **Type of household:** people living on their own have different needs from a family group with children.

Socioeconomic factors
- **Socioeconomic group (SEG):** measured by a mixture of income, education and occupation — different SEGs might read different newspapers.
- **Types of products purchased:** a detailed database may show variation in the timing of purchase and type of product bought.

Psychographics
- **Personality and attitudes:** psychologists identify different types, e.g. early adopters will buy new products as soon as they come out, for a high price.
- **Lifestyle:** full-time workers need different things from those who have retired.
- **Geographical location:** different areas may show different preferences.

Once a segment has been identified, appropriate marketing methods can be used to influence those in the segment to buy.

Portfolio analysis

Portfolio analysis considers the range of products a business produces in the light of the markets it operates in. It considers market growth, market share and segmentation in order to plan the best range of products to meet objectives. The marketing activities can then be applied to this range.

Portfolio analysis can ensure that there is:
- always another product to replace one that is losing sales or market share
- flexibility in a changing market situation
- revenue to cover loss from a failing product

> **Segmentation:** the process of identifying particular groups in a market that have similar needs and wants.

> **Expert tip**
> Do not assume that using marketing methods or selling into a niche market will automatically be successful. Identify the factors on which success may depend.

> **Expert tip**
> When considering any marketing question make sure you determine what the market is and how it might be segmented. Your decisions should then inform your reasons for any marketing activities suggested.

> **Now test yourself**
> 17 Explain the meaning of the following terms:
>   (a) niche marketing
>   (b) segmentation
> 18 Suggest two ways a market may be segmented.
> 19 Give one advantage of portfolio analysis.
> **Answers on p.209**
> Tested

Market research

Primary and secondary research

Market research is the process of gathering information about markets, customers, competitors and the effectiveness of marketing methods.

The purpose of market research

Market research attempts to find out the characteristics, wants and needs of customers in a market. It is invaluable in providing information to enable market segmentation and appropriate marketing methods. It might involve:

- identifying a gap in a market
- forecasting likely demand or sales for existing or new products
- finding information about market trends
- providing information on consumer characteristics
- measuring the effect of marketing methods

It does this by using primary or secondary research methods that generate quantitative (expressed in numbers) or qualitative (expressed in relation to quality, not numbers) information.

> **Market research:** the process of gathering information about markets, customers, competitors and the effectiveness of marketing methods.

> **Now test yourself**
> 20 Suggest four things a business selling a $30 doll might like to find out about possible customers.
>
> **Answer on p.209**

Methods of information gathering

Primary or field research is gathering information for the first time, directly from sources in the market. It is under the control of the business carrying it out so the information should be accurate and relevant. Primary research can be expensive and time consuming so many businesses choose to pay a specialist market research agency to carry it out. **Secondary or desk research** is using information that has been gathered already, either by the business or by other organisations, often for a different purpose.

Any research may be quantitative (seeking information that can be analysed numerically) or qualitative (seeking information about attitudes or opinions).

Primary research methods of gathering information

Primary research involves contacting customers directly. The most common methods are outlined below.

- **Observation** — the researcher watches the behaviour of people via a camera or directly. Observation gives information on how consumers behave when they are deciding what to buy and when faced with, for example, product displays, price information or differing shelf heights.
- **Surveys through questionnaires or interviews** — these may be face-to-face, over the telephone, by post or websites. Questionnaires may have **closed questions** that have a list of possible answers or **open questions** that allow the respondent to reply as they feel. Interviews may be **structured** (the respondent answers specific pre-set questions) and the results are easy to analyse, or **unstructured** (the interviewer may ask any questions and is free to allow the discussion to take a different course) and the results are more difficult to analyse.

Surveys often have a low response rate unless the respondents have agreed to take part beforehand.

> **Primary or field research:** gathering information for the first time, directly from sources in the market.
>
> **Secondary or desk research:** using information that has been gathered already, either by the business or by other organisations.

> **Now test yourself**
> 21 Define the following terms:
> (a) market research
> (b) primary research
> (c) desk research
> (d) qualitative research
>
> **Answers on p.209**

> **Expert tip**
> Make sure you carefully consider the advantages and disadvantages of types of research. Primary and secondary may be applicable in different situations, both give useful information and both may be expensive or relatively cheap.

- **Focus groups or panel discussions** — selected small groups take part in discussion led by a researcher. Typically the group is selected to represent a target market and the aim is often to find out consumer attitudes and views about a new or an existing product.
- **Test marketing** — a new product is actually sold in a small selected area, often before a full-scale launch. Potential problems can then be solved before they become too costly. Test marketing gives information about real buying behaviour.
- **Store cards and databases** — the information from these tells a business exactly what consumers are buying and can be linked to information from other databases to give a detailed picture of customer trends. Sellers can use this to target offers and products to particular people, based on their purchasing behaviour.

> **Now test yourself**
> 22 Identify two disadvantages for each of the following research methods:
>   (a) surveys
>   (b) observation
> 23 Identify two advantages for each of the following research methods:
>   (a) focus groups
>   (b) test marketing
> **Answers on p.209**
> Tested

Secondary research

Secondary research involves using existing information. This may come from:
- government produced data
- trade journals
- internet sites
- business libraries
- company reports
- internal customer and production records

> **Expert tip**
> If you are asked to recommend a method of market research explain at least two and comment on their advantages and disadvantages in relation to the objective of the research, then make a choice based on your analysis of the methods.

Sampling methods
Revised

There are two reasons for not asking everybody from the group of people a business is interested in:
- it is expensive
- not everybody needs to be asked to obtain a statistically valid result

So market research generally uses a sample selection of people drawn from the target group. The larger the sample, the more accurate the results are likely to be. The correct method of sampling (choosing the people to ask) must be used so that the sample represents the group a business is interested in. The target group is the **population** and a **random sample** will mean that every member of the population has an equal chance of being chosen. The sample will then represent the population.

> **Population:** the target group of people for the research.
>
> **Random sample:** a sample in which each member of the population has an equal chance of being chosen, which means the sample will represent the views of the population.

Stratified sampling

Stratified sampling is an attempt to obtain a random sample by dividing the population up into sections (strata) that are distinct. For example, a chair manufacturer may be interested in the views of likely buyers. The population could be divided into a number of strata — by gender (male/female), age (grouped into 10–29, 30–39, 40–49, 50+) and house type (number of rooms). A sample is chosen so that the percentage of people in each strata is the same as in the population. The people who would be asked are then chosen randomly, perhaps by computer.

> **Stratified sample:** a sample formed by dividing the population into groups with shared characteristics so that the number of people chosen reflects the percentage of that group in the population.

Quota sampling

Quota sampling is an attempt to obtain a random sample by dividing the population into a number of similar groups. A quota or set number of people with each characteristic is then decided, e.g. 18 men aged 20–29, 16 women aged 20–29, 29 men aged 30–39, 17 women aged 30–39, giving a sample size of 80. Choosing the individuals can be done in a variety of ways — picking people

> **Quota sample:** a sample in which set numbers of people with different characteristics have been chosen for the sample.

from the street until the quota is reached is less random than using a computer to generate address lists which are then visited.

Choosing a sampling method

There is a trade-off between the cost and ease of gaining a sample and its accuracy. It becomes more expensive to obtain a more random sample. Some methods of choosing who is to be sampled are:

- **Convenience sampling** — researchers choose people in the easiest way for themselves. Not very random.
- **Snowball sampling** — a small number of people are chosen and asked to suggest other people. Not very random.
- **Systematic sampling** — a systematic choice is made, e.g. every tenth house in a chosen street and area. More random.
- **Multi-stage sampling** — a starting selection is chosen. Those who do not respond are substituted by another similar person. Random if systematic methods are used.

> **Now test yourself**
>
> 24 Explain the term 'sampling'.
> 25 Explain the difference between a quota and a stratified sample.
> 26 Explain the importance of obtaining a random sample.
>
> **Answers on p.209–10**
> Tested

> **Revision activity**
>
> 1 Peter Pope is thinking of selling shirts made of a new, expensive, synthetic material that is easy to wash, needs no ironing, wears well and is extremely warm.
>   (a) Suggest two possible objectives for Peter's market research.
>   (b) Produce a table showing the advantages and disadvantages of possible information gathering methods he could use.
> 2 Draw a spider diagram to illustrate the advantages and disadvantages of possible sampling methods.

> **Expert tip**
>
> Do not confuse the method for gathering information with the sampling method used to choose who to ask.

Limitations of sampling

- More random methods will be more expensive but more accurately reflect the population.
- The population may change between selecting a method, carrying out the research and the final results.
- A random sample will take longer than a non-random sample to design and carry out.

> **Revision activity**
>
> Design primary market research to find out the most popular student drink in your school or college. You must choose and explain your choice of gathering information and the sampling method you will use.

Market research results

Revised

Reliability of data collection

The reliability depends on the methods used to collect information. Results will be less reliable if:

- questionnaires had questions that were difficult to understand or led respondents to give certain answers
- interviewers did not have enough training
- respondents deliberately did not give their real views or said what they thought the interviewer or other group members wanted to hear
- the sample size was too small
- the sampling method failed to give a representative sample
- inappropriate analytical methods were used

It is important to consider these when planning market research or analysing results obtained.

Presenting and analysing information

Market research information is usually presented in the form of a report containing graphs, charts, tables and diagrams. Careful choice of the method of presentation will enhance the points being made in the written sections.

Table 1 Presenting and analysing information

Method of presentation	Advantages	Disadvantages
Tables	• Organises large amounts of data • Connections between variables easy to see	• Not visually interesting • Quantity of information difficult to understand
Pie charts	• Easy to see percentage occurrence • Can show absolute values	• Only one variable displayed • Only useful for 3–7 categories
Bar charts	• Visually interesting • Simple to interpret	• Difficult to interpret if more than two variables are shown • Quantity of information difficult to understand
Pictographs	• Easy to read • Connections between variables easy to see	• Absolute numbers difficult to show • May be misleading as 2D illustration may not represent a number exactly
Scattergraphs	• Clear visually • Trends or relationships may be easy to see	• May require complex statistical analysis to detect trend or relationship • Quantity of information difficult to understand
Line graphs	• Clear visually and enable comparisons • Show changes over time clearly and enable forecasts	• Possible to be misled by not checking values of axes • Limited to set values on axes

Now test yourself

Tested

27 Outline two advantages and two disadvantages of using the following methods to display information:

(a) line graph

(b) pie chart

Answers on p.210

> **Expert tip**
>
> The way information is presented is important. The method used must be clear and appropriate for the purpose and the particular business situation.

Analysis of market research results

The important aspects of data are the central tendency and the spread from the highest to the lowest value.

Measuring the central tendency

- **Mean or arithmetic mean** — the mean is calculated by adding up all the numbers in the data and dividing by the total number of numbers in the data, e.g. if there are 20 numbers in a set of data and the total sum of them all adds to 260 the mean will be 260/20 = 13.
- **Median** — the median is the middle number when the numbers in a set of data are arranged in ascending or descending order, e.g. the median of 50 numbers will be a value half way between the 25th and 26th highest or lowest number.
- **Mode** — the mode is the most commonly occurring number in a set of data.

> **Mean:** an average calculated by adding up all the numbers in the data and dividing by the total number of the numbers in the data.
>
> **Median:** the middle number when numbers in a set of data are arranged in descending or ascending order.
>
> **Mode:** the most commonly occurring number in a set of data.

Example

Hours worked by employees in a business

Hours per week	Number employees	Total hours worked
20	3	60
25	15	375
35	24	840
40	12	480
45	6	270
Total	**60**	**2,025**

Mean. The mean hours worked is calculated by finding the total hours worked and dividing by the total number of workers. The total wage column shows the total hours worked at each wage level and these are added to give a total of 2,025 hours. This is divided by the number of workers (60) to give a mean of 33.75 hours per employee per work.

Median. There are 60 employees so the middle number will be between the 30th and 31st employee when arranged in ascending or descending order. This will be in the 35 hours worked per week so 35 hours is the median.

Mode. The most commonly occurring hours worked is 35 per week(24 employees).

Range. The range measures the difference between the lowest and highest values. The lowest hours worked are 20 and the highest are 45 so the range is 25 hours.

Inter-quartile range. The worker one-quarter of the way through the data from the lowest hours worked will be the 15/16th employee and will be working 25 hours. The worker three-quarters of the way through the data from the lowest hours worked will be the 45/46th employee and will be working 40 hours. The inter-quartile range is 40−25 = 15 hours worked.

Measuring the spread

- The **range** — the range is the difference between the lowest and highest values in a set of data. It gives an idea of how spread out the data is.
- The **inter-quartile range** — the inter-quartile range contains the middle 50% of the data. It is the number that is one-quarter from the lowest value subtracted from the number that is three-quarters towards the highest value. A high value for the inter-quartile range indicates more spread out data than a lower value.

> **Expert tip**
> The main focus in examinations is the use of data in providing information to solve a problem, not in carrying out specific calculations. You may be given data in the form of tables or charts and will be expected to apply your analysis to the question set.

> **Range:** the difference between the lowest and highest values in a set of data.
>
> **Inter-quartile range:** the middle 50% of a set of data. It is the difference between the 25% and the 75% numbers when the data is arranged in ascending or descending order.

Revision activity

Weekly spend by consumer households on cosmetics

Weekly spend ($)	Number households	Total spending ($)
0	5	
2	15	
4	18	
6	6	
8	6	

Using the information in the table calculate:

(a) the mean weekly spending by households on cosmetics
(b) the median weekly spending by households on cosmetics
(c) the mode weekly spending by households on cosmetics
(d) the range of weekly spending by households on cosmetics
(e) the inter-quartile range of weekly spending by households on cosmetics

> **Now test yourself**
> 28 Define the following terms:
>   (a) mean
>   (b) mode
>   (c) range
>
> **Answers on p.210**
>
> Tested

Cost effectiveness of market research

Revised

Market research can cost a great deal of money. It may go out of date quickly. The results may be inaccurate and not truly reflect what is actually happening in the market. However, it can give a large amount of information about market trends, customer attitudes and the competition. This means that costs can be saved, products designed to meet needs, and marketing methods can be designed for maximum effect.

Planning is necessary to make sure that the real benefits are realised. This means:
- setting clear objectives
- deciding appropriate methods
- clear presentation and analysis of results

The marketing mix

The **marketing mix** is the combination of product, price, promotion and place (the 4Ps) that is used to make sure that customer requirements are met.

> **Marketing mix:** the combination of product, price, promotion and place that enables customer requirements to be met.

The elements of the marketing mix (the 4Ps)

Revised

Marketing is the process that identifies, anticipates and supplies customer requirements profitably. The elements of the marketing mix must be combined together in an integrated way so that each one reinforces the other three.

- **Product** includes design, function, colour, level of service and quality.
- **Price** may be high or low in relation to costs or competitors' prices.
- **Promotion** is the methods used to inform or persuade consumers, including advertising, offers and sponsorship.
- **Place** is the methods used to get the product to the customer. It includes physical means of transport and where and how customers can obtain the product.

> **Marketing:** the process that identifies, anticipates and supplies customer requirements profitably.

> **Expert tip**
>
> When discussing the marketing mix, make sure that all the elements are integrated, e.g. an expensive jacket is made of high-quality cloth, is sold in exclusive stores and promoted in magazines read by people with high incomes. Showing how marketing mix elements are integrated is analysis.

The role of the customer (the 4Cs)

Revised

The 4Ps deal with the practice of the business. The 4Cs consider the customers' point of view and force the business to give a real reason for people to buy its product. The 4Cs are customer solution, cost to customer, communication with customer and convenience for customers.

- **Customer solution** sets out the customer's perception of the product and the value they place on it.
- **Cost to customer** is not the price but the real cost as the customer sees it. Buying one product means another one will not be bought so a business must offer something more than the competition to make sure the customer sees value in the product and will be prepared to pay for it.
- **Communication** with the customer means not just telling them about a product but engaging in a dialogue and interacting with the customer to form a real relationship.
- **Convenience for customers** means making it as easy as possible for the customer to obtain the product.

> **Now test yourself**
>
> 29 Define the marketing mix.
> 30 State the four elements of the marketing mix.
> 31 Identify the 4Cs.
>
> **Answers on p.210**
>
> Tested

> **Revision activity**
>
> Produce some notes for a new marketing intern in a holiday company to inform him or her about the relationship between the 4Ps and the 4Cs and how these might be used to increase sales.

Table 2 How the 4Cs relate to the 4Ps

4Ps	Meaning	4Cs	Meaning
Product	The product or service produced by the business.	Customer solution/value	The value the customer places on the product.
Price	What the business charges customers for the product.	Cost to customer	The cost the customer sees.
Promotion	What the business tells customers.	Communication with customer	How businesses and customers relate to each other.
Place	Where the business sells its products.	Convenience for customer	How customers obtain products in the easiest way for them.

Ways in which customer relations can be improved

The key to improving **customer relations** is for a business to create a close relationship with its customers. This means more than just integrating the 4Ps and 4Cs. It means a focus on customer-friendly activities and making sure that all employees have a real commitment to customer service. Here are some ways that this can be achieved:

- employees use non-aggressive language in speaking and writing
- clear ordering instructions
- contact pages on websites
- fast answering of e-mails
- free trials of products
- incentives and free gifts

These will create a bond with customers and encourage customers to always think of buying from that business first.

Customer relations: the result of the ways in which a business interacts with its customers.

Now test yourself

32 Identify three ways customer relations may be improved.

Answer on p.210

Tested

Product

Revised

Product includes goods and services and products as well as the many products that include both. A good may be a hat, a pen or a car. A service may be haircutting, insurance or shipping. Products including both may be a restaurant meal, servicing a car or travel with meals provided. All aspects of the product must give customers satisfaction if customer relations are to be good.

Product attributes

Product attributes are the characteristics that make a product what it is. These can be tangible, physical attributes such as shape, materials used or size. They can also be intangible invisible attributes such as quality, how fashionable a product is or customer perception.

Product attribute: a characteristic that makes a product what it is. It can be tangible (physical) or intangible (non-physical).

Table 3 Attributes of an expensive car

Tangible attributes	Intangible attributes
• engine size and power • seat cover material • trunk size	• ownership shows owner is rich • may impress opposite sex • freedom to drive fast

The importance of product development

Product development is the creation of products with new or different characteristics that offer added value to the customer. This can happen either with an entirely new product or through modifying an existing product. Product development can take place with products or services.

Product development takes place:

- to maintain or improve sales or market share in a competitive market
- to build a brand image

Product development: the creation of products with new or different characteristics that offer added value to the customer.

- to make it difficult for competitors to enter the market
- naturally in the case of technology-based products
- due to managers' desire to develop new ideas

Asset-led product development (product-focused)

Product development may be asset led. These products will be developed by research and development within a business and then markets. The business will then seek markets to sell them in.

Market-led product development (customer-focused)

Businesses use market research to find out what customers are interested in. They then design a product that will meet these needs.

Product development is essential in markets where customers' needs are changing and where competitors are always looking for an advantage. Failure to develop new products will mean a business is likely to close unless it constantly re-invents its products in the eyes of the consumer.

> **Now test yourself**
>
> 33 List two possible tangible and two possible intangible attributes of the following products:
>   (a) electric kettle
>   (b) restaurant
> 34 Define product development.
> 35 State two reasons it may be important for a business.
>
> **Answers on p.210**
>
> Tested

Product life cycle

Revised

Product life cycle theory describes five stages from development to decline. Many products fit this pattern but have different time scales. Cassette players lasted 30 years and Coca-Cola is still selling after over 100 years.

> **Product life cycle:** describes five stages from development to decline, showing sales over time.

The stages of the product life cycle

- **Development** — a new product is researched and created but is not put on general sale, though there may be limited test marketing.
- **Introduction** — the new product is launched into the market. Sales will be slow to start with and there may be heavy advertising and promotional costs to make consumers aware of the new product. Price may be high, especially if the product is technologically advanced or very different to existing products. But price may also be set low to encourage consumers to buy. Introductory offers are common. Many products fail at this stage.
- **Growth** — once established, sales increase fast as promotion, media attention and consumer awareness take effect. Profitability increases. There may be the beginnings of significant competition as other businesses see an opportunity for similar products.
- **Maturity** — sales will plateau out as most of the consumers interested in the product are now buying it. There may be intense competition and heavy promotion costs. However, these may actually fall as consumers develop brand loyalty and do not have to be persuaded so much to buy the product. It is likely that a mature product generates significant sales, profits and market share.
- **Decline and extension strategies** — sales fall quickly as consumers are less interested and the product may be becoming replaced by newer technology, increased competition or changing consumer tastes. A business has a choice between:
    - letting decline continue without spending much on marketing. This will still produce profits for a time but may mean consumers associate the firm with decline.
    - stopping selling. This will require other products to be sold to ensure sales and profits continue.
    - engaging in an extension strategy to enable continued or improved sales. This may include special offers or promoting new uses for a product. This will often mean altering the marketing mix by heavy promotional spending to rebrand, e.g. as Lucozade did by changing a drink for sick people into a drink for active trainers.

> **Now test yourself**
>
> 36 Define the term 'product life cycle'.
> 37 State the five stages in the product life cycle.
> 38 What is an extension strategy?
>
> **Answers on p.210**
>
> Tested

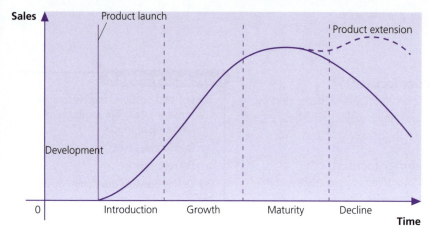

Figure 4 The product life cycle

> **Expert tip**
>
> The product life cycle only gives guidance about how to market a product at each stage. In making a decision other factors must be taken into account.

How product life cycle stage influences marketing activities

The product life cycle gives an indication of what marketing a business might carry out for products at different stages. All the marketing activities should be designed to meet consumer needs and expectations.

Table 4 Product life cycle and possible marketing mix

	Development	Introduction	Growth	Maturity	Decline
Product	Developing ideas and prototypes.	Initial design or service.	• Modified model in light of introduction feedback • More models	Continue existing models, or stop lower selling models, or brand extension to other models.	Possibly sell profitable models only or extend with low cost changes.
Price	N/a	• High (skimming) • Low (penetration) • At going market rate	Possibly lower to attract more sales	Possibly lower to keep sales as competition arrives.	Lowered or heavily discounted.
Promotion	Awareness raising before launch.	Heavy advertising and promotion to raise awareness	Continuing: to capture sales and loyalty.	Possibly heavy to fight competition or less with good customer loyalty.	Much reduced to save costs or special offers.
Place	N/a	Could concentrate on key test areas.	Wider distribution to gain more access to consumers.	Continuing wide distribution or concentrate on profitable areas.	Possibly continued wide distribution or concentrate on profitable areas.

Types of pricing strategies

Revised

A pricing strategy is how a business sets its prices over a medium- to long-term time scale. Demand and supply theory indicates that lower prices will mean more sales, but the reality is more complicated. Prices are linked to consumer perception of quality, and a high price may be seen as showing a quality product so more sales follow. A business can consider setting a price within a range from highest possible (what the market will bear) to lowest possible (just covering costs).

Factors influencing setting a price

Competition: consumers are aware of a range of prices so a business must decide where to place its price in relation to competitors — the same, higher or lower.

- **Costs of production:** a business must set a price that covers the cost.
- **Price elasticity of demand:** the effect on demand of a change in price (see below).
- **Quality:** a higher price can be charged if consumers can be led to see the product is high quality or unique to that business.
- **Demand:** it may be possible to sell a product in high demand at a high price.
- **Pricing strategy:** the overall plan to achieve objectives will include decisions on pricing.

Pricing strategies for new products

Market skimming

A **skimming price** is set very high, well above costs. This strategy is likely to be used for innovative technology based products or fashion items, so lack of competition allows a high price to recover research and development costs. Price can then fall when competition begins.

Market penetration

A **penetration price** is set very low, with low profit margin to attract as many buyers as possible, gain brand loyalty and prevent competition in the market. The price may be raised later. This strategy is suitable for products in a mass market where price is an important factor in the buying decision. An extreme form of penetration pricing is predatory pricing, i.e. selling goods at below cost for a time in order to drive competition away. This may well be illegal in many countries under competition law.

> **Skimming price:** a skimming price strategy sets the price of a new product high to gain high profit margins and allow a price fall as competition arrives.
>
> **Penetration price:** a penetration price strategy sets the price for a new product very low to quickly gain sales, market share and customer loyalty.

Pricing strategies for existing or new products

Competitive pricing

Competitive pricing is setting a price based on what competitors charge. The price may be higher, lower or similar. A higher price, called premium or prestige pricing, is linked to higher quality, a lower price aims to appeal to consumers' desire for low spending, and a similar price will mean other marketing mix elements are important in obtaining sales.

Price discrimination

Price discrimination means setting a different price for the same good to different types of customer. This may be based on

- geography — charging a different price in different regions
- time — charging peak-time users more than off-peak or seasonal variations or by age

This method is only possible when those paying lower prices cannot resell to those faced with high prices.

> **Competitive pricing:** setting a price based on what competitors charge.
>
> **Price discrimination:** setting a different price for the same good to different customers, based on geographical, time or age separation.

> **Expert tip**
>
> Remember the difference between pricing strategies used for a new product and those suitable for a new or existing product.

Cost-based pricing

These methods (full-cost pricing and contribution costing) use cost as a basis for setting a price but market conditions must also be taken into account. It is not effective to add a high mark-up on costs if consumers are seeking very low prices.

- **Full-cost pricing** adds a percentage or fixed amount onto the average full-cost of producing a product. This is simple to calculate and will give a certain profit level assuming the costs are accurately known and all production is sold.

> **Full-cost pricing:** adds a percentage on to the average full cost to give a price.

- **Contribution costing** makes sure all variable costs are covered by adding a percentage or fixed amount onto these costs. It gives a contribution to the fixed costs and often a lower price than full-cost pricing. It is particularly used when there is a wide product range.

> **Contribution costing:** adds a percentage on to the variable cost of producing a good, giving a price that ensures a contribution is made to fixed costs.

> **Now test yourself** — Tested
>
> 39 State two pricing strategies that might be particularly suitable for each of the following:
>
> (a) a new computer operating system
>
> (b) a shirt
>
> (c) a business especially concerned with making sure it covers its costs
>
> **Answers on p.210**

Pricing tactics or methods

Once a strategy has been decided on, a business has to use a tactic to actually set the price over a short time.

- **Loss leaders** — setting the price of some products so a loss is made to encourage consumers to buy additional products. Supermarkets often do this by selling essentials like bread and sugar very cheaply.
- **Psychological pricing** — setting a price just below a whole number to make the customer feel the product is much cheaper, e.g. a price of $3.99 rather than $4.00.
- **Bait and hook pricing** — selling a product at a low price but charging a high price for connected essentials, e.g. printers are cheap but ink cartridges are expensive.

> **Loss leaders:** goods sold below cost to attract customers who are likely to buy other goods.
>
> **Psychological pricing:** setting a price just below a whole number, e.g. $3.99.
>
> **Bait and hook pricing:** selling a product at a low price but charging a high price for essential connected products.

> **Now test yourself** — Tested
>
> 40 Identify two pricing strategies suitable for a new product.
>
> 41 Identify three pricing strategies suitable for an existing product.
>
> 42 State two possible pricing tactics.
>
> **Answers on p.210**

> **Expert tip**
>
> Make sure you are clear on the difference between pricing strategies (medium/long term) and pricing tactics/methods (short term).

Price elasticity of demand (PED) — Revised

A price rise will usually cause a fall in demand, a price fall will usually cause a rise in demand. **PED** deals with how much demand changes when price changes, not whether demand rises or falls.

PED measures the degree of responsiveness of demand for a good to a change in its price and is calculated as follows:

$$PED = \frac{\text{percentage change in quantity demanded}}{\text{percentage change in price}}$$

Demand can be price elastic or price inelastic:

- **Price elastic goods** are sensitive to price changes, that is, a change in price results in a more than proportionate change in demand. The PED of price elastic goods will be greater than 1.
- **Price inelastic goods** are not sensitive to price changes, that is, a change in price results in a smaller proportionate change in demand. The PED of price inelastic goods will be smaller than 1.

> **Price elasticity of demand:** measures the degree of responsiveness of demand for a good to changes in its price. This is percentage change in quantity demanded divided by percentage change in price.

Example

A game player was priced at $100 and it sold 400 units per week in a town. The price fell to $80 and the quantity sold rose to 440 units. The PED is calculated by:

$$PED = \frac{\% \text{ change in demand}}{\% \text{ change in price}}$$

$$PED = \frac{440 - 400/400 \times 100}{\$80 - \$100/100 \times 100}$$

$$PED = \frac{40/400 \times 100}{-20/100 \times 100}$$

$$PED = \frac{10}{20} = 0.5 \text{ (the minus sign is usually disregarded)}$$

So a 20% price fall has resulted in a 10% rise in demand. This means the good is price inelastic, showing a smaller percentage change in demand than the percentage price change.

Expert tip

You need to be able to calculate PED. Practise this until you are confident. Always show your workings as a wrong final answer can still gain some marks if the method shown is correct. You may well have to use the results of your calculation to analyse or evaluate the implications of a price change.

Using price elasticity of demand in pricing decisions

PED tells a business something about its market. A good with a high PED (elastic) is likely to have many possible substitute goods, so a price rise will lead to a large fall in sales and a price fall to a large rise in sales. A good with low PED (inelastic) is likely to be a necessity or have no or few possible substitutes and will continue to be bought even if the price rises.

Table 5 PED and revenue

	Price elastic: price fall	Price elastic: price rise	Price inelastic: price fall	Price Inelastic: price rise	PED = 1 price fall	PED = 1 price rise
Sales quantity	Increases by a bigger percentage than price change.	Falls by a bigger percentage than price change.	Increases by a smaller percentage than price change.	Falls by a smaller percentage than price change.	Increases by the same percentage as price change.	Increases by the same percentage as price change.
Sales revenue (price × quantity)	Increases.	Falls.	Falls.	Increases.	Constant.	Constant.

For example, a product has a PED of 3 (price elastic). If the business cuts its price, sales will rise by three times the price change. This will lead to an increase in revenue. But there are other questions to consider:

- Can the business supply this demand?
- Will average costs rise as production rises?
- Will there be additional marketing costs?
- Will profits also rise?

Businesses are usually keen to try and lower the PED of their products in order to make price increases possible to raise revenue and lower the effects of competition. Methods that may be used to do this include:

- branding to gain customer loyalty
- differentiating products to obtain uniqueness
- using advertising or promotion

Now test yourself

43 A shop selling light fittings has forecast that a price rise from $20 to $21 will result in a fall in sales from 600 to 540.

(a) Calculate PED and state whether this product is price elastic or price inelastic.

(b) Calculate the change in revenue resulting from this price change.

(c) Identify three other possible factors the business might take into account when deciding whether to increase prices.

Answers on p.210

Promotion methods

Promotion is a range of activities that communicate and interact with consumers in order to inform and/or persuade so that attitudes and buying behaviour changes.

Above-the-line promotion

Above-the-line promotion methods use paid-for media space, often in the mass media. Often the purpose is not to persuade a consumer to buy, but to raise awareness of a brand or product and create a desire to buy. It includes:

- **Television advertising** — expensive but reaches a mass audience in a non-selective way, though targeted adverts in the middle of particular programmes may be effective.
- **Newspaper advertising** — less expensive, reaches mass audience, can be kept.
- **Radio advertising** — can target specific groups who listen to particular stations.
- **Magazine advertising** — targets specific groups likely to be interested in the product.
- **Billboards** — large mass audience but little information and likely not to be noticed.
- **Internet advertising** — can target small groups or even individuals but easy for consumers not to notice.
- **Cinema advertising** — only reaches cinema audiences.

> **Promotion:** a range of activities that communicate and interact with consumers to inform and/or persuade to change attitudes and buying behaviour.
>
> **Above-the-line promotion:** marketing methods that communicate with the consumer using paid-for mass media space.

> **Now test yourself**
> 44 Define promotion.
> **Answer on p.210**
> Tested

Below-the-line promotion

Below-the-line promotion is a range of activities that communicate with consumers without paying for media space. It is often more closely targeted at the desired market segment. It includes:

- **Direct selling and direct mail** — direct customer contact face to face in a store, by telephone, home calling or sending material by mail.
- **Point of sale promotions** — in-store posters, displays and demonstrations, flyers, dump bins, and racks all draw the attention of customers to the product or to sales promotions.
- **Sales promotions** — used to persuade a customer to actually buy. Methods include buy one get one free (BOGOF), sales (10% off this week), free gifts and samples, competitions, prize draws, money-back coupons and introductory offers.
- **Sponsorship** — giving money in return for a variety of ways of obtaining recognition, e.g. name/logo on shirts, television credits, product placement and mentions in programmes.
- **Public relations/publicity** — press releases, media stories about the business, conferences with media invited, activities for charity and community.
- **Trade fairs and exhibitions** — attending these can be a way of drawing customers' attention to a business.
- **Packaging** — this is what the consumer sees when they consider buying. Packaging acts as protection, for security, control and transport convenience and giving information about the contents. It can reinforce messages from other promotional methods.

> **Below-the-line promotion:** marketing methods that communicate with the consumer without paying for media space.

> **Now test yourself**
> 45 (a) Explain the difference between above-the-line and below-the-line promotion methods.
> (b) State two methods of each type and list an advantage and a disadvantage for each.
> (c) State three factors that influence the choice of promotional mix.
>
> **Answers on p.210**
> Tested

Factors influencing the promotional mix

The **promotional mix** is the integrated, coordinated combination of promotional methods used to achieve marketing objectives. Factors influencing the choice include:

- **Purpose** — to inform, to persuade, or to build a brand image?
- **Target audience** — consumers in general, a mass market or a niche, household consumers or commercial buyers?

> **Promotional mix:** the integrated coordinated combination of promotional methods used to achieve marketing objectives.

- **Finance** — how much money is available and what is the cost of the methods being considered?
- **Product life cycle** — what stage is the product at?
- **Competition** — how competitive is the market and how are competitors promoting?
- **Legal constraints** — what trade description and similar laws are there?

> **Expert tip**
> Make sure you write about promotional methods in relation to the factors influencing the promotional mix and the objectives of the promotional methods being discussed.

Branding

Branding is creating a name, symbol or design that identifies and differentiates a product or business from others in the mind of the consumer.

Having a brand image means that customers will build up loyalty to the product/business so that a higher price can be charged and/or there will be increased confidence in sales forecasts. It will be easier to get distributors to stock the product and new products can be marketed successfully using the brand name and image, as Mars and other chocolate bar manufacturers have done with their ice cream products. Successful branding takes time and concerted marketing using a coherent integrated marketing mix.

> **Branding:** creating a name, symbol or design that identifies and differentiates a product or business from others in the mind of the consumer.

Place: channels of distribution

Place includes the location where products are sold and the ways in which products are moved from producer to buyer.

Some producers sell directly to customers. Many others use intermediaries through which goods or services pass in a number of stages. Many businesses use more than one distribution method (see Figure 5).

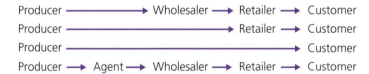

Figure 5 Common channels for distribution

Intermediaries
- **Wholesalers** — link producer and retailer, break large units to smaller units and provide storage.
- **Retailers** — sell directly to consumers, providing storage and an outlet.
- **Agents** — arrange sales without taking ownership of the product, often for import/export.

Advantages of using intermediaries
- Lower marketing costs as sales have to be made to a smaller number of customers.
- Lower storage costs.

Disadvantages of using intermediaries
- Loss of profit to the intermediary.
- Loss of control over selling conditions.

Factors influencing choice of distribution channel
- **Cost** — a short distribution channel will have a lower cost.
- **Product type** — perishable or short shelf-life products must reach customers quickly. Large, bulky products are likely to be sold direct to the customer by the producer.
- **Market type** — mass-market products will need intermediaries, niche products may be sold more directly. National, international and local markets require different approaches.

> **Now test yourself**
> 46 Define the following:
>   (a) wholesaler
>   (b) agent
>   (c) retailer
> 47 Give two reasons why a producer would not sell directly to the public.
>
> **Answers on p.210**

- **Customer preference** — customers want different things, so producers must use channels that appeal to different customer wants, e.g. a luxury car is usually sold via a dealer who can provide after-sales service.
- **Producer preference** — producers may wish to keep control of the selling process or they may wish to hand this over to intermediaries who are more specialised in selling.

The role of the internet is now changing these methods as it enables producers and intermediaries to more easily sell directly to the public.

Selling through intermediaries

Producers who sell through intermediaries must make sure that the selling conditions are right for their product. They can do this by providing:

- product displays and equipment they have designed
- incentives for intermediaries, e.g. prizes for reaching sales targets
- promotional materials for intermediaries to use
- special offers, higher short term commission or discounts
- training in product knowledge or selling

The internet and the 4Ps/4Cs

Revised

The internet has radically changed distribution. Large firms such as Amazon and eBay now provide selling services for businesses and individuals of all types. Internet sales are rapidly increasing in all types of countries and often provide 30–40% of sales revenue for a producer. The internet provides:

- **Online advertising** — pop-ups, banner or hover adverts target particular sites or users.
- **Websites** — these allow online catalogues, product displays, forums and interaction between sellers and buyers.
- **Dynamic pricing** — different buyers are offered different prices, e.g. airline ticket prices may depend on when the booking is made.
- **Direct sales** — digital products can be downloaded directly to buyers and tickets provided online.
- **Social networking** — sites allow easy two-way communication and access to specific consumer groups.

The impact of the internet allows direct communication between producers and customers and increases the importance of the 4Cs.

> **Expert tip**
>
> Make sure that you link together the elements of the marketing mix in a consistent way that is appropriate to the product/service being marketed.

Consistency in the marketing mix

Revised

The marketing mix elements must be integrated and reinforce each other to give the same message. The message must relate to the business, the product and the market to form a coherent whole. For example:

- **Product** — a warm but light shirt made of high tech synthetic material.
- **Price** — more expensive than cotton work shirts and approximately the same price as competitors' shirts.
- **Promotion** — adverts in outdoor magazines, websites, in-store promotion material.
- **Place** — sold online and in specialist outdoor/climbing/sailing shops.

> **Revision activity**
>
> Mr Patel has designed an umbrella that is dark if there is a lot of light and transparent if the day becomes dark or rainy. This feature can also be controlled by the user with a switch mechanism. The umbrella will cost $25 each to manufacture. Draw up a table to show an appropriate marketing mix with reasons for your suggestions.

4 Operations and project management

The nature of operations

Inputs, outputs and the transformation process

Revised

Operations and its role
Operations or operations management focuses on transforming inputs to outputs and covers a range of activities dealing with the practicalities of production including:
- contributing to decisions on product ranges
- implementing production methods
- designing equipment
- selecting suppliers who can deliver the right quality and price
- making sure quality standards are upheld
- ensuring health and safety standards are maintained
- deciding on appropriate levels of stock
- arranging for productivity levels to meet cost targets

Large businesses may have a defined operations department with dedicated managers, while smaller businesses may make these decisions without a formal operations functional area. In all cases, the operations function must work with other areas, e.g. human resources, marketing or finance.

Process: from idea/need to final product/service
Operations deals with the process by which an idea is turned into a finished item or service that is put on sale. A key part is identifying and bringing together all the necessary inputs.

The operations process: from idea to product
The operations process is shown in Figure 1.

> **Operations or operations management:** the designing and controlling of systems that produce goods or services to meet customer requirements.

> **Now test yourself**
> 1 State three processes involved in operations management.
> **Answer on p.210**
> Tested

> **Expert tip**
> Operations is about the way resources are managed, controlled and integrated to achieve business objectives.

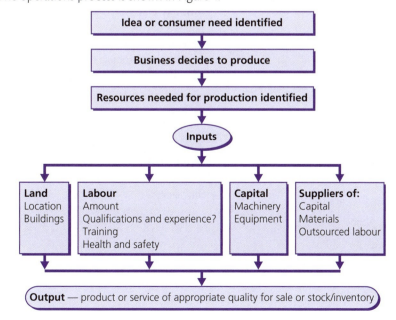

Figure 1 The operations process: from idea to product

The nature of operations 65

Resources: land, labour, capital

Operations deals with the way in which inputs of **land**, **labour** and **capital** are combined to give an output of a product or a service.

- **Land** includes land, buildings, minerals, oil and wood.
- **Labour** is the work done by people, either manually or mentally in managing and decision-making.
- **Capital** is machinery and equipment, including intellectual capital such as qualifications.

Operations determines how the transformation of inputs to an output will take place. It decides how inputs may be combined in different ways and in differing proportions to produce a final product or service.

> **Now test yourself**
> 2 Explain what is meant by the following:
> (a) land
> (b) labour
> (c) capital
> Include an example for each.
>
> **Answers on p.210**
> Tested

The transformation process

Inputs can be combined in differing quantities. **Labour-intensive production** uses relatively more labour than capital so labour costs are a higher proportion of total costs than capital costs, e.g. a craft producer like a potter.

Capital-intensive production uses relatively more capital than labour so capital costs are a higher proportion of total costs than labour costs, e.g. an oil refinery.

The combination of land, labour and capital will determine how the transformation process leads to final product (see Figure 2).

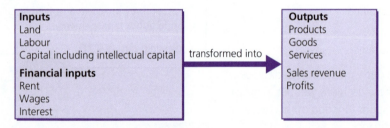

Figure 2 The transformation process

> **Now test yourself**
> 3 Identify two inputs used in the production of each of these products:
> (a) theatre production
> (b) sock manufacturer
> (c) financial adviser
> (d) haulage business
>
> **Answers on p.210**
> Tested

Effectiveness, efficiency and productivity

Revised

Difference between effectiveness and efficiency

Operations efficiency measures the quantity of resources used in producing a given quantity of product. Efficient producers use fewer inputs for a given quantity of output so that unit costs are lower.

Operations effectiveness is a measure of how well the final product meets the needs of customers, e.g.

- **Function** — how well the product does the job for which it is designed.
- **Availability** — how easy it is to obtain the product.
- **Price** — related to efficiency of production (costs).
- **Value for money** — a combination of price and function.

Productivity

Productivity is an efficiency measure usually applied to labour.

$$\text{labour productivity} = \frac{\text{output in units per time period}}{\text{number of employees}}$$

> **Operations efficiency** measures the quantity of resources used in producing a given quantity of product. Efficient producers use fewer inputs for a given quantity of output so that unit costs are lower.
>
> **Operations effectiveness:** a measure of how well the final product meets the needs of customers including function, availability, price and value for money.
>
> **Productivity:** output per worker per time period and measures labour efficiency.

66 Cambridge International AS and A Level Business Studies Revision Guide

A garage employs six mechanics who work for nine hours per day and are paid $60 per day each. In one day they can, on average, repair or service 15 cars. Their labour productivity is:

$$\frac{15}{6} = 2.5 \text{ cars per mechanic per day}$$

Linking productivity and efficiency

Productivity helps determine the costs of production. In the above example the costs are as follows:

$$\text{total cost per day for 15 cars} = 6 \times 60 = \$360.00$$

$$\text{average labour cost} = \frac{360}{15} = \$24 \text{ per car}$$

If productivity rises so that each mechanic can deal with three cars per day the costs are as follows:

$$\text{total cost per day for 18 cars} = 6 \times 60 = \$360.00$$

$$\text{average labour cost} = \frac{360}{18} = \$20 \text{ per car}$$

This means the business has become more competitive and may be able to reduce its price and maintain its profit margin or maintain price and increase profit margin. If any of the factors of production can be made more efficient the same will be true.

Ways to increase productivity

Ways to increase productivity include:
- investing in more efficient capital or better maintenance and use of existing capital
- investing in more training for employees so there are fewer mistakes, faster working and better problem solving. This may be expensive and must be applied correctly
- improving employee motivation
- changing the culture to build efficiency improvements into all processes

All these methods incur costs, i.e. to buy new machinery, training costs, wage increases or implementing change, and to be worthwhile must be chosen correctly and implemented effectively.

> **Expert tip**
> Make sure you remember that productivity is measured over a time period.

> **Now test yourself**
> 4 Define labour productivity.
> 5 Outline two reasons why an increase in productivity may be beneficial.
> 6 Explain three methods to improve productivity.
> 7 Calculate labour productivity for an accountancy business that employs five accountants who each work 40 hours per week and deal with a total of 20 accounts per week.
> 8 What is the difference between efficiency and effectiveness?
>
> Answers on p.210
>
> Tested

Value added

Revised

A business adds value when it transforms inputs to output. At each stage the partly finished good is worth more than at the previous stage. Customers are also looking for their own added value — this is the additional value to the basic product that might persuade them to buy it.

Value added and marketing

Customers see added value as meeting their needs based on:
- improved performance and design
- discounted prices
- extras or accessories, quality assurance
- personal attention and after-sales service

This added value is often what differentiates a product from that of the competition and enables a business to charge a higher price and gain customer loyalty. This can be achieved through the product itself or by promotional activities that make a product appeal to customers.

Value added and the operations process

The operations process transforms a number of inputs into output via a number of stages. Each stage will become more valuable than the previous one because of the work that has been done. These stages may take place within one organisation or across several. For example, selling a cake involves taking basic ingredients, combining them and then arranging for distribution of the finished cake to a sales outlet (see Figure 3). Each stage adds value to the stage before and this is represented by an increase in money value. If the product is sold at one of the stages this added value is represented by sales revenue and profit.

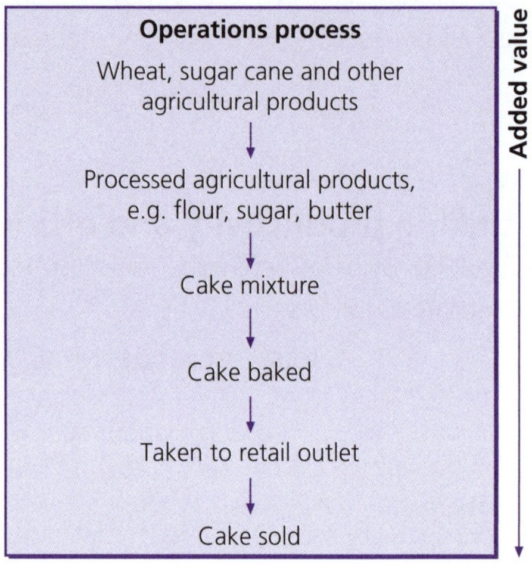

Added value and operations decisions

Operations decisions aim to achieve a target added value or maximise added value so as to:
- increase efficiency and effectiveness
- lower unit costs
- increase sales revenue and/or profits
- meet customers' value added needs

Operations process

Wheat, sugar cane and other agricultural products
↓
Processed agricultural products, e.g. flour, sugar, butter
↓
Cake mixture
↓
Cake baked
↓
Taken to retail outlet
↓
Cake sold

← Added value →

Figure 3 Added value and the operations process in selling a cake

Now test yourself — Tested

9 State two reasons why added value is important for:
   (a) a business
   (b) a customer
10 Explain three ways in which a business might add value to a product.

Answers on p.210–11

Factors in deciding capital versus labour intensity — Revised

Products may be produced with a variety of combinations of capital and labour. Mass-produced cars are built on assembly lines with a large investment in machinery relative to the cost of employing people — robot lines require very few employees. On the other hand, custom sports cars are often built largely by hand with a much higher relative use of labour. The factors that decide the relative amounts of labour and capital include:

- **Production methods/the product** — mass production tends to be **capital intensive**, craft products labour intensive.
- **Relative costs of labour and capital** — low labour costs tend to lead to **labour-intensive production** as in agriculture and factories in developing countries.
- **Business size** — larger businesses tend to have more finance so can afford to be more capital intensive.
- **The level of personal service** involved in the product, e.g. manicures tend to be labour intensive, whilst manufacturing shampoo is capital intensive.
- **Customer's needs** — markets where personal service is important to the customer tend to be more labour intensive; compare a high-class restaurant service with a drive-thru' one.

Labour-intensive production: uses relatively more labour than capital so labour costs are a higher proportion of total costs than capital costs, e.g. a craft producer such as a potter.

Capital-intensive production: uses relatively more capital than labour so capital costs are a higher proportion of total costs than labour costs e.g. an oil refinery.

Expert tip

Businesses can achieve added value and success by choosing a variety of capital intensities. What is most important is that the choice matches the business objectives, market, and product type.

Benefits and limitations of labour-intensive production

Benefits
- Personal services can be delivered well.
- Possible to produce one-off or custom-made products.
- Low start-up costs.
- Lower unit costs if labour is relatively cheap.
- Easy to alter labour force by recruitment or retrenchment.

Limitations
- Difficult to produce on large scale.
- Economies of scale are difficult to achieve.

Benefits and limitations of capital-intensive production

Benefits
- Mass production is possible on assembly line.
- Lower unit costs if capital is relatively cheap.
- Economies of scale are possible.
- Labour force is less skilled so recruitment is easy and labour costs low.

Limitations
- Not suitable for varying product types or short runs.
- Not suitable for personal services.
- High start-up costs due to cost of machinery.
- Machine-dependent so breakdowns are expensive and may stop production.
- Lack of variety might lead to unmotivated employees.
- Cannot vary capital in short run.

> **Revision activity**
> Draw up a table to show the factors that influence a business in the choice of capital intensity for production.

Now test yourself   Tested

11 Explain why the following might be capital intensive:
   (a) a shipyard building ocean liners
   (b) a major sweet manufacturer
12 Explain why the following might be labour intensive:
   (a) an estate agent
   (b) a market stall selling vegetables

Answers on p.211

Operations planning

Operations planning deals with taking decisions about methods of production, process innovation, location and the scale of operation.

Factors influencing operations decisions   Revised

Marketing
Through market research a business gains information to inform the following decisions:
- **Ideas and R&D** — discovering and developing ideas that meet customers' needs.
- **Production methods** — showing what customers will pay and what quality is required. This will inform production methods and the labour/capital balance.
- **Location** — deciding on location in relation to consumer buying patterns and cost constraints.

Availability of resources
Availability of resources at an appropriate cost includes the following:
- The presence of an R&D department will enhance the generation and development of ideas.
- Access to suitable land, labour and capital may be a constraint on production and location decisions.

Availability of technology

Technology is vital in operations decisions, especially IT-based systems. Examples include:
- Computer Aided Design (CAD) is faster and more accurate for design; IT processes marketing information rapidly.
- Computer Aided Manufacture (CAM) links design and production at low cost.
- IT systems reduce labour and payroll costs, make quality consistent, reduce stock and allow more efficient production planning. New materials enable different products.
- Advanced communication systems have enabled many businesses to locate almost anywhere.

> **Revision activity**
>
> Produce a brief report for a business developing a new drill that sets out how the following may influence the operations decisions it has to make:
> - marketing
> - availability of resources
> - availability of technology

Flexibility and innovation

Flexibility is the ability of a production system to adapt to a changing market.

The need for flexibility in volume, delivery time and specification

- **Volume flexibility** is the ability to operate efficiently, effectively and profitably over a range of output. In the short run, this means being able to meet a sudden change in orders, either an increase or a decrease, and still supply quality and at the price the customer requires.
- **Delivery time** — in the long run, this means being prepared for varying demand at different stages of the product life cycle. Flexibility in just-in-time (JIT) production methods and being able to deliver at a time that suits the customer is increasingly important as this flexibility may secure a sale.
- **Specification** — increasingly businesses and consumers demand products that differ slightly from each other, and the ability to provide a range of specifications to order may be vital.

Process innovation

Process innovation is using a new or improved production or delivery method. This may be a new technology, e.g. robots, or a new way of organising production, e.g. cell working. Process innovation:
- lowers total and average cost
- matches product to customer needs more exactly
- motivates employees

However, process innovation requires planning and management for change.

> **Process innovation:** using a new or improved production or delivery method.

> **Expert tip**
>
> Solutions to problems must relate to the business concerned in its specific situation. There are no set answers. The best solutions are supported with sound reasons.

> **Now test yourself**
>
> 13 For each change, state whether it is due to new technology or new organisation:
>   (a) Sales staff use a tablet to send orders and sign contracts on the spot.
>   (b) A school organises students in groups by ability instead of age.
>   (c) CAD/CAM enables designs to be directly produced.
>   (d) A bank offers a loan on the spot instead of referring to a regional office.
> 14 Identify one benefit of each innovation.
>
> **Answers on p.211**

Operations or production methods

Revised

Job production
Job production is producing unique or small-scale products one at a time by skilled workers.

Advantages	Disadvantages
• Flexibility.	• Labour intensive and slow.
• Meets customers' needs exactly.	• High unit costs.

Job production: producing unique or small-scale products one at a time by skilled workers.

Batch production
Batch production is production in stages where several of the same item are put together at the same time. Each batch goes through one stage of the production process before moving onto the next stage, e.g. batches of bread in a bakery. It is a more capital-intensive method than job production.

Advantages	Disadvantages
• Lower unit costs.	• Time taken to reset machines between batches.
• Equipment may be able to produce a range of products.	• Higher inventory costs in batches.
	• Less flexibility.

Batch production: production in stages where several of the same item are put together at the same time. Each batch goes through one stage of the production process before moving onto the next stage.

Flow production
Flow production is continuous production. Products pass directly from stage to stage, often on an assembly line for standardised products.

Advantages	Disadvantages
• Low unit costs.	• High capital start-up costs.
• Quality easy to monitor.	• Limited flexibility.
• Can be mechanised and automated.	• A fault means the whole assembly line stops.
	• Not motivating for workers.

Flow production: continuous production in which products pass directly from one stage to the next, often on an assembly line.

Mass production and customisation
Mass production produces high output at low unit cost using standardised parts, machines and products, usually in flow production.

Advantages	Disadvantages
• Very low unit cost and large volumes.	• Not flexible.
	• Not motivating for workers.

Mass customisation: uses mass production to meet individual customer's needs by setting workstations to produce a range of pre-set options.

To overcome these disadvantages **mass customisation** meets individual customer's needs by setting workstations to produce a range of pre-set options. IT systems enable products to differ as they pass each stage.

Problems of changing from one method to another
Changing from one method to another incurs costs due to:
- redesign of product
- redesign and re-equipping production equipment
- training of employees
- difficulty in meeting quality standards in a different method, e.g. computer screens are batch-produced, taking hours for each coating. Flow production would be very expensive, slow and difficult to standardise.

Expert tip

Decisions on production method and location should involve setting out the appropriate theory and then applying it to the specific situation of a business.

Revision activity

Use a table to set out the advantages and disadvantages of any two production methods for the following:
- a biscuit maker
- a computer keyboard manufacturer

Operations planning

> **Now test yourself** — Tested
>
> **15** Explain the meaning of the following:
>   (a) job production
>   (b) mass customisation
> **16** List two advantages and two disadvantages of each of the following operations methods:
>   (a) job production
>   (b) batch production
>   (c) flow production
>
> **Answers on p.211**

Location — Revised

Location factors depend on the type of business in question. The factors to consider include geographical, demographic, legal, political, availability of resources and the surrounding infrastructure.

- **Geographic factors** — these include climate and the likely occurrence of earthquakes, floods, tornadoes, snow and rain as well as landscape features such as hills, rivers and the coast.
- **Demographic factors** — employees are essential for any business. A chosen location should have enough people who have the right skills, experience and qualifications. Demographic factors may also be important for determining local wages and salary levels.
- **Legal factors** — the legal framework that business operates in varies from one place to another. Laws on tax, government assistance, planning, waste disposal, health and safety, employment and industrial relations are all important for costs or business operation.
- **Political factors** — businesses will take into account political stability and governmental non-interference.
- **Resources** — close access to resources such as raw materials or components reduces transport costs. This is particularly important if these are bulky or expensive to transport. The availability of suitable land may also be a factor.
- **Infrastructure** — infrastructure is the utilities, transport networks, finance, educational and health facilities in a location.
- **Marketing** — being close to the market for products reduces transport costs and finding similar businesses or customers nearby may reduce marketing costs.

> **Revision activity**
>
> The following are about to make a location decision:
> - a furniture shop
> - a furniture manufacturer
> - a steel maker
> - an accountant
>
> Use a table to assess the importance of the factors that influence location.

> **Now test yourself**
>
> **17** Define 'infrastructure'.
> **18** State four factors that help determine a location decision.
>
> **Answers on p.211** — Tested

Relocation and industrial inertia

A relocating business faces the same factors as a new business. But it may choose to stay in the same place because the costs of moving are greater than the benefits of the move. This is **industrial inertia**. Relocating costs include:

- finding and training new employees
- finding new suppliers
- additional marketing costs
- the cost of moving and setting up again

> **Industrial inertia:** when a business stays in its current location even though the factors that led it to locate there no longer apply.

Decisions on location at different levels

- **Local location decisions** — the decision to set up in one particular place is determined by specific factors relating to that place. Considerations include the cost of renting or buying, availability of components, materials and labour and the closeness of the market. Government policy may also be important.

72 Cambridge International AS and A Level Business Studies Revision Guide

- **Regional location decisions** — the same factors operate but at a wider level related to the region and its links with other places.
- **National location decisions** — a business deciding to operate at a national level must make sure that it has sufficient funds for investment and marketing, supply chains, and distribution channels.
- **International location decisions** — firms entering international markets will focus on cost reduction through lower wages and freedom from government regulation (particularly in labour markets), global markets, avoiding/reducing taxes, supply chains, outsourcing possibilities and government incentives. The economic, political and legal environments will also be important factors.

> **Now test yourself**
> 19 Define 'industrial inertia'.
> 20 State three factors that might make it difficult for a business to relocate.
>
> **Answers on p.211**
> Tested

Scale of operation

Revised

The scale is the size of production. An increase in scale is not only an increase in output but a change to a different scale involving an increase in capital.

Factors that influence the scale of production
- Position in the product life cycle — as sales rise, new investment might be needed to provide output to sell.
- Finance available.
- Business objectives — if these do not include expansion there will be no change in scale.
- The market — increasing scale involves increasing output that must be sold.
- The possibility of reducing unit costs.

Economies and diseconomies of scale

Economies of scale are falling **average costs** (costs per unit) as the scale of output increases. This enables lower process or higher profit margins to be achieved and makes it harder for competitors to enter the market. At a certain level of output, the **minimum efficient scale** is reached. As scale and output increase further, **diseconomies of scale** appear. These are increasing average costs as the scale of output increases (see Figure 4).

> **Economies of scale:** falling average costs as the scale of output increases.
>
> **Average costs:** the costs per unit of production. Calculated by dividing total costs of production by quantity produced:
>
> $$\text{average costs} = \frac{\text{total costs of production}}{\text{quantity produced}}$$
>
> **Minimum efficient scale:** the scale of output at which average costs are at their lowest.
>
> **Diseconomies of scale:** rising average costs as the scale of output increases.

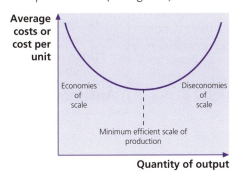

Figure 4 Economies and diseconomies of scale

Causes of economies of scale

Generally, as scale increases fixed costs are spread over more units of output and variable costs may fall as increasing size enables more efficient organisation. Both these will decrease average costs.

Internal economies of scale arise from inside the business
- **Purchasing economies of scale (bulk buying)** — larger orders often attract a discount and this is true for borrowing money. Discounts are also given for orders above a certain size.
- **Technical economies of scale** — new technology or advanced equipment will be more efficient and IT systems enable more efficiency. There are also

physical reasons for economies, e.g. heating 20 tonnes of steel may cost the same per tonne as heating 1 tonne but a 20-tonne block will keep hotter for longer, saving on energy costs, so variable costs per unit fall.
- **Managerial economies of scale** — larger businesses use specialists who are more efficient. They can also afford more expert managers.
- **Administrative and marketing economies of scale** — a particular task often uses the same paperwork or process, whatever its size. Advertising for 20 new staff costs the same as for 100 new staff. Ordering one item costs the same as ordering 1,000. An advertising campaign costs the same if 20 or 2,000 sales result.

External economies of scale arise from outside the business
- **Infrastructure economies of scale** — new infrastructure reduces average costs. Possible examples include faster broadband and new roads or airports.
- **Research and development economies of scale** — access to nearby universities or research facilities can lower average costs.
- **Marketing economies of scale** — similar businesses operating in the same area may need to advertise less as customers visit knowing there will be somewhere to buy from. So individual firms do not need to promote themselves as much. Streets of fast-food shops are an example.

  A promotional campaign by an organisation representing an industry may result in less need for individual businesses to promote themselves. For example, a meat producers' association may advertise the benefits of eating meat, resulting in an increase in demand for all meat producers.
- **Production economies** — if suppliers are nearby, there will be lower transport and communication costs. This explains the concentration of financial services in Singapore and of engineering in Seoul.

Causes of diseconomies of scale
- **Communication difficulties** — as a business grows, communication between all the employees, departments, divisions and functional areas becomes more difficult, slower and requires more resources. This raises unit costs.
- **Duplication and coordination costs** — as size increases it becomes more difficult and expensive to make sure that the same work is not being done in different places, and more resources are devoted to liaison and coordination. Large businesses often have a higher percentage of managers rather than employees directly engaged in production. This raises unit costs.
- **Less motivation and control** — larger firms find it more difficult to motivate employees, as workers feel more remote from managers and the business as a whole. More resources may be devoted to control of employees. Unit costs are raised.

> **Expert tip**
> Economies and diseconomies of scale are a result of the scale of production. They may change as the scale of production changes but are always linked to it, usually through the employment of more capital investment.

> **Now test yourself**
> 21 Explain the difference between:
>   (a) economies of scale and diseconomies of scale
>   (b) internal and external economies of scale
> 22 Identify:
>   (a) three causes of economies of scale
>   (b) three causes of diseconomies of scale
>
> **Answers on p.211**
> Tested

Inventory management

Inventory management deals with the way various types of inventory are held and their levels controlled. Another commonly used word for inventory is 'stock' or 'stocks'.

The purpose of inventory
Revised

Inventory is the raw materials, work in progress (partly finished goods) and finished products. There must be enough inventory to enable production to take place — if there is too much inventory unnecessary costs are incurred.

> **Inventory:** the raw materials, work in progress and finished goods held by a business to enable demand to be met.

- **Raw materials** — these are essential for the production transformation process. They are also held so that a sudden order can be started on without waiting for more raw materials, i.e. they act as a buffer that will enable unexpected orders to be met.
- **Work in progress** — these are goods that are partly finished but are not yet ready for sale, e.g. an assembled car with the wheels still to go on.
- **Finished goods** — these are goods that are ready for sale. Businesses hold them so customers can be supplied immediately, i.e. they act as a buffer that enables demand to be met, e.g. goods in a retail store.

Costs and benefits of holding inventory

All inventory has come from resources used in production that have to be paid for. Inventory does not generate any revenue to recover these costs until it is sold. Holding too much inventory results in unnecessary expense; holding too little may mean loss of customers. Holding inventory is essential for the transformation process and a business has to balance the conflicting costs and benefits.

Costs of holding inventory

These include:

- rent for space or interest on money borrowed for storage costs
- the cost of maintaining storage — employees, equipment and buildings
- insurance and security
- losses due to inventory becoming out-dated and unsaleable at a profit
- inventory may be damaged, stolen or perish
- occupying space that could be used for another purpose — a sign of inertia slowing down needed change

In addition, holding inventory involves the costs of ordering, monitoring, tracking, inspecting and transport.

Benefits of holding inventory

- **Ability to meet demand** — holding inventory means a business is in a position to supply a customer as quickly as possible when an order arrives. Varying demand makes holding inventory essential for flexibility.
- **Ensuring production is not interrupted** — holding inventory enables production and sales to continue even if supplies of raw materials cannot be obtained for a while.
- **Gaining a discount** — economies of scale in transport or bulk buying of raw materials at a discount may save more than the cost of holding inventory.
- **Reducing inflation effects** — buying raw materials before price rises or producing goods before costs rise may produce savings or higher profit margins.

> **Now test yourself**
>
> 23 Define the following:
>   (a) raw materials
>   (b) work in progress
>   (c) finished goods
>
> **Answers on p.211**
>
> Tested

> **Expert tip**
>
> Make sure you can discuss the costs and benefits of holding inventory for each of the three types of inventory.

> **Now test yourself**
>
> 24 Explain three reasons for holding inventory.
> 25 Explain three reasons for holding as little inventory as possible.
>
> **Answers on p.211**
>
> Tested

Managing inventory

Revised

Inventory is a key part of the transformation process. Managing it must be linked to the other functional areas. Sales determine how much production is needed as inventory must be ordered and the number of employees to work must be set. The production process may also determine inventory levels. IT systems enable these functions to be interrelated in the most efficient way, often based on the buffer inventory model. **Buffer inventory** is the minimum inventory that prevents variations in supply, production or demand stopping production or sales.

> **Buffer inventory:** the minimum inventory that prevents variations in supply, production or demand stopping production or sales.

Construction and interpretation of inventory control charts

The buffer inventory model uses inventory control charts that enable sufficient inventory to meet demand while minimising costs. Inventory is used over time; the model assumes this occurs evenly. It assumes a minimum inventory level to be held — the buffer inventory. In order for this to be maintained, inventory must be ordered at the **reorder level**, which will be before the buffer level is reached. The time taken from then until it arrives is the **lead time**. This means that inventory never falls below the buffer level and reordering is triggered when the reorder level is reached. The inventory control chart in Figure 5 shows this graphically.

> **Reorder level:** the level of inventory at which more inventory will be ordered.
>
> **Lead time:** the time taken for inventory to arrive after it has been ordered.

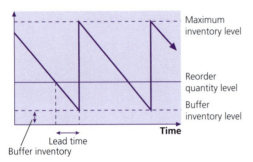

Figure 5 Inventory control chart

> **Now test yourself**
>
> 26 Define the following terms:
>   (a) buffer inventory
>   (b) reorder level
>   (c) lead time
>
> **Answers on p.211**
>
> Tested

Example

A business has a maximum inventory of 3,600 units and a buffer inventory level of 1,200 units. It uses 300 units per week. The lead time for orders arriving is 4 weeks.

This lead time means that the reorder level must be at least 1,200 units (4 × 300) above the buffer inventory level at 2,400 units. This will mean that the new inventory arrives as the buffer inventory level is reached, assuming no delays.

Inventory control methods

There are two principal approaches to dealing with inventory:
- Have inventory at high levels ensuring inventory will never run out — managing levels is easy but it is expensive to hold.
- Have small inventory levels ensuring very small inventory holding costs — high inventory management costs.

Both approaches may be made more efficient by using:
- **Inventory rotation** — old inventory is used before new.
- **IT systems of inventory control** — including electronic point of sale (EPOS), which links sales at the till to stock levels.

Setting a buffer inventory level and using an inventory control chart will be appropriate for either of these approaches. The second approach is typified by just-in-time (JIT) production methods.

Inventory control and just-in-time (JIT)

JIT operates with as low a buffer inventory level as possible. Raw materials are ordered only when needed for production, efficient production methods minimise work in progress and finished goods are supplied immediately to customers, minimising finished goods inventory. JIT requires:
- low reorder level
- low order quantity
- short lead time

> **Revision activity**
>
> 1 Using the information in the example, construct an inventory control chart to illustrate the data.
> 2 Explain the effect of the following changes, each taken in turn.
>   - lead time is reduced to 3 weeks
>   - buffer inventory is increased to 1,600 units
> 3 Explain how using an inventory control chart may reduce costs.

> **Expert tip**
>
> Reducing the costs of holding inventory may involve changes to other areas of operations, e.g. number of employees, different systems of monitoring inventory, new IT tracking systems.

- reliable suppliers for delivery time and quality
- accurate forecasts of customer demand
- integrated production process
- enterprise resource planning (ERP) systems to integrate suppliers, production and customer demand

The result will be very small buffer inventory levels, lead times, order quantities and reorder levels. This applies to raw materials and finished goods. Overall the costs of holding inventory will be small. JIT relies on finding reliable suppliers and integrated processes, linking demand, the production process and the supply chain. It is difficult to reduce inventory to zero but JIT production minimises inventory costs.

> **Now test yourself** — Tested
>
> 27 Outline three reasons why JIT production may reduce inventory costs.
> 28 Identify possible problems for a business using a JIT production system.
>
> **Answers on p.211**

> **Revision activity**
>
> Rush plc manufactures quality motor bike clutches. It sells varying quantities each month. Rush must cut costs because competitors have reduced prices and only goodwill has maintained sales. The business relies on components supplied by a number of firms and holds 4 months' stocks because it cannot afford to lose production time or sales.
>
> Using a spider diagram, analyse the factors that Rush might consider when deciding whether to adopt a just-in-time inventory control system.

5 Finance and accounting

The need for business finance

Start-up capital and capital for expansion

Revised

Business start-up
When a business is first set up, the owners will need finance to buy premises (if not renting), equipment and/or raw materials. Service businesses will also need some initial finance. For example, a business consultant is likely to require an office that will need to be furnished and equipped, perhaps with chairs, desks, telephones and computers. These need to be purchased or leased; either way money will be needed.

Businesses usually experience other expenses such as wages before any income is received. Sufficient finance must be available to cover these initial costs. This is known as '**start-up capital**'.

> **Start-up capital:** the money that a business requires to begin operating, e.g. to purchase or rent premises, to purchase equipment or raw materials.

Business expansion
Established businesses frequently make the decision to expand. This might be acquiring additional premises or equipment. In some cases, finance might be required in order to buy another existing business. This differs from start-up capital because this type of finance is only required after the business is operational.

Different needs require different sources of finance
The need for finance might be for a long-term project and therefore long-term sources of finance are likely to be used. For example a business may need finance for:
- new product development
- the exploration and development of new markets
- an increased level of promotion in response to the arrival of a potentially serious competitor — this could be a long-term issue for a business if the competitor stays in the market

Alternatively the need for finance might be related to temporary short-term shortages of finance, for example while waiting for payment from customers, causing short-term sources of finance to be more appropriate. For example to:
- purchase materials
- pay wages or utility bills
- pay for promotional activities

The amount of money required, regardless of the length of time involved, might also influence the source of finance that would be used.

> **Now test yourself**
> 1. Define the term 'start-up capital'.
> 2. Explain why the reason that finance is required might influence the source of finance used.
>
> **Answers on p.211**
>
> Tested

> **Expert tip**
> In answering any question related to this topic make sure that you take note of the reason why the business needs finance, i.e. for start-up capital or to expand an existing business. This will influence the sources of capital that would be used. Take note also of the size of the business and its form of ownership as this also influences sources of finance.

Working capital

Revised

The meaning and significance of working capital as a source of finance

- **Working capital** is used to finance the day-to-day activities of a business. It finances the purchase of materials and the payment of wages to the employees. Working capital is current assets minus current liabilities.
- **Current assets** consist of **liquid assets**, i.e. inventory (stock), trade receivables (debtors) and cash and cash equivalents.
- **Current liabilities** consist of trade and other payables (creditors) and overdrafts.

> **Working capital:** the excess of current assets over current liabilities: also known as net current assets.
>
> **Liquid assets:** the assets that can be quickly and easily converted into cash. For example, bank accounts and stock although stock is the least liquid of the current assets.

Positive working capital

Where a business has positive working capital this means that the business has more current assets than current liabilities. Too much working capital means that the business has assets that are not working hard enough. It could be that too much money is tied up in stock and is therefore creating an opportunity cost. The money held in stock could be used more productively elsewhere in the business.

Negative working capital

In this situation, current liabilities exceed current assets. Too little working capital could mean that the business is unable to pay its **short-term liabilities** such as suppliers and wages. This could lead to the business becoming illiquid and ultimately failing. Liquidity means the ease with which an asset can be turned into cash.

> **Short-term liabilities:** debts that are expected to be repaid within a 12-month period.

A shortfall in working capital is often resolved by agreeing an overdraft to enable the business to continue to function.

Many businesses fail due to a lack of working capital even though they are profitable.

Now test yourself

Tested

3. Explain what is meant by the term 'working capital'.
4. Explain why too much working capital might cause problems within a business.
5. State one disadvantage and one advantage of positive working capital.

Answers on p.211

Revision activity

Make a list of the current assets and current liabilities that a shoe retailer might have.

The working capital cycle

Many businesses carefully monitor their **working capital cycle** which is shown in Figure 1.

> **Working capital cycle:** the time between purchasing stock and/or raw materials and the receipt of payment from customers for the goods or services received.

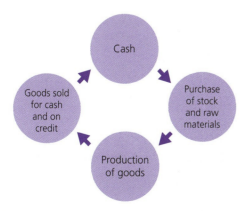

Figure 1 The working capital cycle

The need for business finance

Ways of improving the cycle

These include:
- Shortening the time customers take to settle their debts.
- Speeding up the production process so that the time between receiving materials and delivering products to customers is shortened. The length of time goods are in production before being sold will affect the working capital cycle.

Remember that a positive working capital does not always mean that a business has lots of cash to spend. Although it means that current assets are greater than what the business owes in the short term, high levels of inventory (stock) are included in the working capital figure and a business cannot use that stock to pay the wages of its workers or to settle its debts with suppliers.

Significance of the distinction between revenue expenditure and capital expenditure

Revenue expenditure

Revenue expenditure is expenditure on everyday running costs within a business. Such costs might include the purchase of raw materials, the payment of wages to employees or the payment to an electricity company for the power to run the machinery. They are generally items that will be used in the short term. Revenue expenditure is shown as an expense in the income statement (profit and loss account).

Capital expenditure

Capital expenditure is expenditure on non-current assets (fixed assets) such as buildings or machinery. These items will be used in the business for a long time. It is recorded in the statement of financial position (balance sheet).

If a business purchases new machinery and pays for it with cash, the payment will show as a reduction in the cash balance of the business. If a bank loan is used to pay for the machinery, then this will be seen as an increase in the non-current liabilities (long-term liabilities).

The new machine will also appear as an increase in the non-current assets (fixed assets) of the business.

> **Revenue expenditure:** money used to pay for everyday running costs of a business such as raw materials and wages. They are short-term costs.
>
> **Capital expenditure:** money used to acquire non-current assets (fixed assets) that will be used in the business over a long period, e.g to purchase machinery or premises.

Now test yourself

6 Explain the difference between revenue expenditure and capital expenditure.

Answer on p.211

Tested

Revision activity

Make a list of items that might be included in revenue expenditure and another list of items that might be included in capital expenditure. Do this for a retail business and a manufacturing business.

Sources of finance

Legal structure and sources of finance

Revised

The sources of finance available to a business can be influenced by the legal structure of an individual business, the size of the business and the reason for which finance is required, and the amount required and the length of time for which the finance is needed.

A sole trader or a partnership would not have access to share capital unless they changed the structure of their business to a private limited company or a public limited company. Remember that the sale of shares in a private limited company is limited and it cannot be sold to members of the public. A public limited company is able to sell shares to anyone through the **stock exchange**.

> **Stock exchange:** the place where stocks and shares are bought and sold.

Short-term and long-term sources of finance

Revised

Distinction between short- and long-term sources of finance

- **Short-term finance:** usually defined as being repayable within 12 months, e.g. an overdraft or short-term bank loan.
- **Long-term finance:** repayable over terms as long as 10 or 20 years, e.g. a mortgage or a long-term bank loan.

The sources of finance can be internal or external to the business.

> **Short-term finance:** money that is to be repaid within one year.
>
> **Long-term finance:** money that is repaid over several years.

Internal sources of finance

Revised

Internal sources of finance are those sourced within the business itself. Examples include retained profit, working capital and the sale of assets. Table 1 outlines the advantages and disadvantages of the various kinds of internal sources of finance.

Table 1 Advantages and disadvantages of internal sources of finance

Source	Advantages	Disadvantages
Retained earnings (retained profit) Profit earned by the business in previous years of trading.	• Does not require interest payments to be made. • Does not have to be repaid to anyone. • Is instantly available. • Does not create a debt to anyone outside the business.	• Is dependent on previous years having been profitable. • If shareholders prefer larger dividends, they might not agree to its use.
Sale of assets Assets that are no longer used by a business can be converted into money to provide finance for other projects. Some assets can be sold without the business losing the use of them. If assets are sold and then leased back the initial inflow of funds must be balanced against the lease payments that will have to be made. The business must be sure that it does not need to own the asset that is to be sold.	• The finance does not have to be repaid to anyone — it is a permanent source of finance. • It does not incur interest payments. • It can be a fast method of obtaining finance although this depends on the asset being sold, e.g. buildings can take some time to be sold.	• The amount raised might not be large; if a business no longer needs the asset will it have a high value? • The asset and its use is permanently lost to the business. • If the asset is sold and leased back this will require regular payments to be made by the business in the future.
Working capital This source of finance can be made available by ensuring that credit customers settle their debts. Inventory can be sold off perhaps on special terms in order to increase the amount of working capital available.	• It is a permanent source of finance. • By having a special sale, old inventory can be sold off, making room for more up-to-date stock. • It can be a fast way of raising finance.	• The current assets might be reduced to a point that makes it difficult to cover current liabilities. • Customers might not be happy about being asked to settle their debts earlier than usual. • Potential new customers might prefer to deal with a business that offers a longer credit period. • It might not produce a large amount of finance.

Internal sources of finance might be insufficient to satisfy the financial needs of the business. If the finance is required for a large project then it is possible that internal sources alone will not be sufficient.

It is possible that a business might have sufficient **retained earnings** to finance a large project, but most businesses will have been using their retained earnings to help to generate larger future income rather than letting it accumulate.

> **Retained earnings:** retained earnings are the profit earned by a business in previous years.

> **Now test yourself** *Tested*
>
> 7 Explain what is meant by 'short-term finance'.
> 8 State two reasons why a business might prefer to use long-term rather than short-term finance.
> 9 Identify one advantage and one disadvantage of using working capital as a source of finance.
> 10 Outline two advantages of using retained earnings as a source of finance.
>
> **Answers on p.211–12**

External sources *Revised*

Examples of external sources of finance include overdrafts, bank loans, mortgages, introduction of new partners or sale of shares. Table 2 outlines the advantages and disadvantages of these sources of finance.

Short-term sources

Table 2 Advantages and disadvantages of short-term sources of finance

Source	Advantages	Disadvantages
Bank overdraft The bank agrees to allow a business to draw money greater than the amount in the account. A limit is placed on the additional amount that can be drawn. Overdrafts should be agreed before they are used. An unagreed overdraft is likely to carry even higher interest rates.	• Usually quick to put in place. • There is no loss of ownership or control. • Flexibility — business does not need to use the full amount of overdraft agreed and will not incur charges for the unused amount.	• Often expensive due to high rates of interest being charged. • Overdrafts can be recalled at short notice — this might mean the business is unable to meet its short-term financial obligations. • The business will need evidence that it will receive funds shortly, e.g. from customers. • The final amount to be repaid is often uncertain.
Short-term bank loan Money loaned to a business to be repaid usually within 12 months.	• Security (collateral) is not always required. • Usually a cheaper option than an overdraft. • The term of the loan will be fixed and stated. • Regular repayments aid budgeting.	• The amount agreed cannot be varied unlike an overdraft. • Interest is payable on the whole amount. • Early repayment might incur a financial penalty.

> **Now test yourself** *Tested*
>
> 11 A business sells its good on credit and is awaiting payment from a number of customers. It is short of funds to pay the wages of its employees. Explain which source of finance you would recommend the business uses to pay the wages.
> 12 Identify one advantage and one disadvantage of using a short-term bank loan as a source of finance.
> 13 Identify two possible sources of short-term finance.
>
> **Answers on p.212**

Long-term sources

Long-term sources of finance are often used when finance is required for a project that is likely to take a long time before it becomes profitable. These sources can be permanent or non-permanent sources of funding. Some sources will require repayment at some time in the future, whilst other do not require any repayments to be made. Table 3 outlines the sources of long-term finance and their advantages and disadvantages.

Table 3 Advantages and disadvantages of long-term sources of finance

Source	Advantages	Disadvantages
Introduce new partners A source of long-term permanent finance. A sole trader might become a partnership or an existing partnership might invite additional people to join the business. If a new partner is admitted, the existing partners must agree.	• Usually a quick method of acquiring additional finance. • It is a permanent source of finance.	• Some ownership and control of the business is lost. • A sole trader taking in partners loses some independence.
Share capital Available to incorporated businesses and can involve the sale of shares to new or existing shareholders. Sale of shares results in the sale of part of the ownership of the business. *Private limited company:* existing shareholders must agree if shares are to be sold to new shareholders. *Public limited company:* shares may be bought by new or existing shareholders through the stock exchange and can be sold to the general public.	• It is a permanent source of finance and does not have to be repaid. • It can potentially raise large sums of money.	• The ownership of the company is diluted if new shareholders are introduced. • The amount of authorised share capital will limit the amount of shares that can be issued.
Long-term loans Usually used for large and/or expensive projects when it might take a long time before the sum borrowed can be totally repaid. The higher the risk to the lender, the higher will be the rate of interest that must be paid on the money borrowed.	• The amount and time of the loan is fixed. • There is a possibility a fixed rate of interest can be agreed, removing the threat of future interest rate increases. • Ownership and control of the business is unaffected. • The regularity of payments aids budgeting.	• Interest must be paid. This varies according to the risk involved, the length of the loan and current rates of interest. • Repayments usually begin as soon as the loan is taken, but some projects might not yield returns for some time. • Lenders require a guarantee, i.e. security or collateral. • Assets used as security will be seized and sold if the loan is not repaid as agreed.
Mortgages Usually used for the purchase of premises. They are often repaid over 20 or 30 years or even longer. The security to the lender will be the value of the premises being purchased and perhaps other property owned by the borrower until the value of the mortgage is fully repaid. The borrower has full use of the property throughout the term of the mortgage.	• Large amounts can be raised. • Ownership and control remain unaffected. • The asset can be sold but the mortgage debt must be cleared. • Once the value of the asset exceeds that of the amount borrowed, an additional mortgage might be possible if extra funds are required.	• If the value of the asset falls below the value of the original loan, the full value of the mortgage is still due. • Interest payable on the loan will be determined by the current rate of interest unless on a fixed term agreement. • Mortgage payments must be made whether or not a profit is made. • The asset can be seized if repayments are not made as agreed. If the amount recovered is less than the outstanding debt the borrower is liable to pay the difference.
Debentures Debentures do not give the holders any ownership in the business. They are issued for a specified time period and yield a fixed rate of interest each year. The capital sum is repaid to the investor when the maturity date is reached.	• Ownership and control is unaffected. • Large amounts of finance can be raised. • Repayment of the loan is not made until the maturity date.	• A fixed rate of interest must be paid whether or not the business is profitable. • A debenture might be linked to a specified asset that can be sold if the business is unable to repay the lender at the maturity date. • A large amount of finance raised through the issue of debentures (non-current liability) might deter other potential lenders.

Continued

Continued

Source	Advantages	Disadvantages
Venture capital Venture capitalists are generally associated with riskier ventures that other lenders might avoid. Although more willing to take risks, they might demand a higher return on their capital. Venture capitalists will often require some share in the ownership of the business in order to protect their investment.	• Business advice is also frequently available as well as the finance. • The loan might be a permanent source of finance or is only repayable if the venture is profitable. • It provides a last resort for businesses that are unable to provide proof of their ability to repay a loan, e.g. new business.	• There might be some loss of ownership and control. • The venture capitalist might want the business to take a direction about which the original owner(s) is not happy. • Future profits might have to be shared with the lender.
Government grants and loans A grant does not have to be repaid unlike a loan. Governments use grants to stimulate specific aspects of an economy, e.g. to encourage employment or to stimulate activity within, say, the building sector of an economy.	• Permanent finance. • Grants do not have to be repaid. • Loans can have a lower rate of interest than loans from a bank. • Can be available to businesses that might not be able to get finance elsewhere.	• There could be strict guidelines about how the money can be spent, e.g. to purchase new equipment. • The business might be required to relocate to an area of high unemployment. • Loans have to be repaid with interest.

> **Expert tip**
>
> There is often confusion over whether or not the sale of shares is an internal or an external source of finance. Shares are an external source of finance because they are purchased with money drawn from accounts outside the business.

> **Now test yourself** *Tested*
>
> 14 Identify two possible sources of long-term finance.
> 15 Explain why a business might decide not to use venture capital.
>
> **Answers on p.212**

> **Authorised share capital:** the total amount of shares that a business is allowed to issue.
>
> **Debentures:** long-term loans made to a business, which earn annual interest and the capital sum is returned to the lender at the maturity date.
>
> **Venture capital:** money received from individuals who are willing to take a risk in offering financial support to a business.

Factors influencing the sources of finance and the selection of the source of finance

Revised

Different sources of finance are appropriate in different circumstances. The chosen source of finance might be for many reasons:

- **The financial history of the business.** The financial history of the business includes the length of time that the business has been in existence and also the evidence that shows how well or not the financial affairs of the business are and have been managed. A business that already has high levels of debt will be considered too great a risk for a lender to agree to any additional finance.
- **Whether the finance is required for the short term or the long term.** A short-term need for finance would be advisable, for example, to pay suppliers and wages until customers settle their debts. The time for which the finance is required should be matched by the repayment period of any loan.
- **The use to which the finance will be put.** Large projects, such as the building of a new factory, are usually financed by long-term sources because it is likely to be a long time before profits from the new factory are gained.
- **Need to retain control.** Ownership and control of a business must also be considered. Current owner(s) might prefer to choose a source of finance that does not involve any dilution of ownership and control, in which case options such as issuing shares would be ignored.

> **Now test yourself**
>
> 16 Describe one example when short-term finance would not be appropriate.
>
> **Answer on p.212**
>
> *Tested*

- **The cost of various options.** The rate of interest to be paid is an obvious consideration. Fixed interest loans are sometimes available, but if interest rates in general were to fall then the loan repayments will be higher than they might have been if a variable interest rate loan had been taken. Debentures incur lower payments initially because only interest is paid until the maturity date when the capital sum must also be repaid to the holders of debenture certificates.
- **Flexibility.** A bank loan is likely to offer more flexibility in the ways that the money can be used than a government loan or grant. Governments often insist that a business receiving a government loan or grant meets certain criteria. For example, the business might be required to locate in a specific area to help to reduce unemployment. The business might also be given finance on the understanding that it is used for building new premises or for purchasing new equipment.

Flexibility can also be required by a business in terms of how and when it can repay the debt. Some businesses might ask to delay the start of any repayments until the project has begun to yield some returns. A business might also want the flexibility to repay the debt earlier than agreed without any penalty, although some banks will penalise early repayment of loans by requiring interest that would have been paid for part of the remaining duration of the loan to be added to the final payment.

> **Expert tip**
>
> The context in a question should be considered when suggesting various sources of finance. Is the project short or long term? Is the business a sole trader, partnership, private limited company or public limited company?

> **Revision activity**
>
> 1. Analyse the sources of finance that a sole trader might consider when requiring some extra finance to pay wages for the next month.
> 2. Analyse the sources of finance available to a private limited company that wants to build new premises and launch a totally new product.
> 3. Analyse the sources of finance that a public limited company might use if it finds that it has insufficient funds to pay the suppliers this month.

Forecasting cash flows and managing working capital

Purposes of cash-flow forecasts

A **cash-flow forecast** is produced to estimate or predict the amount of cash that a business can anticipate having in a particular period. It helps a business prepare for times when it might experience a shortfall in cash and can therefore make arrangements for an injection of cash in time to cover the shortfall.

The estimate could prove to be inaccurate. A cash-flow forecast is not based on cash inflows and outflows that have already happened. It is an educated guess about what can reasonably be expected to happen in the future.

> **Cash-flow forecast:** a prediction or estimation of future inflows and outflows of cash to a business during a specific future time period.

Difference between cash and profit
- **Cash** is money in the form of notes and coins or money held in bank accounts that is readily available to pay for a business's purchases.
- **Profit** is the difference between sales revenue and costs. Profit is not necessarily money that is available to spend because some sales might have been credit sales and payments have not yet been received. Some customers might never settle their debts and therefore that 'profit' will never be available for the business to spend.

> **Expert tip**
>
> Make sure you do not confuse a cash-flow forecast with a cash-flow statement. A cash-flow statement is a record of transactions that have already taken place.

The importance for a business of holding a suitable amount of cash
- Cash allows a business to pay for items such as wages and payments to suppliers. Employees would not continue to work for a business that did not pay their wages and suppliers would not continue to supply a business that did not settle its debts.
- A business must have access to sufficient cash to enable it to meet short-term financial obligations.

- A profitable business can be declared insolvent if it cannot honour its short-term liabilities.
- Holding too much cash creates an opportunity cost because the money might have been used in a way that produced a beneficial outcome for the business, e.g. investment in new equipment or by placing it in an interest yielding account.
- It is the production of a cash-flow forecast that allows businesses to monitor the level of cash in the business and to take timely action to ensure that an appropriate level of cash is maintained.
- A profitable business can fail because it has a cash-flow problem. New businesses are particularly vulnerable due to suppliers refusing to sell on credit terms until the business is more established. However, the customers of the business are likely to expect credit terms to be given to them, causing a cash-flow problem.

Now test yourself

17 Explain the difference between cash and profit.
18 Explain two reasons why businesses need to hold some cash.
19 Explain one disadvantage of holding too much cash.

Answers on p.212

Cash-flow forecasts in practice

Uses of cash-flow forecasts

- **To predict times when there might be a shortage of cash in the business.** This is particularly important when a large payment has to be made, for example, the premises insurance. Regular weekly or monthly payments do not tend to have a disruptive effect on cash flow, but a large quarterly, half-yearly or annual payment might be forgotten, and therefore not planned for, causing a shortfall in the cash balance of the business. Businesses must be prepared for these less regular payments.
- **To plan for foreseeable variations in cash flow.** Seasonal variations can have a large impact on the cash flow of some businesses, e.g. those involved in the tourist industry. Fixed costs will still have to be paid, whilst the inflow of cash is severely reduced at certain times of the year.
- **To set targets.** A business can set reduced targets for spending to ensure that outflows do not exceed inflows. Expenditure can perhaps be delayed until the cash situation is improved.
- **To show to a potential lender.** When a business requests an overdraft or a bank loan, the lender usually needs proof that the business will be able to make the repayments. A cash-flow forecast can be used to show that the cash flow is sufficient to allow the loan repayments to be made.
- **To undertake 'what if' analysis.** The potential impact of predicted changes to sales and/or costs can be anticipated. It could also illustrate the impact of changing the credit terms given to debtors or received from creditors.

Now test yourself

20 Explain two reasons why a business might construct a cash-flow forecast.
21 Identify one possible cause of a shortfall in cash within a business.

Answers on p.212

Construction of cash-flow forecasts

Various formats are used for cash-flow forecasts. A simple example of what is contained in a cash-flow forecast is shown below.

	$
Cash inflows	
Payments from customers	3,500
Bank loan	10,000
Cash injection from owner	4,000
Total cash inflow	**17,500**
Cash outflows	
Rent	3,400
Purchase of vehicle	9,500
Payments to suppliers	2,800
Wages	3,500
Total cash outflow	**19,200**
Net cash flow (total cash inflow – total cash outflow)	(1,700)
Opening balance	2,000
Closing balance (net cash flow + opening balance)	300

> **Net cash flow:** total cash inflows minus total cash outflows.

> **Expert tip**
> Be prepared to fill in some missing figures from a prepared cash-flow forecast.

> **Revision activity**
> Practise finding missing figures by removing random figures from cash-flow forecasts that you have prepared in class and completing the forecasts again.

Note that:
- The closing balance becomes the opening balance for the following month.
- Cash-flow forecasts are usually constructed on a month-by-month basis to cover a 12-month period.
- Cash-flow forecasts are based on historic fact and what is expected to happen in the future, e.g. the arranged purchase of a new vehicle or an insurance premium that must be paid annually. Some figures will have to be estimated, e.g. the cost of raw materials or transport costs that might be subject to change due to market forces such as demand, supply or inflation.
- A new business faces a particular difficulty because it does not have the previous financial data on which to base its forecasts.
- Cash-flow forecasts must be as realistic as possible because they are often required by banks when a bank loan is being requested. They can also mislead a business owner into overspending if the forecast was too optimistic.

> **Now test yourself**
> 22 A business has a net cash flow of $3,000 and a total cash inflow of $12,000. Calculate the total cash outflow for the business.
> 23 The total cash inflow of a business is $15,000, the net cash flow is $4,000, the closing balance is ($1,000). Calculate the total cash outflow and the opening balance for that month.
>
> **Answers on p.212**
> Tested

Interpretation of simple cash-flow forecasts from given data

A cash-flow forecast allows businesses to assess the following:
- Are there likely to be times when a cash shortfall is expected?
- How long is a shortfall predicted to last?
- How big is the shortfall expected to be?
- Can a cause for the shortfall be identified?
- Are there any months in which the business has a cash surplus?
- How large are the surpluses forecast to be?

Businesses must have strategies to deal with cash-flow issues. For example:
- If there is a predicted cash surplus, make sure that surplus cash is put to profitable use rather than lying unused in the business.
- If there is a predicted cash shortfall (this will be a negative figure shown in brackets):
  - Arrange funds to cover periods of cash shortfall, e.g. arrange an overdraft or short-term bank loan.
  - Check to see if any cash inflows are being delayed, e.g. payment from credit customers.
  - Perhaps postpone any planned spending or arrange a longer credit period with suppliers.

– Do nothing. It might be that the cash shortfall is expected to be very short term and will be compensated for in the following months.

Amendment of cash flow in the light of changed circumstances

Forecasts are predictions or estimations of what can reasonably be expected to happen in the future. However, the future is never certain and therefore assumptions made might have to be changed in the light of changing circumstances. Forecasts, predictions and estimations that might change include:
- the forecast value of sales
- the credit terms offered to customers
- the credit terms from suppliers
- price changes either of own goods/services or those of suppliers
- wage rates
- interest rates
- requirements for new equipment, e.g. a new delivery van

The more realistic a cash-flow forecast is, the less need there might be to make amendments to the estimated figures. It is generally accepted that some changes are beyond the control of the business, e.g. the price of suppliers' goods.

> **Expert tip**
> Be prepared to comment on trends shown in a cash-flow forecast, e.g. an increasing or decreasing cash shortfall, and what steps can be taken if any action is required.

Methods of improving cash flow

Revised

Short-term methods

Reduce the credit period given to customers (debtors)
- Ask customers to pay more quickly, e.g. reduce the credit period from 60 days to 28 days. Businesses would have to be prepared to lose customers to businesses that offer a longer credit period. They might not want to lose the business of customers placing very large orders and might consider a longer credit period for them.
- Discounts for earlier payment can be offered but this means that the total amount received will be reduced by the amount of the discount.

Reduce costs
Reducing cost may mean renegotiating prices with suppliers or finding cheaper suppliers. For example, Carole and Dougie run a small building company and their supplier had just announced a 10% increase in the price of bricks, cement and sand. Carole found another supplier that could supply them at the original price for the same quality materials. A quick phone call to the original supplier resulted in the prices charged to Carole and Dougie being unchanged.

Increase the price of goods or services sold
The success of this action is likely to depend on the reaction of customers. If price elasticity of demand is inelastic, an increase in price will lead to an increase in sales revenue, i.e. increased positive cash flow. If there are a lot of competitors then a price increase might result in a substantial fall in sales and sales revenue.

Increase sales revenue
This might need an initial cash outflow. For example, if sales are low due to a lack of awareness in the market, advertising expenditure might be needed. However, if the resulting sales revenue is greater than the advertising expenditure then cash flow will be improved.

Existing old inventory (stock) can be sold at a reduced price. It may be better to sell at a low price and receive cash than to have the goods sat in storage incurring storage costs.

> **Expert tip**
> If you are asked to comment on a cash flow problem make sure that you identify the potential cause and then that your suggested solutions are consistent with your stated cause and with the business context given.

Extend credit periods to creditors (suppliers)
A balance must be achieved between the credit period given to customers and that received from suppliers. If a business allows customers 45 days in which to pay for goods but pays its suppliers in 30 days, a potential for a cash shortfall is being created.

Suppliers might also experience cash-flow problems and therefore would be unlikely to agree to an extended credit period. They might prefer that the business obtained its materials elsewhere. This is likely to depend on the size of orders being placed.

Debt factoring
The debts of credit customers can be sold to a third party who will then recover the value of the debt. The business selling the debts will receive a proportion of the original invoice value with the **debt factor** keeping the remainder.

Customers might resent having their debts sold to another business, and therefore this can cause a lack of trust between a business and its credit customers, resulting in the loss of some customers.

Debt factor: a business or individual that buys the outstanding invoices from a business. The debt factor will pay a proportion of the invoice value to the seller of the debts and then recover the debt from the debtor.

Longer-term methods of improving cash flow
Sometimes a longer-term approach to improving cash flow is required:
- **Sale and leaseback:** assets can be sold to another business but then leased back from the purchaser in return for regular payments. The seller will receive an inflow of funds but will not lose use of the equipment. However, lease payments will form a regular cash outflow in the future.
- **Leasing:** leasing equipment means that the business never owns the asset — it remains the property of the lease company — but it has full use of the asset in return for regular payments.
- **Sale of assets:** unused or under-used assets can be sold if the business is certain that it will not need them in the future.
- **Hire purchase:** instead of paying the full cost of an asset at the time of acquisition, the asset can be paid for over an agreed period. The business will make agreed regular payments until the asset plus interest is paid in full. At this time the business becomes the owner of the asset.

Now test yourself
24 Explain one short-term and one long-term method of improving cash flow.
25 Explain why it might not be advisable for a business to sell outstanding invoices to a debt factor.
26 Explain why suppliers might not be willing to extend their credit period.
27 Explain two ways of improving cash flow into a business.

Answers on p.212

Tested

The link between cash flow and working capital
Working capital is current assets minus current liabilities. Current assets consist of inventory, **trade receivables (debtors)**, bank balances and cash in hand. Current liabilities consist of short-term loans and **trade payables (creditors)**.

The effective management of working capital can help to improve cash flow. For example:
- the amount of inventory is restricted
- debtors are carefully monitored
- the best possible credit terms are agreed with suppliers — this can also include renegotiating loan or overdraft agreements

Trade receivable (debtor): a customer of a business that has purchased goods on credit terms and will pay at a later date.

Trade payable (creditor): a business that has allowed another business to obtain goods and/or services on credit terms — the debt will be settled at a later date.

Situations in which various methods of improving cash flow can be used
Steps taken to improve cash flow or working capital will be dependent on the perceived cause of the problem. For example:
- Debtors delaying payment might require stricter control over which customers are given credit.
- If the problem is increasing costs, then cheaper alternative suppliers might be the answer or some other cost-cutting measures, such as taking steps to reduce wastage of resources.
- A review of marketing strategies might solve a problem of falling sales revenue.

Revision activity
Draw up a table listing all of the methods of improving cash flow. Use three headings: method, advantages, disadvantages. List the advantages and disadvantages of each method. Consider each method in as many business situations as you can.

Costs

Cost information

Revised

Costs are the financial payments for resources used in production. The level of costs is a measure of efficiency.

The need for accurate cost data

For pricing
Businesses need to make sure that the price charged will cover all costs and, hopefully, provide some profit for the business.

To calculate profit
Profit = total revenue − total costs
(revenue = price × number sold; total costs = fixed costs + variable costs)

Inaccurate cost information might lead a business to anticipate a profit when, in reality, the revenue received will not cover the total costs of producing the product or providing the service.

Accurate cost information might also alert a business to the fact that it is spending too much on a particular aspect of producing its product or in the provision of its service. It also allows a business to calculate the impact of a change in price of its own product/service or of those supplied to the business.

To prepare cash-flow forecasts
A cash-flow forecast is a prediction and therefore might prove to be inaccurate. That possibility increases if the cost information on which the forecast is based is not accurate. This could lead a business to prepare for a shortfall or a surplus of cash that does not happen. An overdraft facility might have been agreed that would be insufficient to meet the actual needs of the business, which could cause severe liquidity problems.

When preparing final accounts for a business
The annual financial statements of a business must give a true representation of its financial position. This cannot happen if the business is using inaccurate cost information. This can give a misleading picture to possible investors and to all of the stakeholder groups linked to the business.

For comparisons of cost information over time
It will be impossible to make an accurate comparison of costs over different time periods if one or other of those periods was using inaccurate cost data.

Types of costs
- **Fixed costs (FC):** these do not vary with the level of output. Fixed costs must be paid regardless of whether any output is produced or not. Examples include rent, rates and salaries. A landlord will still want his rent for the factory even though production has not taken place.
- **Variable costs (VC):** these change or vary according to the level of output. Examples include raw material costs and the wages of workers paid by piece rate.
- **Marginal cost:** the change in the total cost of producing one additional item of a product or of providing a service to one extra person.
- **Direct costs:** these can be linked directly to the making of a specific product or provision or a specific service. Examples include the raw materials used in a product or the direct labour costs (rate paid per unit produced).

> **Fixed costs:** costs that do not vary according to the level of output, e.g. salaries and rent.
>
> **Variable costs:** costs that vary directly according to the level of output, e.g. raw materials, piece rate payments.
>
> **Marginal cost:** the cost of producing one additional product, e.g. the cost of the extra raw materials.
>
> **Direct costs:** costs that can be specifically linked to the production of a particular item, e.g. raw material or direct labour costs.

- **Indirect costs:** these costs cannot be attributed to the making of a particular product or provision or a particular service. Examples include the wages paid to administrators in the business.

> **Indirect costs:** costs that cannot be linked to a specific product or service, e.g. wages paid to administrators.

Now test yourself
Tested

28 Define 'fixed costs'.
29 Explain what is meant by variable costs, giving an example.
30 Explain what is meant by direct costs, giving an example.

Answers on p.212

Revision activity

1 Make a list of possible costs that occur in your school or college. Divide your list into fixed costs and variable costs.
2 Make a list of possible fixed costs and a list of possible variable costs for a business that manufactures mobile (cell) phones.

Problems of allocating costs in given situations

- **Semi-variable costs:** some costs contain a fixed and a variable element. An electricity bill generally consists of a standing charge (FC) and a charge for the amount of electricity used (VC).
- **Multi-product businesses:** a business that produces a variety of products might find it difficult to know exactly how much of the administration costs have been incurred by one specific product. In such cases, businesses will usually decide to apportion a part of the costs to each product based on factors such as factory space used or the number of employees involved.

> **Expert tip**
> The situation described opposite is 'apportioning' of costs. Try not to confuse this with 'allocation' of costs which, in accounting terms, means that a portion of costs can be linked to a specific product and is therefore allocated to that product.

Uses of cost information
Revised

Cost information for decision making

Whether or not to produce a particular product
Before committing to the production of a product, businesses calculate the likelihood of a profit being made. In order to be profitable, the price that can be charged should be sufficient to cover all the production costs and provide some profit. The **total cost** divided by output gives the **average cost**, which must be lower than the price to be charged if a profit is to be made.

> **Total cost:** fixed costs plus variable costs.
> **Average cost:** total costs divided by output.

Special order decisions
Occasionally a business receives a one-off order for its products but at a lower price than usual. The order should be accepted if the extra cost of making the additional goods is lower than the price being offered. The business would take into account the additional materials costs, labour costs and transport costs. Fixed costs need not be part of the calculation if they are already covered by the orders from existing customers.

Should a business cease trading?
The relationship between costs and revenue can determine whether or not a business continues to exist. In the long term, revenues must cover costs for a business to survive. Businesses might look at the trend of costs when making such a decision — are they rising or falling? An unprofitable business with a trend of falling costs might be profitable in the long term and should probably continue.

How costs can be used for pricing decisions
In the short term, it is essential that variable costs are covered, but in the longer term, fixed costs must also be covered by the revenue received. Pricing decisions are usually based on average cost i.e. (FC + VC) ÷ output.

For example, a business that produces bicycles has fixed costs of $200,000 per annum and variable costs per bicycle of $50. If the business produces and sells 3,000 bicycles each year the average cost per bicycle would be (FC + VC) ÷ output:

$$\frac{200{,}000 + 150{,}000\,(50 \times 3{,}000)}{3{,}000} = \$116.67$$

The desired profit of the business would then be added to determine the price of each bicycle, e.g. if $15 per bicycle is the desired profit, the price of each bicycle might be rounded to $130.

How an analysis of costs can help in the calculation of payments for resources

Analysis of costs can identify where costs are rising, perhaps unnecessarily. Increases in the cost of raw material might be removed by renegotiating with suppliers, by finding new suppliers or by using a lower standard of material. The decision between labour and capital might be reviewed and a change in policy might result in more machinery and fewer employees being used. High levels of wastage might be identified as a contributor to cost increases, and therefore appropriate measures would be introduced to reduce this.

How costs can be used to monitor and improve business performance

When costs and profits can be identified accurately within a specific part of business activity, the business might be divided into **cost centres**, each being responsible for their own costs, and **profit centres**, each of which must be able to demonstrate that it is profitable.

> **Cost centre:** a section within a business for which costs can be identified.
>
> **Profit centre:** a section within a business for which the profit can be calculated.

The performance of each cost and profit centre can then be measured usually against pre-set targets. Senior management can then take action against a specific part of the business that is judged to be underperforming.

Part of a business that is unable to control its costs or to produce the required level of profit is likely to be required to improve quickly or the management within those sections might be replaced.

Now test yourself

31 Explain two occasions when cost information would be used in business decision making.
32 From the following information calculate total cost, average cost and profit.
   Fixed cost = $100,000, variable cost = $5 per unit, output = 4,000, and price = $36.

Answers on p.212

Breakeven analysis

Determination of the minimum level of production needed to break even

Breakeven analysis is a means of calculating the level of output at which the business makes neither a profit nor a loss and at which total costs equal total revenue. It can also be used to calculate the amount of profit made at a specified level of output.

Production of output above the breakeven level will yield a profit, while production levels below the breakeven level will produce a loss for the business.

The breakeven level of output can be found by calculation or by using a graph.

> **Contribution:** the difference between selling price and variable costs that can then be used as a contribution towards covering fixed costs.

Contribution method

The information required is the selling price, the variable cost per unit and the total fixed costs.

If the contribution method is used to calculate the breakeven level of output the following formula is used:

$$\frac{\text{total fixed costs}}{\text{contribution per unit (selling price per unit – variable costs per unit)}}$$

For example, if the fixed costs for a product are $28,000, variable costs per unit are $10 and the selling price is $17 then the breakeven level of output will be:

$$\frac{\text{total fixed costs (28,000)}}{\text{contribution (17 – 10)}} = 4,000 \text{ units}$$

Formulaic method

Breakeven level of output can be calculated using the simple formula of TC = TR.

Total costs = fixed costs + variable costs (variable costs per unit × quantity produced)

Total revenue = price per unit × quantity sold. As the quantity is still unknown we can call that Q.

Using the same figures as for the contribution method the calculation would be:

TR = TC
$17Q = 28,000 + 10Q$
$17Q - 10Q = 28,000$
$7Q = 28,000$
$Q = \frac{28,000}{7}$
$Q = 4,000$

This business will break even when 4,000 bicycles are produced and sold.

By diagram

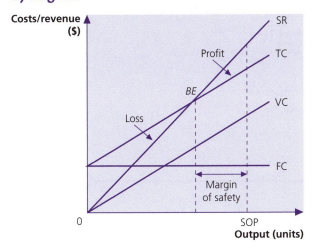

Figure 2 Breakeven

Figure 2 illustrates breakeven. When drawing a breakeven diagram, you need to:
- Give it a title, e.g. 'Breakeven diagram for the Belltyre Bicycle Co. Ltd'.
- Make sure that you label the axes and each of the lines.
- Label the breakeven point.

> **Expert tip**
>
> If an examination question requires you to calculate a breakeven level of output, using a calculation method is usually much quicker than drawing a diagram, and can therefore save valuable time.

> **Now test yourself**
>
> 33 Explain what is meant by the term 'breakeven level of output'.
> 34 Give a formula that can be used to calculate the breakeven level of output.
>
> **Answers on p.212**
>
> Tested

> **Revision activity**
>
> Practise drawing breakeven diagrams and then change the price or one of the costs and redraw the lines to find the new breakeven level of output.

> **Expert tip**
>
> There will not be sufficient time in the examination for you to be asked to draw a complete breakeven diagram but you should be able to redraw any line and to identify the impact of any changes on the breakeven point.

- Mark the **margin of safety** (the difference between the achieved level of output and the breakeven level of output when the achieved level of output is higher than the breakeven level of output).
- Check your breakeven point by also using a calculation method.

> **Margin of safety:** the amount of output produced above the breakeven level of output.

Calculation of the margin of safety
Using the examples of bicycles again, if the current level of output at the factory was 6,500 bicycles each year, then the margin of safety is 2,500 bicycles. This means that if the sales of bicycles fell by 1,000 units per annum then the business would still be profitable because the fall in sales is within the margin of safety.

Uses of breakeven analysis
- To calculate the level of profit achieved at any given level of output.
- To calculate the level of output that would be required in order to achieve a specific level of profit.
- It allows the calculation of the impact of any changes to price and/or costs on the breakeven level of output.

> **Revision activity**
> Practise drawing and labelling breakeven diagrams using a variety of figures (a diagram without labels is of little use). Practise checking your breakeven level of output by using a calculation method. Once learned, this is a quick method of checking the accuracy of your graphs.

The limitations of breakeven analysis
- It is assumed that all output is sold when in reality businesses often have unsold finished goods held in stock.
- The accuracy of breakeven calculations is dependent on the accuracy of the cost and revenue information. Inaccurate data will result in an inaccurate breakeven calculation.
- The cost and revenue lines are assumed to be linear when, in reality, they might not be. For example, a customer might receive a discount on the price if a large order is placed. In addition, as output increases, bulk purchases of materials might be made, therefore variable costs might reduce.
- Fixed costs can also increase over time due to increased production levels requiring the purchase of additional equipment.
- Breakeven analysis is only useful for one product. For a multi-product business, breakeven analysis would be very complex to achieve.

> **Now test yourself**
> 35 Define the 'margin of safety'.
> 36 Outline one use and one limitation of breakeven analysis.
>
> **Answers on p.212**
> Tested

Accounting fundamentals

Accounting is concerned with the accurate recording of the financial transactions of a business (financial accounting) and the use of this information in decision making (management accounting). Different stakeholders will be interested in different aspects of accounting.

Income statement
Revised

An **income statement** (profit and loss account) records the revenues and expenses of a business over a period of time, usually 1 year, and shows if the business is making a profit or a loss. An income statement has the heading 'Income statement for the year ended DD/MM/YYYY'. It is a financial statement of what has actually happened in the stated period of time. This means that the figures are not estimated; they are fact.

> **Income statement:** the document that shows the costs and revenues for a business and the profit or loss achieved in a given time period (usually 1 year).

Contents of an income statement
An income statement shows the gross profit and the profit for the year (net profit) and the way in which any profit or loss has been calculated.

The **trading section** shows gross profit. This is calculated by:

	$	$
Sales revenue		xxxxxx
Opening inventory	xxxx	
Purchases	xxxx	
	xxxx	
Closing inventory	(xxx)	
Cost of sales		(xxxx)
Gross profit		xxxx

Cost of sales is calculated by adding purchases to opening inventory and subtracting closing inventory.

All other expenses, e.g. transport costs, wages and rent etc., are deducted from gross profit. This gives us the profit for the year (net profit).

	$	$
Rent	xxxx	
Heat and light	xxx	
Wages	xxxx	
Office expenses	xxx	(xxxx)
Profit for the year		xxx

> **Trading section:** part of an income statement that shows the gross profit by recording sales revenue and the cost of goods sold.

> **Now test yourself**
> 37 State two items that are in the trading section of an income statement.
> 38 State two items that are deducted from gross profit to give net profit.
>
> **Answers on p.212**
> Tested

The profit for the year is used to cover any interest payments due and any tax on profits that must be paid to the government. Dividends will then be paid to shareholders. The remaining amount is **retained earnings** (retained profit).

The final section of the income statement shows how the profit after tax is shared between the shareholders and retained profit.

	$
Profit before interest and tax	xxx
Interest	(xx)
Profit (before tax) for the year	xxx
Tax at say 20%	(xxx)
	xxx
Dividends paid to shareholders	xxx
Retained earnings	xxx

> **Retained earnings** (also know as retained profit): the amount left in the business after all expenses and interest and tax obligations have been met.

> **Now test yourself**
> 39 Define retained earnings.
>
> **Answer on p.212**
> Tested

The statement of financial position (balance sheet)

Revised

A statement of financial position (balance sheet) documents the net worth of a business including a list of the values of the assets and liabilities. The assets and liabilities are recorded as either short term or long term. The balance sheet values are correct on one particular day, usually the last day in the business's financial year. The heading is 'Statement of financial position at DD/MM/YYYY'.

Contents of a statement of financial position (balance sheet)

- **Non-current assets (fixed assets):** examples include premises, equipment and vehicles that will be in use for more than 1 year.
- **Current assets:** examples include inventory, trade receivables and cash and cash equivalents — items that are expected to be used within 1 year.
- **Non-current liabilities (long-term liabilities):** examples include a mortgage or long-term bank loan, which would be repaid over a period in excess of 1 year.

> **Asset:** something that the business owns or is owed to the business, e.g. equipment, inventory or trade receivables (debtors).
>
> **Liability:** something that the business owes to another person or business, e.g. overdraft or trade payables (creditors).

Accounting fundamentals

- **Current liabilities:** debts to be repaid within 1 year, for example, an overdraft or trade payables.

From this information the net assets (total assets − total liabilities) and the working capital (current assets − current liabilities) of a business can be calculated.

Reserves and equity
- Comprises all permanent share capital (ordinary shares and preferred shares) and all reserves.
- Revenue reserves are profits retained out of 'normal' trading activities; capital reserves are profits retained from capital transactions and adjustments to the capital structure of the company.

Example

Statement of financial position (Balance sheet) for XXX plc at 31 May 2013

	$000s
Non-current assets	
premises	xxx
equipment	xxx
vehicles	xxx
	xxxx
Current assets	
inventory	xx
trade receivables	x
cash and cash equivalents	xx
	xx
Total assets	xxxx
Non-current liabilities	
long-term bank loan (repayable 2032)	(xxx)
Current liabilities	
overdraft	(x)
trade payables	(xx)
	(xx)
Total liabilities	(xxx)
Net assets	xxx
Equity	
ordinary shares	xxx
preferred shares	xxx
reserves	xxx
	xxx

Now test yourself

40 State two items that are current assets and two that are non-current assets.

41 State two items that are current liabilities.

42 Explain the difference between an income statement and a balance sheet.

Answers on p.212

Ratios

Ratios are a way of using the financial statements of a business to assess and compare its performance either with earlier years or with other businesses in the industry.

Liquidity ratios and how they are used

Liquidity ratios are a measure of the ability of a business to meet its short-term financial obligations and, for example, show if it is able to pay its suppliers for materials.

Current ratio

The **current ratio** is calculated by taking the total of all current assets and comparing them to the total of current liabilities. It is calculated using the formula:

current assets (CA) : current liabilities (CL)

or

$$\frac{\text{current assets}}{\text{current liabilities}}$$

> **Current ratio:** a comparison of the assets that are expected to become cash within 1 year with the liabilities that are due to be paid within 1 year. This measures a business's ability to meet its short-term debts.

The result shows how many times the current assets could cover the current liabilities. If the result is 3, this indicates that for every $1 of current liabilities there is $3 of current assets: the ratio is 3:1.

The current ratio figure will vary according to how much credit businesses extend to their customers. A business that deals mainly in cash can safely have a lower current ratio than one that allows all customers to purchase on credit.

Acid test ratio

The **acid test ratio** ignores the value of inventory due to the possibility that these assets might be difficult to turn into cash. The acid test ratio is calculated by:

current assets less inventory : current liabilities

or

$$\frac{\text{current assets less inventory}}{\text{current liabilities}}$$

> **Acid test ratio:** compares current assets minus inventory (stock) with current liabilities, and measures a business's ability to meet its short-term debts.

A low figure may indicate that a business could have difficulty in paying its bills or meeting its short-term debts.

> **Now test yourself** — Tested
>
> 43 A business has inventory of $1,000, trade receivables $2,500 and cash equivalents of $1,000 with an overdraft of $1,000 and trade payables of $2,000. Calculate the current ratio for the business.
>
> 44 Using the figures given in the question above, calculate the acid test ratio.
>
> 45 Explain the significance to a business of the difference in the results from questions 43 and 44.
>
> **Answers on p.212**

Profitability ratios and how they are used

Such ratios can be used to analyse the quality of the profit of a business. The two profitability ratios are the **gross profit margin** and the **net profit margin**. These figures can then be compared with those of previous years and with other businesses. This can determine if the profit is good, acceptable or unsatisfactory. Profitability ratios give more information than a mere statement of profit in dollars.

> **Gross profit margin:** measures gross profit as a percentage of sales revenue.
>
> **Net profit margin:** measures net profit as a percentage of sales revenue.

Gross profit margin

The formula used to calculate gross profit margin is:

$$\frac{\text{gross profit}}{\text{sales revenue}} \times 100$$

Gross profit margin will be affected by changes in the cost of sales and/or the price charged by the business.

Net profit margin

The formula to calculate net profit margin is:

$$\frac{\text{profit for the year}}{\text{sales revenue}} \times 100$$

Net profit margin will be influenced by any changes to the level of expenses incurred by the business. For example, an increase in wages paid to employees or an increase in the cost of electricity would reduce the net profit margin.

The profitability ratios can show the ability of a business to reward its shareholders by the payment of dividends. Potential lenders are likely to use both liquidity and profitability ratios to judge the ability of the business to make regular repayments (liquidity) and the ability of the business to generate profits (previous profitability ratios).

> **Expert tip**
>
> You are unlikely to be asked to calculate a ratio without commenting on the significance of the result. Make sure that your comments are meaningful. To say a ratio is 'good' or 'bad' does not convey any real meaning. To say it is 'better' or 'worse', showing an increasing or decreasing trend, than the previous year gives more useful information.

> **Now test yourself** — Tested
>
> 46 Calculate the gross profit margin for a business that has sales revenue of $80,000 and a gross profit of $30,000.
>
> 47 Calculate the net profit margin for a business that has sales revenue of $75,000 and a net profit of $15,000.
>
> **Answers on p.212**

Practical use of ratio analysis — Revised

Comparisons between businesses

A business can compare its ratios with those of other businesses and assess whether or not it is performing as well as other businesses in the same industry. Negative differences might indicate that action must be taken if the business is to remain competitive. It might need to look more closely at the expenses incurred and see if there are any inefficiencies that are causing costs to be higher than necessary.

A lower-than-average gross or net profit margin could be as a result of the price charged by the business being too low.

Comparison with previous years

Information is obtained from a comparison between the ratios from previous years. Net profit margin is used as an indication of how well a business is controlling its expenses. Trends in the profit margins might signify an improving or a worsening business situation.

For example, if the trend showed that the net profit margin was decreasing, then the business might need to take action to control its expenses. The shareholders might look at the final accounts to judge the impact of an investment project on the overall profitability of the business.

To get financial support

When a business is asking for a bank loan it is likely that the lender would look at the liquidity ratios in order to judge the ability of the business to repay the loan.

If a business is seeking additional funds from shareholders, the investors would possibly analyse the profitability ratios as they would be looking for a reasonable return on their investment.

Limitations of accounting ratios

- They are based on past information and might not be a good indicator of future performance.
- The interpretation of ratios can be influenced because published accounts give the detail required by law but avoid information that is not required and which might help a business's rivals.
- Ratio analysis is a quantitative technique and other qualitative factors might also need to be considered.

- Ratios measure an outcome of business performance but do not convey information about the possible causes or solutions to any potential problems.
- The use of different accounting techniques can make comparisons between businesses difficult. Different techniques mean that you cannot compare like with like.
- The published accounts are an overview of a whole business and do not reveal departmental performance.
- The statement of financial position (balance sheet) records the value of assets and liabilities on a particular day, but those values tend to vary throughout the year.
- Other factors, such as the relative size of a business, can make the comparisons difficult or of less value for reasons such as the ability to bulk buy or not.

> **Now test yourself**
>
> 48 Briefly explain two possible uses of financial ratios.
>
> 49 Explain two possible limitations of using financial ratios.
>
> **Answers on p.212**

Main users of accounts

Identification of the information that stakeholder groups might seek

The owners of a business

Sole traders and partnerships will use their financial statement to calculate the amount of tax that is due to be paid, as well as for checking that they have been running cost effectively.

The shareholders of a private limited company or a public limited company will use the final accounts to see the profit that has been made and to assess the likelihood of them receiving a dividend on their investment. They can also assess the efficiency of the management team in managing the business.

Lenders of finance

It is usual for a potential lender to ask to see the financial statements of a business in order to assess its suitability for a loan. They would want to assess the ability of the borrower to repay the loan in the time allocated. The lender would look for evidence, most probably the cash-flow forecast and income statement, that the potential borrower manages all financial aspects of the business efficiently.

The government

The government will want to assess the amount of tax due to be paid by the business. The financial statements might also be used to ensure that the business is worthy of an investment if the government is considering awarding it a grant. It is likely that the income statement would be of most interest to a government.

Customers

Customers are reassured if they can see that a business is going to survive. People might be concerned about buying goods from a business that appears to be on the edge of financial disaster.

Local community

Locals seeing an expanding business might welcome some reassurance that employment will remain in the area and, hopefully, that more workers might be required in the future.

The managers of the business

The managers of a business are likely to use the income statement and the statement of financial position (balance sheet) to assess the performance of the business. They are likely to compare the performance of their business with that of other businesses in the industry. Their aim will be to outperform the industry average. Managers might fight to reduce costs if they can see that other similar businesses are more effective is that area.

Suppliers
Suppliers will use final accounts to assess the liquidity of businesses seeking credit, i.e. to see if a business is in a position to pay for any goods or services supplied to it.

The limitations of published accounts

- Published accounts cannot be taken as an accurate predictor of the future because they are based on past data and future trends might be very different.
- The financial statements contain quantitative information and not qualitative aspects of the business. Information about the motivational levels of the employees cannot be deduced from financial statements.
- **Window dressing** of the accounts might present an unrealistically positive set of figures. For example, a business might sell off some assets so that it appears to have a lot of cash in the business.
- A weak performance in one department might be masked by an outstanding financial performance in another department. The final accounts give an overview of the business as a whole.

Distinction between financial and management accounting

Financial accountants keep accurate records of all financial transactions within the business. They are also responsible for producing the final accounts to portray a 'true and fair' picture of the financial performance of the business and to provide the financial information to the shareholders and the managers of the business.

Management accountants are users of financial information as a basis for future business decisions. The information might be used for monitoring and evaluation purposes.

> **Now test yourself**
>
> 50 Identify two possible users of financial accounts, and explain how the accounts would be of use to them.
>
> **Answer on p.212**
>
> Tested

> **Window dressing:** presenting accounts in such a way that they seem more attractive to users.

> **Now test yourself**
>
> 51 Briefly explain two limitations of using published financial statements.
>
> **Answer on p.213**
>
> Tested

> **Revision activity**
>
> Using any sets of financial accounts that you can obtain, practise calculating the financial ratios covered in the syllabus. Analyse your results and try to explain the possible significance of them for future business activity.

AS questions and answers

This section contains exam-style questions for each AS level topic followed by example answers. The answers are followed by expert comments (shown by the icon e) that indicate where credit is due and areas for improvement.

1 Business and its environment

Paper 1-style questions

Question 1

(a) State two qualities of an entrepreneur. [2]

(b) Explain two business objectives that an entrepreneur might have when starting his or her new business. [3]

Candidate answer

(a) Creativeness and confidence in their ability.

e This answer scores the full 2 marks for two accurate qualities. The candidate has merely stated the answer and has not wasted time in giving an explanation that is not required by the question.

(b) The most important objective is survival in the short term. If the business does not survive the early stages then other possible objectives, e.g. profit maximisation, cannot occur.

A second objective might be to obtain a specific market share. For a new business enterprise this objective might be to gain a 10% share of the market within 2 years. This could depend on the strength of competition already in the market.

e This answer scores 3 marks. The candidate gives two clear objectives and an appropriate explanation of each of them.

Question 2

Discuss the possible effects on stakeholder groups of a large manufacturing business planning to scale down its operations on two of its five sites. [20]

Candidate answer (extract)

A stakeholder is anyone who has an interest in the activities of a business.

The effects on stakeholders of the proposed scaling down will depend on how much the two sites are to be reduced. Are they to close completely? If the two sites are to close, then employees would be concerned about their jobs. Some might hope to move to one of the other sites. Their reaction would depend on how easily they might get another job in the area. If jobs are hard to find, trade unions might try to persuade the business to help save as many jobs as possible, perhaps by offering to transfer workers to other sites.

Shareholders would worry that the business is in financial difficulty and that profits are likely to be reduced. This would mean that shareholders might receive lower or no dividends.

The local community might suffer because the job losses in the area could result in less money spent in the local area, causing local businesses to suffer as a result. This could have a downward spiral effect on the local economy.

The extent of the impact on any stakeholder group would depend on how much the sites are scaled down. If the scaling down is very minor then the impact might be minimal.

e This extract shows good practice by defining stakeholders at the start of the answer. Three stakeholder groups are mentioned, which is sufficient unless a question states that more should be discussed. The answer is analytical and makes a judgement. The candidate concludes correctly that the effect on stakeholders would be dependent on how big the scaling down was. The complete answer would gain a grade A and would be awarded marks in the top level, e.g. 17–20 marks.

Paper 2-style question

Question 3

Superior Cosmetics Ltd (SC)

SC Ltd manufactures a range of cosmetics and skin care products. Following an investigation by a national newspaper, a recently published article accused the business of using unacceptable methods of testing its products and also questioned the safety of some of the ingredients used in its skin care range. The mission statement for the business is 'To provide the best and purest products to the population'. The article claims that the business is not an ethical one and that its customers are being misled because its behaviour contradicts its mission statement.

Discuss the extent to which SC Ltd should be concerned about the newspaper article and the dangers of being seen as an unethical company. [10]

Candidate answer (extract)

Ethical behaviour is not always governed by law but also by what is morally acceptable and what is perceived as good and fair practice. SC Ltd needs to worry about the newspaper article if it believes customers buy from it because of its claim to be an ethical company. However, if it believes that customers buy their products for other reasons, e.g. low prices, then perhaps it should not be too worried. It might feel that customers will continue to purchase SC Ltd's products because they are cheaper than substitute goods available in the market.

However, if SC Ltd's customers are very aware of business ethics, then the business would need to take action to prevent sales from falling. This could depend on how many people read the article. If the newspaper is popular and is read by many of SC Ltd's customers then it needs to act quickly to get its side of the story published. If the allegations are true, then SC Ltd needs to change its testing methods and ingredients quickly and make customers aware of the changes. It takes years to build a good reputation but it can be destroyed in days. Therefore SC Ltd must thoroughly investigate its testing methods and ingredients. It must ensure it conforms to its customers' expectations and that it does not contradict its mission statement. More customers are aware of ethics in the modern business world, therefore these allegations need to be dealt with quickly. The internet allows news to spread globally very quickly. Therefore, if SC Ltd sells worldwide, it might not be only readers of the newspaper in their own country that are made aware of the issue. Sales could fall in other countries too.

e *This extract has analysis and judgement in both paragraphs. Note: not all evaluation is at the end of answers. The candidate questions correctly the number of people who might see the article and whether or not the allegations are true. The extract then discusses the need for action and also introduces the idea of how far news can travel via the internet. This is a well-balanced answer that focuses directly on the issue in the question. If all of the answer is of this quality, the candidate would score the full 10 marks.*

2 People in organisations

Paper 1-style questions

Question 4

(a) **Explain what is mean by 'worker participation'.** [2]

(b) **Explain why employees who are viewed as Theory X might not welcome the introduction of worker participation.** [3]

Candidate answer

(a) Worker participation means to involve employees in decision making in the business.

e *This answer gains the 2 marks, although an example could have been given, e.g. the use of worker directors.*

(b) Theory X workers resist responsibility and prefer to be given clear instructions about what is required of them. They do not want or seek responsibility that would include any involvement in decision making.

e *This is a short but clear answer showing good understanding of Theory X and how this relates to worker participation. The full 3 marks is awarded.*

Question 5

Discuss the importance of a human resource management department in helping a business to achieve its objectives. [20]

Candidate answer (extract)

A business needs to have the best employees in order to achieve its objectives. The right number of workers with appropriate skills and experience are required and they must be in the right place at a time. The HRM department finds out what workers are currently employed and then compares that with the workers that are required to meet business objectives. The department then either makes workers redundant if the business has too many or it recruits workers if the business does not have enough. The HRM department does the recruitment and selection of new workers.

The HRM department gives induction training to new employees so they can quickly become familiar with the business and its systems. It also keeps records of employee performance. It works with line managers to organise extra training if any workers needed it.

Without the HRM department, a business might not be able to achieve its objectives because it might not have the right quantity and quality of employees to meet departmental targets. However, if the business is small it might not need a HRM department to make sure that it has the most appropriate employees as this could be done by the owner or a production manager.

e *This extract shows the candidate is focused on the question throughout the answer. He or she restricts the answer to the HRM activities that are most relevant to the question and does not deviate into a discussion of functions, such as the management of grievance and disciplinary issues. The candidate stresses the importance of the role of HRM in ensuring that the business has the right quantity and quality of employees to allow its objectives to be achieved but also recognises that a small business might not have or need a HRM department. The complete answer would achieve marks in the top level, i.e. 17–20 marks, due to its analytical and evaluative content.*

Paper 2-style question

Question 6

Best Bakery Ltd (BB Ltd)

Robert and Cecilia have run BB Ltd for 10 years, employing 10 local people in the bakery and shop.

The gradual increase in trade over the years means that their current site is now too small. They plan to relocate BB Ltd to a larger town 30 minutes drive from the current site. Some of their employees are unhappy about the move and are not sure that they can continue to work for the business.

Discuss the incentives that Robert and Cecilia might consider using to persuade their workforce to move with them to the new site. [10]

Candidate answer (extract)

Robert and Cecilia could offer financial or non-financial incentives. They might realise that their employees could be worried about the costs involved in travelling to the new bakery and could offer extra money to cover the transport costs or provide daily transport to the new site. They could also offer promotions to their loyal staff; the expansion of the business might mean that they also need to employ more people. This increase in status might persuade the promoted employees to move with them.

They might consider increasing the wages of employees to reward their loyalty. The incentives used will depend on what motivates their workers. If their employees are driven by money, the increased wage and/or help with transport costs might be sufficient. However, if money is not the main motivator, the offer of promotions might be the best incentive.

It is possible that the staff will not be motivated by the same thing. Therefore, Robert and Cecilia might have to use a range of incentives to encourage employees to make the move.

e *This extract retains focus on the question set and does offer some judgement at the end. The extract does not investigate all incentives but concentrates on those that directly relate to the situation in the scenario. The suggested incentives are explained in context throughout which adds to the quality of the answer. The complete answer would be given full marks for knowledge and application and 5/6 marks for analysis and evaluation. To gain full marks the candidate could have discussed the incentives in terms of if Robert and Cecilia could afford financial incentives. In total this response would be awarded 9/10 marks.*

3 Marketing

Paper 1-style questions

Question 7

(a) **Define the term 'market segmentation'.** [2]

(b) **Briefly explain two advantages of segmenting a market.** [3]

Candidate answer

(a) The way businesses identify particular groups in a market that have similar wants and needs.

e *The candidate gives a clear definition with two key points about wants of particular groups (2 marks) although he or she could have commented that individuals in the groups share similar characteristics.*

(b) Promotion costs are lower because advertising is limited to places the target segment looks at. Competition may be less as many firms aim at other segments or the whole market, so sales may be higher.

e *Two clear statements (2 marks) are given with an explanation of why these are advantages (3 marks).*

Question 8

Discuss the most appropriate methods of market research a shoe manufacturer might use when developing a new fashion shoe. [20]

Candidate answer (extract)

Market research is gathering information about markets, customers and their reaction to the marketing mix. It involves setting an objective. Developing a new shoe involves finding out what potential customers are looking for, what price they will pay and where they might buy the shoe.

Primary research is gathering information directly; secondary research is using information already gathered. As it is customer focused, primary research will be essential, though it may be useful to look at catalogues and information from competitors.

Primary research methods include observation (not applicable here), questionnaires, interviews or focus groups. A suitable number of customers of varying ages, gender and socioeconomic groups can be chosen, or particular types. They can be questioned using closed or open questions, or using structured or unstructured interviews. It would be best to do this face to face, over the telephone or using the existing website for a questionnaire. This will give information about the type of shoe that is demanded. A focus group would be more useful once a particular design is available based on the initial research.

The questions must be easy to understand and not lead respondents in a particular direction.

The sample must be large enough to represent the whole of the target market — a random sample, e.g. a shoe is aimed at rich females, aged 30–55. The sample could be stratified (divided into distinct section) — age ranges (30–39, 40–49, 50–55), gender (female) and income (high).

A shoe based on this research and made at a cost that suits the target customer may be test marketed: sold for real to a small part of the market. Changes can be made to the marketing mix to improve sales.

e *This extract contains definitions of key terms, gaining knowledge marks. It is organised and contains key research methods, with explanations and comments as to their advantages or disadvantages. The methods are explicitly related to a shoe firm and there are comments as to their appropriateness. The complete answer would achieve marks in the top level, i.e 17–20 marks.*

Paper 2-style questions

Question 9

Paper Systems plc

Paper Systems makes paper products for packaging and protection. These include envelopes, bags, and crushproof fillings sold to retail shops. The chair opened the last board meeting by saying: 'We cannot continue as we are. We import raw materials and these are rising in price. Interest rates are rising and all our costs have gone up. The economy is slowing and businesses are selling less; demand for our products is falling and sales revenue is likely to fall. Reducing prices by 10% could lead to an increase in sales of 15%.'

The marketing director responded: 'I agree broadly we must change. Market research shows retail shop sales are falling but e-commerce is growing. We must change to supplying businesses selling goods through the internet. These are likely to want lower prices, better quality and certain delivery.'

(a) Calculate the price elasticity of demand for the products of Paper Systems. [3]

(b) Explain how Paper Systems might use this PED information when setting prices [3]

Candidate answer

(a) PED = % change in q/% change in price = 15/10 = 1.5

e *The definition of PED gains 1 mark and a correct answer 3 marks. One error, e.g. PED = 15/10 = 1.2, is likely to gain 1–2 marks. Always show your workings.*

(b) PED of 1.5 is elastic. If prices are reduced, sales revenue will rise, so if Paper Systems is concerned about falling revenue it should reduce price assuming all other factors, such as competitor behaviour, are the same.

e *This response shows understanding of the implications of PED for revenue change and notes the possible relevance of other factors. It gains all 3 marks.*

Question 10

Discuss how Paper Systems might respond to these market changes by altering its marketing mix. [10]

Candidate answer (extract)

A marketing mix is the combination of product, price, place and promotion that meets consumers' needs. The market changes include rising costs, a slowing economy and the replacement of retail shops by online selling. Paper Systems could consider promoting its products to online sellers rather than street retailers. The potential clients are not final consumers, so general advertising is not effective. Advertising could take place in e-commerce trade journals. Personal selling by visits to online retailers is more likely to result in sales. For the first buyers, discounts or free sample offers with each purchase is recommended. Rising costs make it difficult for price and quality to match expectations, so a USP could be the quality of the products. Adverts and publicity material should emphasise this. Public relations may play a big role as it is cheap and articles in the trade press using Paper Systems products could be set up. E-commerce businesses are likely to use social media so these could be used to generate interest by setting up online events or invitations to try samples. Suitable e-commerce trade conventions could be attended.

It is important not to neglect existing customers. Personal selling and offers may be important in keeping them and delivery times must be reduced. A different direction may be to offer products to consumers. This could be gift-wrapping paper, document storage systems, filing, photograph boxes etc. This would mean promoting in a different way, to reach individual customers.

Changing the marketing mix will be successful if the product matches the promotion. Sales will increase but it will be important to respond to the competition.

e *This extract starts well with definitions. It is structured, with all components of the marketing mix explained with relevant possible examples. These are linked to the target market and its needs and are integrated (analysis). An attempt is made to qualify points and explain factors that success might depend on (evaluation). Comments show the likelihood of success (evaluation). The complete answer would be expected to score 8–10 marks.*

4 Operations and project management

Paper 1-style questions

Question 11

(a) Explain the term 'flow production'. [2]

(b) Briefly explain two advantages of flow production. [3]

Candidate answer

(a) Continuous production on an assembly line for standard products.

e *The candidate gives a clear definition (2 marks) but could have referred to cumulative stage-by-stage processing.*

(b) Low unit costs due to mechanisation, quality easy to check as on line.

e *A brief and accurate response that gains all 3 marks.*

Question 12

Discuss the factors managers of a chocolate-making business should consider when deciding where to locate a new factory in their country. [20]

Candidate answer (extract)

Employees with the right skills and experience are essential so the availability of these is important. Chocolate making may not require highly skilled people initially so it is more important that there are people. The managers must consider any local laws that might affect the operation of the factory. Infrastructure is crucial — materials must be able to reach the factory cheaply and products must be able to be sent to market easily. There must be power and other utilities as well as the availability of financial advice. State assistance in the form of tax incentives, low rent or training costs may be important. There must be land with planning permission. Finally, from a marketing view, the factory must be able to send products to market easily and quickly.

e Relevant factors are listed in this extract with brief comments. Some attempt is made to explain why these are important or not but little detail or application to chocolate manufacture is given. The complete answer could be expected to score 11–15 marks. Ranking factors or discussion of chocolate as a consumer product and the nature of materials or market conditions would increase the score.

Paper 2-style questions

Question 13

Office Ideas Ltd

Office Ideas produces a range of custom-built office furniture. It buys in components and basic raw materials such as wood, screws and metal sheets. It uses these to produce its products to order, selling from a shop, the internet and a catalogue. Eight employees can usually produce 36 typical fittings per week. The firm is finding it increasingly hard to compete on price. To gain discount prices Office Ideas hold between 8 and 40 weeks' worth of sales in different materials.

(a) Calculate the labour productivity in Office Ideas. [3]

(b) Comment on the significance of this figure for Office Ideas. [3]

Candidate answer

(a) 36/8 per week = 4.5 fittings per week.

e The workings are shown, the calculation is correct and time period is indicated. This response gains all 3 marks.

(b) Labour productivity measures the efficiency of the workforce. Office Ideas needs to lower costs and if productivity can be increased from this figure costs will fall, orders can be completed quicker and its competitiveness will improve.

e The candidate demonstrates knowledge of the term, with two reasons why it might be important, in general and as applied to Office Ideas. It gains all 3 marks.

Question 14

Discuss why Office Ideas might change to just-in-time inventory control. [10]

Candidate answer (extract)

Just-in-time inventory control is operating with as low a level of inventory (raw materials, work in progress and finished goods) as possible. It means only ordering materials when they are needed for production, working efficiently and sending finished goods immediately to customers. This means that inventory is held at a minimum level. This lowers all the costs of holding it, e.g. storage costs, insurance, security, space and the possibility of loss or damage. But JIT does mean that sudden orders may not be able to be met, production could be disrupted and it would not be possible to buy materials in advance of price rises. Office Ideas does take advantage of discounts for large orders and the materials are durable and unlikely to perish. However, it does build to order and could get the precise inventory it needs for each job without having to incur the costs of holding it; 8–40 weeks is a long time. A considerable saving would follow if inventory was reduced to 4 weeks' worth of sales or less. Office Ideas needs to lower costs and assuming it can train its employees and have reliable suppliers it would be advantageous to move to JIT inventory control.

e JIT is explained in this extract and some of its advantages and disadvantages are discussed with particular application to Office Ideas. Judgements are made, supported by reasoning (evaluation). The complete answer would be expected to score 8–10 marks.

5 Finance and accounting

Paper 1-style questions

Question 15

(a) **Define working capital.** [2]

(b) **Explain two reasons why a new business might use a cash-flow forecast.** [3]

Candidate answer

(a) Working capital is the money used to finance the day-to-day activities of a business. It is calculated by subtracting current liabilities from current assets.

e *This is a short but precise answer to the question. The candidate clearly understands what working capital is and gains both of the 2 marks.*

(b) To apply for a bank loan. New businesses often need bank loans for part of start-up capital. Bank managers often ask for a cash-flow forecast to see whether the business will be capable of making the required repayments. To make sure that the business will not run out of cash.

e *This answer gains 2 out of 3 marks. The first reason given is correct and well explained. However, although the second reason is correct the candidate has not offered any explanation. This answer would have scored the full 3 marks if the candidate had explained that the predicted inflows and outflows of cash could help to predict any times when there might be a shortfall of cash so that early preventative action could be taken.*

Question 16

Many small businesses fail in their first year of business. Discuss the arguments that a government might consider when deciding whether or not to give grants and/or cheap loans to small businesses in its country. [20]

Candidate answer (extract)

Many small businesses do fail in the first year but many others survive and make a contribution to the economy. They provide jobs, service the needs of larger businesses and, if profitable, contribute to the tax revenue of the government. In a country experiencing high levels of unemployment, the government might believe that helping small businesses is the quickest way to get people into work because once set up they will hopefully employ others.

Governments need to consider other demands on their spending and whether money given or loaned to large businesses might be more beneficial to the economy. However, large businesses might buy more machinery with the money, making some workers redundant. Small businesses are more likely to employ people rather than machines because of limited finance in the early years. If it is the aim of the government to increase employment it might be better to give or loan the finance to the smaller businesses.

Governments need to know that grants and loans given to small businesses will benefit the economy. If giving loans then they need to be sure that small businesses will be able to make the necessary repayments. Given the high failure rate of small business, giving loans might be risky — some loans might never be repaid.

When giving grants to any business, large or small, the money is not required to be repaid, therefore the government must have sufficient funds to be able to make the finance available.

e *This extract shows a clear focus on the question. It refers to both grants and loans and considers small businesses throughout. The second paragraph offers some analysis of the possible impact of providing finance to small or large business and ends with a judgement that links to what the government might hope to achieve. An answer that demonstrated this quality throughout would be expected to score marks in the highest level (17–20 marks).*

Paper 2 style question

Question 17

Homely House Builders Ltd (HHB Ltd)

Cash-flow forecast for HHB Ltd

Item	Month 1 ($000s)	Month 2 ($000s)	Month 3 ($000s)
Cash inflows	500	475	525
Cash outflows	450	530	615
Net cash flow	50	(55)	???
Opening balance	110	160	105
Closing balance	160	105	???

(a) Calculate the net cash flow and closing balance for month 3. [2]

(b) Discuss the significance of the cash-flow forecast to HHB Ltd and to its plans to apply for a long-term bank loan to finance a new house building project. [8]

Candidate answer

(a) The net cash flow for month 3 is ($90,000) and the closing balance is $15,000.

e *This answer scores the full 2 marks. The calculations have been completed accurately and the amounts are correctly written as being $000s.*

(b) The cash inflows appear to be unstable and there is an estimated upward trend in the cash outflows. As a result, the net cash flow is predicted to worsen each month causing the closing balance to reduce each month. The business might need to prove to the bank that this trend is not expected to continue. The bank might worry that the business will be unable to meet the repayments if a long-term loan was given to HHB. The bank's decision might depend on other factors. For example, if the house building project is expected to be completed quickly and the houses are predicted to sell quickly for a large profit, the bank might not place too much importance on the cash-flow forecast.

e *This is a good answer showing a clear understanding of cash-flow forecasts and the link with a loan application. There is some analysis of the trends shown and the significance of them to the loan application. An answer of this quality is awarded marks in the top level, i.e. 7/8 marks.*

6 Business and its environment

Business structure

Local, national and multinational businesses

Revised

Main differences between local, national and multinational business

Local businesses are active in a specific town, area or region within a country. They tend to be small- to medium-sized businesses that meet local customer needs, e.g. hairdressers, independent food shops and repair shops, such as radio and television repairs.

National businesses operate on a country-wide basis and might have branches in many regions of a country. Due to operating in several parts of a country, these businesses tend to be larger than the majority of local businesses. Although branches might exist to serve a small area, the business itself is one of national standing.

Multinational businesses operate in more than one country. They frequently produce and sell products in several countries, sometimes adjusting their products to meet the specific preferences of different countries. Multinational businesses produce and trade across national boundaries.

> **Multinational businesses:** operate in more than one country. The head office is located in one country but branches of the business exist in several countries.

The growing importance of international trade links and their impact on business activity

International trade links can be formed between businesses or as a result of governments reaching trading agreements. Links will be pursued and agreed when both parties believe that they can benefit. For example, coffee growers will form links with a coffee processing business if they can secure a market for their coffee beans at a fair price. The coffee processing business will benefit from knowing that they have a secure supply of coffee beans and of a quality that they can trust.

Governments might reach trade agreements with different countries in order to enlarge the potential market for goods produced in their own countries.

The benefits to business of international trade links
- A larger potential market — possibly a global market.
- The potential for growth of a business.
- Economies of scale.
- Possibly fewer restrictions placed on the import/export of goods to and from other countries.
- Lower import duties might be agreed by the participating governments.
- There could be a beneficial sharing of expertise.

Possible disadvantages to business of international trade links
- Businesses are likely to be exposed to competition from businesses in other countries. For example, if import duties are reduced, then overseas businesses will be able to sell goods at a cheaper price than previously. This

can put pressure on the price that the national businesses can charge. This can potentially reduce their profit.
- Meeting the needs of a wider variety of customers might mean a greater variety of products need to be produced, causing a lack of economies of scale.
- Some countries have lower wage rates than others, therefore this is likely to influence the price charged for finished goods that might be significantly cheaper than home produced goods. This could lead to a loss of jobs in some countries.
- Not all goods are acceptable for sale in all countries, e.g. alcohol. Therefore, businesses must be fully aware of any restrictions on the type of goods that can be sold.

> **Now test yourself**
>
> 1 Distinguish between a national and a multinational business.
> 2 Briefly explain one advantage and one disadvantage of the development of international trade links
>
> **Answers on p.213**
>
> Tested

Multinationals

Revised

Multinationals and the state: advantages and disadvantages

Benefits to a country
- The multinational business might bring substantial investment into a country in terms of technology and skills development.
- Increased employment if the multinational recruits locally.
- The infrastructure might be improved to accommodate the multinational business. It might make some improvements as part of an agreement with the host government.
- An increase in the variety and possible quality of goods offered for sale in a country.
- Lower prices for goods produced or sold by the multinational.
- If the multinational is profitable, the host country can benefit from an increase in tax revenue paid to the government. Tax paid can be income tax from employees as well as tax on profits.

Disadvantages to a country
- The arrival of a multinational business might prevent infant industries in the host country from becoming established.
- The multinational might demand tax concessions for locating in a particular country, therefore depriving the government of potential tax revenue.
- Multinationals often bring their managerial staff with them and therefore the jobs offered in the local market might only be the lower-skilled ones. This can dilute the benefits to the host country in terms skills development.
- Some multinationals have a larger turnover than the gross domestic product (GDP) of some host countries. This can produce an unequal balance of power in favour of the multinational that might cause some governments to allow activities that would otherwise not be acceptable. For example, a multinational that breaches employment legislation or causes pollution might not suffer the same consequences that a smaller business might. The multinational might threaten to withdraw from the country.

> **Now test yourself**
>
> 3 Briefly explain one reason why a government might encourage a multinational to locate in its country.
> 4 Identify one disadvantage to a country of a multinational locating there.
>
> **Answer on p.213**
>
> Tested

Privatisation/nationalisation

Revised

In recent years it has been more usual, in most countries, for **privatisation** to occur rather than **nationalisation**. In virtually all economies there are now privatised and nationalised businesses/organisations.

Many governments prefer market forces to determine business activity providing that all relevant laws are complied with. This means that business activity that previously took place under public ownership now occurs in the private sector. Examples in the UK include the production and supply of gas, electricity and telecommunications.

Advantages and disadvantages of privatisation or nationalisation

Advantages of privatisation
- When a previously state-owned business is not privatised as one business, increased competition between the smaller privatised units should result and that should improve the service and drive down prices to customers.
- Privatisation allows access to different sources of finance through the stock exchange and banks.
- The sale of state-owned businesses provides an inflow of finance for the government that can be used to meet other priorities.

Disadvantages of privatisation
- Once the business is sold to the private sector, and if it becomes highly profitable, that revenue is lost to the government.
- Privatised businesses will be run to make a profit and the needs of customers might not be a priority. This is particularly possible when there is a lack of competition within an industry or when movement between businesses is difficult.
- Once a state-owned business has been sold, the government no longer has control over how it operates and what its objectives are.
- Economies of scale might be lost as large and perhaps unwieldy businesses are broken up into smaller units.

Advantages of nationalisation
- Essential goods and services can be provided at a price that the population can afford.
- Strategic industries, such as the provision of electricity or gas and the defence industry, can be kept under state control, removing the possibility of them being controlled by a hostile country.
- Employment levels can be influenced by the number of jobs provided through state-owned businesses.

Disadvantages of nationalisation
- Decision making can be very slow due to the involvement of government departments.
- The businesses might not be run as efficiently as possible because a priority is the provision of essential goods and services rather than the profit motive.
- Any funding will be provided by the government, which reduces the amount that can be spent elsewhere. This will probably be taken from tax revenues.

> **Privatisation:** the transfer of ownership and control of a business/organisation from the public sector to the private sector (from government ownership into ownership by private individuals).
>
> **Nationalisation:** the transfer of ownership and control of a business/organisation from the private sector to the public sector (from private ownership to government/state ownership).

> **Now test yourself**
> 5 Identify one advantage and one disadvantage of nationalisation.
> 6 Briefly explain why a government might not want to privatise a strategic industry.
>
> **Answers on p.213**
> Tested

Public/private partnerships

Revised

Governments in many countries have seen the benefits of some businesses/organisations being jointly owned and controlled by the government and private organisations. These are known as public/private partnerships.

Public/private partnerships are appropriate in cases where a privatisation would not be in the best interests of the population but where some input from private businesses can be beneficial. The benefits can be in terms of business skills or in the form of financial support.

The nature of public/private partnerships including private finance initiatives (PFI)

In many countries, the provision of services such as health, education and transport have been judged appropriate for joint ventures between the state and private businesses/individuals.

Some organisations are funded by governments but the day-to-day activities are carried out by private organisations. For example, some health provision is sub-contracted to private individuals or organisations but the funding is provided by the government. This removes the government from the need to provide the actual services on a daily basis. The private sector has been judged to be more efficient in the provision of some services.

Some agreements involve government initiatives being funded by money from the private sector. For example, some schools and colleges in the UK have been funded by private investors.

> **Revision activity**
>
> Draw up a table with three categories across the top: healthcare, education and transport. For each category, list as many advantages and disadvantages (a) of it being purely state-owned and controlled and (b) of it being totally privately owned and controlled.
>
> Finally, list the possible impact on each of these services of public/private partnerships and/or PFI.

Size of business

External growth

External growth is usually a faster means of expansion than internal growth. It involves either **mergers** with other businesses or **takeovers** of other businesses. Growth achieved in this way is often referred to as horizontal integration or vertical integration.

Many modern businesses have grown in a way that has allowed them to diversify and therefore gain some protection from a downturn in one particular market. Other businesses have sought to secure their supply chain by merging with or by taking over their suppliers.

> **Merger:** the joining together of the ownership of two or more businesses with the full consent of all the businesses involved.
>
> **Takeovers:** when the ownership and control of a business is acquired by another business. The takeover can be by agreement or can be a forced or hostile takeover.

The different types of merger and takeover

Horizontal
Horizontal growth is the merging with or taking over of a business in the same economic sector, e.g. if a tea packaging business merged or bought out a coffee packaging business and if a chain of restaurants merged with another restaurant chain. The merger of two restaurant chains might, for example, make them stronger and more likely to survive.

Vertical
Vertical integration takes place between businesses in different economic sectors, e.g. if a coffee processing business merged or took over a coffee plantation or if a furniture manufacturer merged with a large forestry business. In both of these cases, the joining of the businesses would be to ensure a supply of the raw materials by the manufacturer and might equally be to secure a market for the raw materials on the part of the primary sector business.

Conglomerate
Conglomerate integration is when businesses from different industries and often also from different stages of production merge or are taken over.

Integration does not need to be within the same industry. A clothes retailer could decide to diversify and buy an existing chain of coffee shops — different type of business but both in the tertiary sector.

A clothes retailer could decide to buy into a forestry business because it believes forestry to be profitable. There is not any link between the businesses other than their common ownership.

Friendly and hostile takeover
A merger is a joining of two or more businesses when both sets of owners consent. A takeover can be either agreed by all parties involved, a friendly takeover, or it can be against the wishes of the owners of the business being bought, i.e. a hostile takeover. A friendly takeover occurs with the

knowledge and often the agreement of the owners of the business that is being taken over. However, a hostile takeover is seen as an aggressive act on the part of the business that is forcibly acquiring another business. This can be achieved by buying sufficient shares on the stock exchange to gain a controlling interest in the other business. A business can buy shares in another business often without the target business being aware that a takeover is in progress until it is too late and the predator business has acquired sufficient shares to gain control, though there may be laws that require the predator to declare its intentions once a certain percentage of shares have been purchased.

Impact of a merger on the various stakeholders

Table 1 Potential impacts on some stakeholders of a business

	Owners	Managers	Employees	Suppliers	Customers
Advantages	• More status. • Larger more competitive business. • Realisation of capital gain.	• Promotion. • More responsibility. • More status.	• Status of working for a larger business.	• Potential for larger orders.	• More variety. • Lower prices as economies of scale are gained.
Disadvantages	• Some loss of control. • Relocation — the merging businesses might relocate on one site.	• Fear of job loss as fewer managers might be required. • New, unfamiliar systems might be introduced.	• Fear of losing job. • Employment practices might change. • Location of job could change.	• Suppliers of the other business might be retained.	• Product quality might change. • Product range might change.

Now test yourself — Tested

7 Briefly explain the difference between a merger and a takeover.
8 Give one disadvantage of a takeover to the employees of a business.

Answers on p.213

Expert tip

Questions often ask you to give advantages or disadvantages to a business or to the employees or other stakeholders. Make sure that you take note of that focus in your answer. Students frequently explain advantages when disadvantages are required. This does not seem to happen the other way round as often!

Revision activity

Draw up a table with stakeholders not in Table 1 and list the possible advantages and disadvantages that they might experience as a result of a merger.

Why a merger may or may not achieve objectives

A merger might be successful because:

- The new, larger business can achieve economies of scale and become more competitive due to:
  - more purchasing power with suppliers
  - managerial economies, e.g. the new, larger business would only require one finance director
- The status of the business might be raised in the eyes of customers, making their products more appealing.

A merger might not be successful because:

- The larger business becomes difficult to control, i.e. diseconomies of scale are experienced.
- The feeling of insecurity among employees might continue as new systems are introduced, perhaps leading to a higher labour turnover.
- The businesses might find that their cultures are too different to allow effective collaboration.

Now test yourself

9 Briefly explain one reason why the merger of two businesses might not be successful.

Answer on p.213

Tested

The importance of joint ventures and strategic alliances as methods of external growth

An alternative means of growth that does not involve any change in ownership is the formation of joint ventures and strategic alliances. These occur when two or more businesses believe that working together, perhaps only on one specific project, can be beneficial to each business.

Joint ventures can involve businesses sharing resources to produce a product for sale or to provide a service. The venture must yield benefits to all the businesses involved in order to be worthwhile.

A **strategic alliance** would also be mutually beneficial but it might, for example, be in the form of medical care and education being provided to a part of the world that a business relies on for some of its materials. This form of alliance benefits the local inhabitants because they receive better education and healthcare. The business benefits because the local community is healthier and better educated. The business can also ensure that the local labour force is educated in the skills that are required by the business.

The businesses can benefit from:
- pooling their financial resources
- sharing expertise that each business individually might not have
- gaining access to different markets, e.g. if an alliance was formed between a business in the UK and one in India or China

One example of a strategic alliance that might be formed is between a coffee processor and some of the farmers growing the coffee. By forming this alliance:
- The coffee growers can be given the financial help and perhaps some additional input of expertise to enable them to increase the amount and the quality of their crop.
- The coffee processing business might provide the initial cost of planting and of some of the equipment that can improve the growing and harvesting process.
- The coffee processing business would be having some control over the quality of the coffee beans that it received as well as some assurance that the coffee grower could continue to grow the beans.

> **Joint venture:** when two or more businesses contribute their expertise to a business venture. The businesses do not merge but work together for the purpose of the separate business activity/project.
>
> **Strategic alliance:** an agreement between two or more businesses or organisations to link their activities as in the example of the coffee processor and the coffee growers.

Expert tip

A joint venture or strategic alliance allows each business to remain as a separate operation, able to withdraw or change the relationship if needed.

Revision activity

Think of other businesses that might benefit from joint ventures or strategic alliances and make notes of the ways in which the arrangement might be mutually beneficial.

Now test yourself

10 Outline one benefit of joint ventures.

Answer on p.213

External influences on business activity

External influences affect the business environment and determine the framework businesses operate in. They include the actions of the state and governments and their associated policies, relevant laws and international agreements, technology, and social and environmental factors. Businesses have to take all these into account when making decisions. Analysts use the acronym PESTLE to summarise these influences:
- **P**olitical
- **E**conomic
- **S**ocial
- **T**echnological
- **L**egal
- **E**nvironmental

Economic constraints and enablers

The role of the state

The state and government play a major role in determining the business environment. Governments have large spending programmes and these have to be financed from taxes and borrowing. A government has a responsibility to make sure that the country it is governing has an appropriate environment for businesses to operate in, e.g. that the population is well educated, prices are not rising too fast, infrastructure is in place and relations with other countries are good. Objectives like these are **macroeconomic**, i.e. concerned with managing the overall economic conditions. Governments can also act to create the right conditions for individual businesses and consumers at their level.

Macroeconomic: describes decisions or objectives that relate to the economy of a country as a whole and deal with the overall framework of economic activity.

How the state might intervene to help or constrain businesses

Macroeconomic level — helping businesses
Governments try to create the right conditions for businesses by ensuring that:
- the finance system is able to make money available to businesses
- the right number of educated workers are available
- prices do not rise too fast
- consumers have enough income to spend on goods
- exchange rates do not vary quickly or too much
- different regions do not differ too much in terms of income or unemployment

> **Expert tip**
> In many countries there is an assumption that the private sector produces goods and services most effectively. There must therefore be a reason why the state would provide these goods and services or intervene to regulate or support private sector businesses.

Individual businesses level
At an individual business level, governments will help businesses by providing:
- grants, subsidies and low-cost loans for investment
- roads, railways, airports and broadband
- skilled government consultants and agencies to assist with business problems
- advice to different sized businesses or those in rural or high unemployment areas

State intervention to constrain businesses
State intervention and constraints on business include:
- taxes, which reduce profits or increase costs
- laws to promote or enforce health and safety and consumer protection
- regulations on presenting fair and accurate accounts

> **Now test yourself**
> 11 Give two reasons why the state might intervene to help or constrain businesses.
> **Answer on p.213**

How the state might deal with market failure
Market failure occurs when the price mechanism and the laws of supply and demand fail to produce an outcome that is socially desirable. Examples include:
- education for all
- streetlights
- refuse collection
- utility networks
- consumer protection and labelling
- medical and hospital services for everyone
- roads, railways, ports and airports
- a legal system and police forces
- defence and national security
- public open spaces

Market failure: occurs when the price mechanism and the laws of supply and demand fail to produce an outcome that is socially desirable.

> **Now test yourself**
> 12 Identify three areas of market failure.
> **Answer on p.213**

In all these cases, it is very unlikely that a privately owned business will be able to provide these facilities and make a profit. The state will step in and be the provider. It can do this directly by providing these things as in the case of a national health service, an army or local government taking rubbish away. Another option is for the state to use private businesses to provide these services by contracting out (outsourcing), franchising or licensing.

6 Business and its environment

Governments' key macroeconomic objectives and their impact on businesses

Governments set objectives for the economy, which they try to achieve by using policies. The priority placed on each objective will determine which policies are implemented, when and by how much. It is this implementation that is important for businesses rather than just the setting of objectives. Important government objectives include achieving:

- low **unemployment**
- low **inflation**
- stable **exchange rates**
- **growth**
- **transfer of wealth**

Low unemployment

People who want to work should be able to find work. The reason governments have an objective of low unemployment is because high unemployment is a cost to a country as it causes:

- a waste of human resources that lowers overall production and economic growth
- social problems like drug taking and personality problems
- a cost to the whole country in benefits, lost taxation and increased crime levels

Possible impact of high unemployment on businesses

High unemployment means there are relatively more workers seeking the available jobs. In turn this causes:

- a low consumer income, which means sales are lower and competition is greater, leading to low output, low profits and pressure to cut costs and lower prices
- redundancies and rationalisation
- a consumer switch to lower-priced, lower-quality products
- employees fearing the loss of their jobs, which means they will work harder and complain less
- easy recruitment of already skilled employees
- low wages as scarcity of jobs means workers will work for less
- investment falls

Low inflation

Inflation is a persistent increase in the general level of prices. Rising prices mean that the value of money in a country falls. The reason governments have an objective of low inflation is that a high level means uncertainty because it:

- erodes the value of savings and makes borrowing more attractive
- makes planning and fixing contracts difficult
- might lead to hoarding

Possible impacts of high inflation on businesses

Possible impacts of high inflation on businesses are:

- increased borrowing for investment as asset values will rise with no effort
- increased costs of materials, fuel and labour
- it is easier to increase prices and pass on price rises of materials and labour
- consumer spending lowers as prices rise
- price becomes a more important marketing mix element
- increased pressure from employees for higher wages
- increased difficulty in tracking and setting prices
- a country's products become less competitive and less attractive to foreign investors

---

Unemployment: occurs when some workers who want to work cannot find jobs.

Inflation: a persistent increase in the general level of prices.

Exchange rate: the price of a currency in terms of other currencies.

Growth: an increase in economic activity, usually measured by a rise in gross domestic product (GDP).

Gross domestic product (GDP): the total value of the output of a country in 1 year.

Transfer of wealth (or wealth redistribution): when governments use taxes, subsidies or regulation to move wealth from one group in society to another.

Now test yourself

13 Identify and define three key government macroeconomic objectives.

Answer on p.213

Tested

Revision activity

Use a flow diagram to show how rising unemployment might affect a garage selling petrol.

Expert tip

Remember that a decrease in inflation means that prices are rising less quickly, not that they are falling.

Now test yourself

14 Define inflation.

Answer on p.213

Tested

Revision activity

Write a short article for your school/college magazine to explain how a business selling accountancy services might react to a period of high inflation.

Stable exchange rates

The exchange rate of a country's currency is its price in terms of other currencies. A stable exchange rate means that this price is remaining the same over time so that the price of exports and imports will not keep changing. This makes planning easier. Exchange rates are only one factor in decisions on exporting and importing.

Possible impact of unstable exchange rates on businesses

Stable exchange rates make planning easier and more certain for importers and exporters.

- Rising exchange rates mean that exporting businesses become less competitive. Prices of exports rise in the importing country and the volume of exports falls. The extent of the fall will depend on the price elasticity of demand.
- Rising exchange rates mean that importing businesses become more competitive. Prices of imports fall and the volume of imported goods increases. The extent of the increase will depend on the price elasticity of demand.
- Falling exchange rates mean the reverse of the above.

Growth

Growth is an increase in economic activity, usually measured by a rise in gross domestic product (GDP). Economic growth means there is more wealth, and on the whole consumers will be able to buy more and governments can provide more facilities such as education, health services and infrastructure. Growth can be achieved by more use of resources, higher investment, a more skilled workforce, higher exports, or higher consumer spending.

Possible impact of economic growth on businesses

- sales and profits increase as consumers' incomes rise
- sales of luxury items rise relatively more than basic products
- new product launches are likely to increase
- investment and more new technology is more likely
- employment increases, unemployment falls
- tax revenues increase
- it may be more difficult to recruit suitable skilled labour

Transfer of wealth or redistribution

Governments are concerned not just with the level of GDP and income but with which groups in the country have the wealth and income. Governments generally have objectives related to this. For example, they might wish to:

- pay benefits to those on low incomes, the unemployed or disabled
- get those on high incomes to pay relatively more taxes
- transfer wealth and income from richer to poorer parts of the country
- provide cheap housing for those on low incomes
- encourage or discourage certain products or industries

Possible impact of wealth transfer on businesses

- Income tax, wealth/property taxes and benefits will redistribute income and wealth from richer to poorer and spending patterns will alter.
- Profit taxes may vary by the amount of profit made.
- Businesses in areas of low unemployment may be able to receive subsidies or grants.
- Certain industries may get subsidies, e.g. renewable energy suppliers, or have to pay more taxes, e.g. fossil fuel businesses.
- Groups who gain or lose will have certain spending characteristics and these will affect businesses in those areas.

Now test yourself

15 State the effect on prices for each of the following changes:
  (a) price of imports if exchange rates rise
  (b) price of exports if exchange rates rise

Answer on p.213

Revision activity

Use a spider diagram to show the possible effects on a business selling furniture domestically and for export of a rising exchange rate for its country's currency.

Now test yourself

16 Explain economic growth.

Answer on p.213

Revision activity

Economic growth is rising rapidly. Construct a table to show the different effects of this on a yacht manufacturer and a match manufacturer.

Expert tip

You need to understand economic theory and use it to explain the impact of change on businesses and the decisions they make.

Now test yourself

17 Outline two reasons why a government might wish to transfer wealth from one group in the country to another.

18 For each of your two reasons, give an example of how two specific groups might be affected.

Answers on p.213

External influences on business activity

Changing macroeconomic objectives

Revised

Governments face different situations at different times so their objectives will change. An economy with full employment and economic growth is more likely to emphasise objectives such as low inflation or wealth transfer. An economy with low unemployment, some inflation but facing wildly changing exchange rates might focus on stabilising the exchange rate. An economy with high inflation may focus on this first and see growth and employment fall.

A complicating factor is that macroeconomic objectives often conflict. It is very difficult to achieve all five objectives at the same time, as a policy to achieve one often leads to being unable to achieve another.

Typical conflicts in achieving objectives
- Achieving low unemployment may mean high growth but also high inflation.
- Transferring wealth from rich to poor may mean it is not worth low-income groups working so unemployment rises.
- Achieving low inflation may mean low growth and high unemployment.
- Stabilising exchange rates may mean low growth.

> **Revision activity**
>
> List the current macroeconomic objectives of the government in your country. Can you identify any conflicts in these objectives?

Policy instruments used to achieve macroeconomic objectives

Governments have a range of economic policies they can use to achieve objectives but these mostly fall into monetary, fiscal or exchange rate policies.

Monetary policy

Monetary policy is using government controls over interest rates or the amount of money (money supply) to achieve policy objectives. The rate of interest is the price of money. Changing interest rates will alter the cost of borrowing for those who wish to take out a loan. If rates rise, it will be more expensive to borrow so less will be borrowed. This has the effect of:

- Reducing investment spending because it is more expensive to borrow to pay for the money to fund machinery or equipment.
- Reducing consumer spending because interest on mortgages, credit cards and loans will increase and so fewer goods will be purchased. Repayments of existing loans, such as credit cards, rise so there is less money left over for spending. In addition, saving will become more attractive so less will be spent.
- Raising exchange rates because rising interest rates will make a country more attractive for foreign financial institutions to put money into.

> **Monetary policy:** using government controls over interest rates or the amount of money (money supply) to achieve policy objectives.

Changing the amount of money in the country will also influence the total available for banks to pass on for consumer spending or investment. Increasing the money supply can be done by:

- Selling more government debt to the banks (quantitative easing) to enable more money to be available to businesses.
- Reducing the amount of secure reserves banks need to hold, so freeing up more money for lending.
- Lowering restrictions on bank lending.

Lowering interest rates or expanding the money supply will lead to increased consumer spending and investment and higher economic growth. Inflation may increase if this growth is small, and the effect on exchange rates will depend on by how much imports increase as growth may lead to greater exports too.

Fiscal policy

Fiscal policy is the use of taxation and government spending to achieve economic objectives. Governments can choose from a range of possible taxes, each one with its own effect on different groups. Major taxes include:

> **Fiscal policy:** the use of taxation and government spending to achieve economic objectives.

- income tax on individuals
- profit taxes on businesses
- taxes on sales or value added
- taxes on particular goods, e.g. alcohol, petroleum, carbon or tobacco duties

Major government spending areas include education, health, defence, transport and benefits to individuals. Businesses may gain from subsidies or grants.

Increasing taxes will have the effect of taking money out of the economy so growth is reduced, unemployment may grow and inflation may fall. Increasing government spending may result in inflation, growth and a fall in unemployment. The precise effects depend on what taxes are changed and which areas of government spending change.

Exchange rate policies

Exchange rate policies are actions taken to influence the exchange in a desired way. Monetary policy will have an impact on the exchange rate because lowered interest rates will make a currency less attractive to foreign investors. They take money out of the country's banks so the exchange rate will fall. It is possible for a government to use exchange controls to limit the amount of money moving in and out of a country, but in today's global world this is effectively very difficult. Some countries tie the value of their currencies to stronger currencies or use public relations to try and influence opinion about their strength.

Exchange rate policies: actions to influence the value of the exchange rate.

Table 2 The effects of exchange rate changes on business

	Effect on exporters	Effect on importers	Effect on domestic market
Exchange rate rises	• Export price rises. • Sales volume falls. • Sales value change depends on price elasticity of demand.	• Import price falls. • Import quantity rises. • Sales value change depends on price elasticity of demand.	• Import price falls. • Lower costs for imported materials. • Increased competition for domestic producers.
Exchange rate falls	• Export price falls. • Sales volume rises. • Sales value change depends on price elasticity of demand.	• Import price rises. • Import quantity falls. • Sales value change depends on price elasticity of demand.	• Higher import prices. • Higher costs for imported raw materials. • Decreased competition for domestic producers.

Choice of policy instrument

Governments have to address economic issues they currently face and choose appropriate policy instruments. First, the cause of the problems must be established before choosing a policy to address the cause. These decisions are usually difficult and have different possible solutions to achieve the objectives. Other possible policies include **supply side policies**. These focus on freeing up businesses to become more efficient by relaxing regulations, providing efficient infrastructure and helping provide a well-trained, skilled workforce. The key thing for business studies students is to consider what effect a given policy might have on businesses.

Supply side policies: policies that attempt to make businesses run more efficiently and have lower costs. They include: better infrastructure, relaxing regulations, lowering trade union influence, grants and subsidies for investment and helping provide a better skilled workforce.

The effect of changes in macroeconomic performance and policies on business behaviour

There are infinite combinations of macroeconomic variables and policies. It is important to look at the effects of each variable on its own, assuming all other variables are constant. Table 3 sets out some possible effects of changes in macroeconomic variables and policies but there are many others.

Expert tip

When analysing the effects of changes in the economic environment consider one change at a time and imagine that all other factors are constant.

Table 3 Possible effects of macroeconomic changes and policies on business behaviour

Macroeconomic change	Possible policy	Effect of policy	Possible business behaviour
High unemployment or economic growth	Monetary — lower interest rates or increase money supply	• Loans become cheaper. • Households spend more as borrowing becomes cheaper and more spending money is available. • Exchange rate falls as foreign money leaves banks.	• More investment. • More borrowing. • Production increases to meet extra demand. • More employees are hired. • Exporters face higher prices. • Importers face lower prices.
	Fiscal policy	• Lower income taxes so households spend more, especially on luxury products.	• Increase production to meet demand. • Producers of luxury goods increase production.
		• Lower sales taxes so prices fall.	• Increase production to meet demand.
		• Lower profit taxes.	• Lower prices. • Production increases to meet demand.
		• Higher government spending leads to an increase in consumer demand and government contracts.	• Production increases, especially government contractors. • Businesses move to seek government contracts.
High inflation	Monetary policy — raise interest rates	• Borrowing becomes more expensive. • Households spend less as borrowing gets more expensive and less spending money is available.	• Production falls. • Marketing increases. • Prices are reduced. • Search for new markets.
	Fiscal policy	• Higher income taxes so households spend less.	• Prices fall to encourage purchases. • Production falls. • Marketing increases. • New products. • Search for new markets.
		• Higher sales taxes cause price rises.	• Lower profits. • Cost cutting.
		• Higher profit taxes.	• Profits fall. • Investment falls. • Cost cutting. • Relocation to lower tax country.
		• Decreased government spending causes less consumer demand and government contracts.	• Profits fall. • Redundancies/rationalisation in government suppliers. • Search for new markets.

Revision activity

1 Use a diagram to show how lowering interest rates might help a government to increase employment.
2 Explain how lowering interest rates might conflict with an objective of lowering inflation.
3 Produce notes to show the effect of lowered interest rates on a medium-sized producer of electronic consumer goods that exports 30% of production.

Now test yourself

19 A country is facing high unemployment, low growth, low inflation and a stable currency.
   (a) Identify two appropriate macroeconomic objectives for the government.
   (b) Outline two policies a government may adopt to achieve these objectives.

Answer on p.213

Tested

Corporate social responsibility (CSR)

Corporate social responsibility is the actions, legally required or voluntary, needed for an organisation to act responsibly to all its stakeholders. CSR includes acting in an ethical way, respecting the people, communities and the environment that the business affects and balancing the claims of stakeholders. Acting on CSR might:

- reduce environmental problems such as pollution and climate change
- mean long-term needs are put ahead of short-term goals
- be behaving in the right way
- reduce exploitation of one group by another, e.g. profits for shareholders may mean very low wages for employees

CSR includes:

- accurate accounting procedures that reflect the true value of assets and cash flows
- not paying bribes to win contracts
- paying a fair wage and providing healthy and safe working conditions
- buying raw materials from sustainable sources
- acting to reduce pollution beyond the legal requirements
- making suppliers conform to an ethical code of conduct
- not outsourcing to poorly paid or child workers or where low health and safety standards operate
- a social audit or CSR report of stakeholder objectives, establishing CSR indicators, measuring these and regularly reporting on them

Arguments for CSR

- Better financial performance as customers are attracted and costs are looked at carefully.
- Can be a marketing advantage in brand image and reputation.
- Lower costs, e.g. recycling or lowering waste.
- Customer loyalty.

Arguments against CSR

- Expensive and raises costs and prices.
- Makes businesses uncompetitive, especially in a global marketplace.
- Stakeholders cannot agree on ethical/socially responsible behaviour.
- A luxury in a time of recession.
- It is a fashionable, cynical way to market a business.

> **Corporate social responsibility:** the actions, legally required or voluntary, needed for an organisation to act responsibly to all its stakeholders.

> **Now test yourself**
> 20 Explain the meaning of corporate social responsibility.
> 21 Identify three stakeholders in a business manufacturing shoes, including at least one external to the business.
> 22 Give one reason why it might be difficult for a business in a developing country to act in a socially responsible way.
>
> Answers on p.213

> **Expert tip**
> Many profit-making businesses also have some social objectives. Achieving these may incur costs but may give marketing advantages.

Political and legal influences on business activity

Government and the law

Governments have a responsibility to make sure that the business environment is one where competition is fair, workers have healthy and safe conditions, consumers are given accurate information and are protected from faulty or dangerous products and that businesses are encouraged to set up in the best places to contribute to the life of the country. They do this through passing laws and using regulations to achieve these objectives. Much of this is aimed at the primary objective of improving the way that markets work so that they are fair to everyone involved — producers, suppliers, advertisers, consumers, employees, investors, society as a whole.

Employment and conditions of work law

Employment law varies from country to country, but most countries have laws that deal with most if not all of these topics:

> **Expert tip**
> Laws vary from one country to another. Make sure that you understand the areas of law that governments use and how laws in general might affect business activity. You do not need to know specific details of particular laws, but you might want to check out the law in this area in your own country to gain a deeper understanding.

- protection of health and safety of employees
- minimum pay or wage levels
- contracts of employment, unfair dismissal and redundancy arrangements
- prevention of discrimination against certain groups of people based on their characteristics, e.g. disability, age, religion, gender, sexual orientation
- parenting rights and workplace harassment/bullying
- membership of trade unions

These laws add costs, and create the need for record keeping and employees to monitor them, but they also lead to more committed and secure employees and less costs as there will be fewer accidents, legal costs and court cases.

Marketing behaviour — consumer protection law

Businesses are very often large or small enough to disappear easily if there is a problem. This means that compared to consumers, they have a lot of power if there is a problem. Businesses may be tempted to sell faulty or unsafe products or to use persuasive unethical selling techniques to get consumers to buy. Most countries have laws that relate to these areas ensuring that:

- goods are not faulty, are safe and are fit for the purpose for which they are sold
- goods and services provided are as they are described
- weights, measures and sizes are accurate
- food products are safe to eat and prepared in hygienic conditions
- advertising gives accurate descriptions of the products or services and does not exploit anyone, e.g. children

These may add costs or limit the way a business may behave, but governments have a responsibility to make sure that consumers are protected. Having laws means businesses quickly adapt to the requirements and consumers can have more confidence when they buy.

Competition law

Goods and services are sold in markets where there is competition between providers. Businesses might be able to limit competition to their own advantage, e.g. by getting together and all agreeing to sell at a high price, forcing consumers to pay more than if there was real competition. **Competition law** aims to bring about as much competition as possible so that suppliers are encouraged to become more efficient, lower costs and prices, and provide choice to consumers. Competition law usually deals with fair trading requirements and pro-competition laws.

> **Competition law:** aims to produce as much competition in markets as possible by banning anti-competitive practices and encouraging competition.

Fair trading requirements banning unfair practices

Unfair practices include:
- price fixing and price agreements
- information sharing agreements
- producers refusing to sell to retailers unless minimum prices are set
- sole supplier arrangements — suppliers only supply if no competitors are allowed
- predatory pricing

Pro-competition laws

These include:
- banning cartels
- investigating monopolies to make sure that these are not acting against consumer interest
- investigating proposed mergers and takeovers to make sure they will not result in unfair monopoly power

Competition law is a cost to government and businesses that have to check they are in line. It requires sophisticated analysis of markets and may take time to be introduced in a way that works.

Other laws, including location decisions and particular products

Governments have a range of other laws that affect businesses. For instance, there may be planning requirements to be met when setting up a factory, office or shop. There may be restrictions on pollution that require equipment to clean up smoke or chemicals. There may be noise limits on industrial premises, limits to lorry movements or business operations may be restricted to daytime hours.

Particular products may have specific laws that apply to them, e.g. explosive substances, drugs, chemicals that require safe particular storage solutions.

The impact of international agreements on businesses

Most countries have signed up to a number of international agreements setting up common regulations and behaviours. Businesses must then act in line with the agreements. Examples include:
- World Trade Organization or regional trade agreements on freeing trade
- United Nations-based Kyoto agreement on restricting carbon emissions
- International Labour Organization standards on employment conditions
- United Nations Law of the Sea setting out mineral rights, fishing rights and ownership rights
- internationally agreed accounting standards

Particular examples include businesses having to:
- design products to meet particular standards of safety
- reduce pollution or use less energy
- set out their accounts to include corporate social responsibility factors

> **Now test yourself**
> 23 Give two reasons why governments have passed laws that affect business behaviour.
> 24 Identify two areas of business activity that are affected by law.
>
> **Answers on p.213**

Technological influences on business activity

Technology is now key to business success in all areas.

Production
- Design based on information collected from market research using IT and the internet.
- Computer-aided design.
- Manufacturing using computer-aided manufacturing and robotics.
- Fracking to produce previously unobtainable gas supplies.
- Genetically modified plants and animals.
- 3D printers.

Operations
- Enterprise resource planning.
- Electronic point-of-sale systems to link sales, stock and ordering.
- Access to online information and data.

Communications
- Mobile computing and home working.
- Video conferencing.

Marketing
- Databases to sell to particular identified groups or individuals.
- E-mail and social networks to communicate with customers directly.
- E-commerce — global on-line sales outlets.

External influences on business activity

Table 4 The benefits and problems of introducing technological change

Benefits	Problems
More efficiency, less waste.	Cost of researching new technology.
Improved products and services directly tailored to consumers' needs.	Cost of new technology that may date quickly.
New materials, designs, products.	Investment in wrong technology is easy and expensive.
Faster more detailed instant communication.	Jobs disappear; retraining and new skills needed; resistance from employees.
Increased quality and quality control.	More pressure on employees.

> **Revision activity**
>
> Draw up a list of the benefits and problems for a supermarket considering introducing a point-and-press scanning system for shoppers, which will record all purchases and generate a detailed database of purchases linked to payment methods and e-mail addresses of customers. It will mean that nearly all the tills will not be needed.

Other businesses and business activity

Businesses are constrained by and rely on other businesses

Businesses never operate on their own. They are always part of a supply chain, either as a supplier or purchaser. They may rely on agency staff, use marketing agencies, consultants, energy suppliers and transport businesses. They will use internet providers, search engines and telephone networks. The actions of competitors will affect their behaviour and plans. Government agencies may place legal requirements on activities and pressure groups, trade unions and consumer groups may have a large influence.

Social influences on business activity

The need to consider the community and pressure groups

Businesses operate in a society that may be affected by business activity. Society is a stakeholder and increasingly acting as an influence on business decision making. Businesses are not separate from social change and have to take account of social needs including:

- the changing role of women
- environmental issues
- sustainability and energy concerns
- ideas of fairness and equality
- perceptions about wealth and income distribution

Many of these needs are reflected and articulated by pressure groups such as Greenpeace, Oxfam or a trade union. These groups gain publicity in the media that both reflects and affects consumers' buying behaviour. It may be in the interests of a business to engage with pressure groups and work with them to change so that social needs and attitudes are reflected better. Failure to engage may lead to the government forcing change by passing laws following lobbying by pressure groups. Examples might include the pressure for:

- more women to enter the workforce.
- a higher percentage of women to become senior managers
- more environmentally friendly processes of production

Failure to respond may lead to fewer sales and less profit, lowered employee motivation, difficulty in recruitment, poor public relations and internal conflicts.

Many businesses are finding that having an ethical approach or engaging in corporate social responsibility has a positive effect on sales, consumer perception and the employees, and use this as a marketing tool, e.g. line caught tuna fish is sold as a sustainable catch and fair trade products appeal to an increasing number of consumers in richer countries.

Demographic change and business activity

How a business might react to a given demographic change

Demography is the study of population structure and its changes. It is concerned with age, gender, ethnic origin, migration and education levels. It deals with how birth and death rates and migration affect these. Demography is vital to business activity because it is related to patterns of demand and employment.

Demand and demography

People with different characteristics, such as age or gender, have different demands for products — men and women buy different types of clothes and read different types of books.

Effects of age

A society with increasing percentages of older people will:
- spend relatively more on holidays and travel, health products and eating out
- need more care homes and medical services but spend less on music, electronic goods and entertainment
- require governments to pay more pensions so taxes may rise

On the other hand, a society with a high percentage of people aged under 15 will:
- have relatively high demand for toys, baby food and children's clothes
- face increasing demand over time for products appealing to young adults then families

Effects of changing ethnic mix

A more ethnically diverse population will demand a wider range of clothing, food and possibly of religion related products.

The demographics in a particular country will affect the opportunities for business activity, some firms will find their products in a declining market, some in a growing market

Employment and demography

Effects of age

- Older workers tend to be loyal to the employer, have experience, be less likely to move jobs or location, and are possibly more reliable and less likely to be absent.
- Younger workers tend to cost less, be flexible, willing to move and able to learn new skills but may need more family/parenting leave.

Effects of education levels

A society with a low percentage of people with school or university qualifications will have a low-skilled inflexible workforce that forces employers to offer training programmes.

Effects of changing ethnic mix and migration

- Different ethnic groups may have different expectations regarding facilities at work, or working hours.
- Immigrants may have different skills or be willing to work for lower wages.

> **Demography:** the study of population structure (age, gender, ethnicity, education levels) and its changes.

> **Revision activity**
> A country has a high and growing percentage of population aged 45 and over. Prepare a table that compares the effect this might have on the following:
> - a furniture manufacturer
> - a hotel chain
> - a childcare provider

> **Expert tip**
> It is important to be able to understand that demographics affect demand and employment patterns and to be able to apply this understanding to a specific situation involving a specified business.

> **Revision activity**
> Use a spider diagram to explain possible consequences for the labour market in a country with a high immigration rate.

Influence of environmental issues on business activity

All business activity will change the physical environment. Concerns are growing that this process has reached a point that is not healthy for human beings or the planet. There are many pressure groups acting to try and reduce the impact on the global and local environment, and governments are passing laws and putting pressure on businesses to try to reduce the impact of business activity on the environment.

Ever more businesses are changing their policies and practice to reflect these concerns and regulations. Examples include:
- A more explicit focus on corporate social responsibility in relation to pollution, waste disposal and recycling.
- Building environmental audits into planning.
- Focusing on environmental policy in marketing material.
- Changing to obey new environmental laws and regulations.
- Engaging with and responding to environmental campaigners and pressure groups.
- Developing more energy-efficient, sustainable solutions to raw material supplies, operations planning and product design.

> **Revision activity**
>
> Prepare notes for a presentation to the board of directors of the following companies on how their operations might be affected by a greater concern for the physical environment:
> - a computer manufacturer
> - a law firm
> - a forestry company

7 People in organisations

Human resource management

Measures of employee performance

Revised

Staff appraisal

Staff appraisal plays a key role in measuring the performance of employees. The appraisal is usually carried out by the line manager. Performance is assessed, targets can be set and training needs and the potential for career progression identified. The HRM department is where all records of such appraisals are kept.

> **Staff appraisal:** when the performance of employees is measured against pre-set targets or expected outcomes.

Appraisals are carried out at agreed intervals — quarterly, half-yearly or annually — and measure:

- the extent to which pre-set targets have been met
- the achievement of key competencies
- the successful undertaking of identified training needs

The benefits of staff appraisal

- Training needs or a need for new equipment might be identified.
- Possible ambitions of employees, for example for promotion, might be identified and perhaps appropriate actions can be taken to help the employee to progress.
- Pay levels and incentives can be adjusted appropriately.
- Bonus payments can be determined based on the extent to which targets have been met or exceeded.
- The causes and consequences of poor employee performance can be set out (see Figure 1).

> **Now test yourself**
> 1 Outline two advantages of using staff appraisal.
>
> **Answer on p.213**
>
> *Tested*

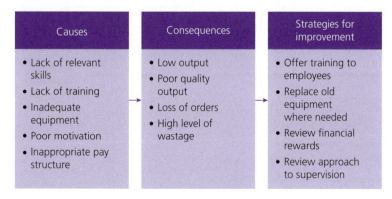

Figure 1 Causes and consequences of poor employee performance

Management by objectives (MBO)

Revised

Implementation of MBO

Staff appraisal is usually part of the **management by objectives** process. The appraisal session is when future objectives will be agreed. The objectives can be:

- agreed between the employee and their manager or set by management without discussion with the employee

> **Management by objectives:** an approach used to ensure that employees are all working towards the overall business objective. Objectives for individuals are either agreed or imposed by managers.

- individual or for a whole department
- direct from senior management or as part of a departmental target

The objectives should be achievable and realistic if they are expected to motivate. There is a view that objectives are more likely to be met when they have been agreed rather than imposed. Generally, all objectives should be:

- SMART if they are to be an effective management tool
- in line with the overall business objectives
- able to be monitored and measured so that immediate action can be taken if targets are likely to be missed
- recognised when met so that appropriate reward or recognition can be given. This is an encouragement to all other employees to meet or exceed their targets too

The usefulness of MBO

- Employees feel involved when objectives are discussed and agreed.
- Having specific objectives to achieve can be motivating.
- Employees are more likely to be committed to objectives/targets that they have been involved in agreeing.
- Employees know exactly what is expected of them and how they are contributing to the overall business objectives.
- Employees are likely to be motivated by having their training needs and potential for promotion recognised.

Possible disadvantages of using MBO

- It is time consuming.
- A business might not want to discuss some of its overall objectives with all employees.
- Employees might suggest and agree very easy targets to ensure that financial rewards will be achievable.
- Targets that are too difficult to achieve can be demotivating. Any forecast of what is to be achieved must be as accurate and reasonable as possible.
- It can be inflexible because any change in the business environment might require agreed targets to be changed, e.g. the recent worldwide financial crisis.
- Any discussion of training needs might make employees feel inadequate or might give them unrealistic expectations of future promotion.

> **Revision activity**
> A clothes manufacturing business has decided to introduce management by objectives. Make notes that could be given to supervisors working in the business to help them understand the benefits that both they and the business could hope to gain.

> **Now test yourself**
> 2 Explain what is meant by the term 'management by objectives'.
> 3 Outline two ways in which MBO might help a business to achieve its objectives.
>
> **Answers on p.213**

Labour legislation

The need for labour legislation

Labour legislation governs how employees are to be treated. Workers are given some protection against exploitation and employers are given some form of legal support if employees fail to meet their contractual terms. The adherence to labour legislation is monitored by the HRM department, who will also deal with issues arising when laws may have been broken.

Without legislation, some businesses might expect workers to work in an unsafe environment that could put their health and physical safety at risk.

Broad principles underlying labour legislation

The broad principles for labour legislation are shown in Table 1.

Table 1 Areas for labour legislation

Issue	Content
Hours of work	Maximum hours work allowable per week or averaged over a given time period. Age restrictions also apply to hours worked in some instances. Legislation will also outline exemptions, e.g. armed forces.
Remuneration issues including minimum wage	Outlines the national minimum wage if there is one. Also details how and when employees should expect to be paid and the rate at which any overtime should be paid.
Discrimination issues	Designed to prevent employees experiencing discrimination for reasons of gender, race, religion, disability or sexual orientation. In some countries, employees cannot face discrimination due to trade union membership, political affiliation or being HIV positive.
Health and safety	Designed to protect employees while at work. Legislation ensures a safe and healthy working environment, outlining the steps that can be taken when a business fails to meet the legal requirements.
Employment contracts	Legislation outlines the required details of employment contracts and how and when they might be terminated.
Holiday entitlement	Some governments will dictate a minimum holiday entitlement. Employers may give more as an incentive, but must at least meet the minimum required.
Employment relations	Covers the right to be a member of a trade union. Can also include details of national collective bargaining agreements. Legislation would also outline the type of action that workers can take.
Minimum age issues	This can limit the type of work that can be done below a stated age. All work is prohibited below a certain age in some countries.

> **Now test yourself**
>
> 4 Briefly outline two reasons why labour legislation is necessary.
> 5 Explain what is meant by anti-discrimination legislation.
>
> **Answers on p.213**

Cooperation between the management and the workforce

The benefits of cooperation

- Employees and managers might learn to respect and understand each other.
- It can produce a useful exchange of ideas.
- It helps to remove the feeling of 'them and us'.

Methods of achieving cooperation

Cooperation can be achieved:
- through the use of worker participation
- by recognising the value of input from employees that can lead to a more motivated workforce

Workforce planning

Workforce planning is the process of deciding how many workers will be needed and what skills are required to allow the business to meet its future business objectives.

Reasons for and role of workforce planning

Workforce planning:
- avoids having too many employees, resulting in a wasted human resource
- improves the potential for the business to run efficiently because the right numbers of workers with the right skills are employed

> **Workforce planning:** the process of deciding how many workers will be needed and what skills are required to allow the business to meet its future business objectives.

7 People in organisations

What does workforce planning involve?
- A clear idea of what is to be achieved in order to determine accurately what workforce is needed.
- An audit of the current workforce to determine if the business has too many or too few workers, and whether the employees have the skills required to meet the business objectives.

What steps can be taken if the business does not have enough employees with the right skills?
- Recruit more staff — permanent or temporary, full- or part-time.
- Retrain existing staff.

What steps can a business take if it has too many employees?
- Make some existing workers redundant.
- Perhaps do nothing. Workers might leave or retire and reduce the workforce to the desired size naturally.
- Make sure that the employees needed by the business are kept — persuade them to stay.

> **Now test yourself**
> 6 Explain what is meant by 'workforce planning'.
> **Answer on p.213**
> Tested

The role of trade unions in HRM — Revised

Purpose and value of trade unions
A trade union works on behalf of its members to protect their rights at their place of employment. It is intended to create a balance in the power between workers and their employers. Trade unions might:
- represent their members at meetings with business representatives
- seek changes if a business is requiring its employees to work outside legal guidelines, e.g. to exceed regularly the number of hours that should be worked
- work to resolve grievances between workers and their employers

Reasons for joining a trade union
- To gain the protection of a larger organisation that speaks on behalf of employees.
- To benefit from legal advice, support and representation when needed.
- To benefit from the improved conditions of employment that a trade union might negotiate with businesses.
- Trade unions will negotiate on behalf on an individual, all the employees of a particular business or the whole union membership.

> **Now test yourself**
> 7 Explain two reasons why a worker might choose to join a trade union.
> **Answer on p.213**
> Tested

Negotiation — Revised

Main processes involved in negotiation
- Deciding what is the actual issue for discussion.
- Deciding who should be involved in discussions.
- Deciding the procedures to be followed.
- Gathering information from all parties involved, perhaps including legal advice.
- Following procedures until agreement is reached.

Situations in which negotiation might be effective
- Determining wages and conditions of employment.
- Resolving grievance issues.
- Determining redundancy strategies.
- Discussing proposed changes in company policy.

Collective bargaining

Collective bargaining means that discussion takes place between trade unions, on behalf of employees, and management. This means that discussions with individual employees are not required.

Benefits of collective bargaining
- The business deals with one party rather than individual employees.
- The trade union can intervene to resolve problems with employees.
- Employees can benefit from having a representative to present their views to management because the trade union representatives would be more skilled in such situations and might therefore achieve a better outcome.
- Sometimes a good working relationship can build up between the business and the trade unions enabling some issues to be discussed and resolved amicably and not always requiring a formal approach.

> **Collective bargaining:** where discussions take place between businesses and trade unions on behalf of a whole group of workers.

The processes involved in conciliation and arbitration

An impartial outside view can sometimes help towards a speedier resolution of problems between a business and its employees. **Conciliation** is where an independent outside body enters the discussion in an attempt to help negotiations and suggest a way in which a satisfactory outcome can be reached. Solutions reached through conciliation are not binding and are merely suggestions.

However, **arbitration** involves an outside, independent body in making the final decision about how a dispute should be resolved. In such cases, both the management and the trade unions are bound by the agreement. The parties involved must agree to arbitration as they will be bound by the decision of the arbitrator.

In the case of a dispute between the managers or owners of a business and its employees the following stages might occur:
- The managers and workers would try to reach an agreement between them.
- If agreement is not reached they might seek the help of an intermediary (conciliation).
- The intermediary attends a meeting with representatives from both sides of the dispute present or meets with each party separately.
- If a face-to-face meeting is not appropriate, the intermediary might convey information from one group to the other.
- Conciliation aims to find some compromise and common ground that can allow agreement to be reached.
- If the dispute cannot be resolved by conciliation, arbitration might be used.
- Both sides need to agree to arbitration.
- The arbitrator will examine all of the facts of the dispute and make a judgement that can be binding if both parties have agreed to abide by the decision.
- In the UK, conciliation and arbitration is provided by ACAS (Advisory, Conciliation and Arbitration Service) which offers help and advice to prevent or resolve workplace disputes.

> **Conciliation:** an impartial, outside body assists employers and employees, by facilitating negotiations and suggesting a solution to the problem.
>
> **Arbitration:** an impartial, outside body makes a decision after hearing evidence, which will be binding between employers and employees.

Now test yourself

8. Distinguish between 'conciliation' and 'arbitration'.

Answer on p.213

Revision activity

1. Make a list of possible situations that can be the cause of a dispute between employers and their workers.
2. Draw up a table outlining the advantages and disadvantages of trade union membership for both employers and employees.

Situations in which either conciliation or arbitration might be useful
- Resolving disputes about pay issues.
- In disagreements about proposed redundancies.
- In cases where an employee believes that he or she has been dismissed unfairly.
- When a disagreement has arisen and the employer and/or the employees believe that they cannot find a solution without outside help.

Single union deals

Revised

The meaning of single union deals
A business that recognises and deals with only one trade union is said to have a single union agreement. This is usually the largest union that works on behalf of workers in that particular industry.

Why they might be used
- Discussions only need to be held with one trade union.
- It might increase the potential for reaching agreement as only two parties are involved.
- Once agreement has been reached, the deal would be binding on all employees.

However, members of trade unions that have not been included in a single union deal might feel that they are not fully represented.

Now test yourself
9 Briefly explain why a business might prefer to have a single union deal.

Answer on p.213

Tested

Organisation structure

Relationship between business objectives, people and organisation structure

Revised

An organisation structure should be designed to meet the changing needs of the business in terms of growth and development and should allow levels of **authority** and **responsibility** throughout the organisation to be identified.

An organisation chart will give an overview of the number of levels within a business and the scope of responsibility at each level.

Authority: the power to direct and control the actions of others.

Responsibility: being accountable for any action taken.

Purposes and attributes of an organisation structure
An organisation structure provides a framework for decision making, allowing flexibility, growth, development and a structure for meeting the needs of a business. In particular, an organisation structure:
- illustrates who is responsible for whom and who is accountable to whom within a business
- allows employees to know which task should be their priority when given work from more than one person
- shows who the decision makers are in an organisation
- shows the official **chain of command**
- illustrates the official channels of communication
- can also show the different functional departments/divisions within a large business
- gives employees some idea of their promotion or progression route within a business

Chain of command: the route through which orders will be passed down from senior managers to employees on the lower levels of the hierarchy.

Types of structure

Revised

The performance of a business can be influenced by the type of organisation structure it adopts.

Factors influencing choice of organisation structure
- Some businesses organise their structure according to the functional activities taking place within the organisation, e.g. production, finance,

human resource management or marketing. Each department has a clear function and its own internal hierarchy.
- Other businesses divide the organisation into product groups or geographical regions depending on the nature of the business involved. A multi-product business might have a structure for each product, whereas a business operating in several geographical regions might have a separate structure for each region, e.g. North America, Europe and southeast Asia.
- The structure must be appropriate for the size of the business. Larger businesses tend to need functional departments. An organisation structure can demonstrate the relationship between departments and the levels of authority within and across departments.
- An organisation structure must be compatible with the aims and objectives of a business. For example, if the overall aim of a business is growth, the organisation structure must allow growth to take place without sacrificing any level of efficiency. When frequent changes need to be made to an organisation structure this can be very unsettling for many employees.

Functional structure

Figure 2 shows a functional organisation structure.

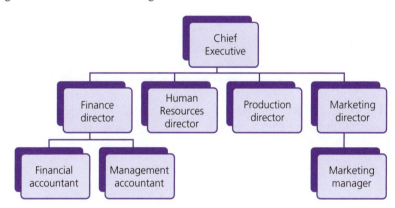

Figure 2 A functional organisation structure

Advantages and disadvantages of a functional structure

Advantages of a functional structure
- Specialists will be employed for each functional area.
- There will be a clear hierarchy and chain of command in each department.
- Employees will know how they contribute to the overall business structure.

Disadvantages of a functional structure
- Communication between departments can break down.
- A lack of communication between departments can lead to a lack of coordination and a duplication of effort.
- It is possible that employees focus only on their department, meaning that an understanding of the whole business is not developed. In some cases, actions taken by one department can have a detrimental effect on another department without the consequences having been considered.
- Competition between departments can develop which might not be in the best interests of the business as a whole.

Organisations structured by product

Many multi-product businesses create cost and profit centres for each product, with each product having its own organisation structure and specialist teams to support it.

Advantages of structure by product
- Employees become specialised in one product.
- It is straightforward to allocate costs and revenues to a particular product.

Disadvantage of structure by product
There is duplication of effort if each product or area has its own specialist finance or marketing department. These specialist departments could work across different products or could serve more than one geographical region.

Organisations structured by geographical region

Advantage of structure by geographical region
A business with a division dedicated to one geographical region is more likely to understand the needs of the local customers.

Disadvantages of structure by geographical region
- The business might not gain the maximum possible benefit from economies of scale if business activity is divided between different regions.
- Local influences might cause geographically remote divisions to move away from the intended image for the business as a whole.

> **Now test yourself**
> 10 Identify two functions of an organisation structure.
> **Answer on p.213**
> Tested

Hierarchical structure

Revised

A hierarchical structure demonstrates the levels of authority in a business, with those with the most authority at the top of the structure and those employees with the least authority and responsibility placed at the bottom. It can be either narrow (tall) or flat.

Narrow (tall) organisation structure
This structure is associated with bureaucratic organisations and has many levels, typically with a small number of personnel reporting to each line manager (see Figure 3). Examples might include organisations such as the armed forces.

> **Span of control:** the number of people directly reporting to one person.

Advantages of a narrow (tall) organisation structure
- There are several levels with delegated decision making.
- Several levels in the structure mean that employees can progress in small steps towards higher levels of responsibility.
- There is usually a narrow **span of control** for each manager/supervisor. The ideal span of control depends on the skill of the employees and the type of work being undertaken. Highly skilled workers tend to need less supervision than unskilled workers and therefore could work under a wide span of control.
- Senior management has some of the burden of decision making taken on by managers below them in the hierarchy.

Disadvantages of a narrow (tall) organisation structure
- Some loss of control by senior managers.
- Poorer decisions may be made at lower levels.
- The bureaucratic nature of tall structures requires communication through several levels, which can be very slow and time consuming.

Figure 3 Example of a narrow (tall) organisation structure

- Higher levels of management can become distanced from lower levels and might be unaware of issues concerning employees on the lower levels of the hierarchy.
- Due to the many layers through which communication must pass, there is a danger that some communication is ineffective, leading to lack of contact and/or some duplication of effort or lack of coordination.

> **Now test yourself**
>
> 11 Identify one advantage and one disadvantage of a tall organisation structure.
>
> **Answer on p.214**
>
> Tested

Flat organisation structure

Revised

A flat structure is frequently found in new businesses, which have small numbers of employees (see Figure 4). Alternatively, delayering might have produced a flat structure due to the removal of some management levels.

Advantages of a flat organisation structure
- A flat organisation can aid fast decision making because communication has to pass through fewer levels.
- The feeling of 'them and us' can be reduced because there is a closer link between senior managers and the lower levels.

Figure 4 Example of a flat organisation structure

Disadvantages of a flat organisation structure
- There are limited opportunities for promotion.
- Usually a flat organisation structure means a much wider span of control. Managers might find it difficult to communicate directly with a large number of staff without holding frequent meetings.
- The decision-making responsibility rests with a smaller number of managers, which might prove to be a great burden.

> **Now test yourself**
>
> 12 Identify one advantage and one disadvantage of a flat organisation structure.
>
> **Answer on p.214**
>
> Tested

Formal and informal organisations

Revised

Features of a formal structure
- A formal structure is hierarchical. All relationships and levels of authority and responsibility will be illustrated by the structure. The person with the most power will be at the top of the hierarchy and the people with the least power will be at the bottom.
- The chain of command will be that which passes from one level to the level immediately below in the hierarchy. This will also be the official channel of communication.
- The organisation structure can also illustrate the route for delegated tasks. Tasks should only be delegated to those working on the level immediately below. Tasks should not usually be delegated across departmental lines.
- An organisation structure also illustrates the centralised or decentralised nature of the business. Centralised structures involve decisions being made at the top of the organisation, while a decentralised organisation has some decision-making power delegated to the lower levels.

Features of an informal structure
- Relationships may develop that do not conform to the official chain of command or channels of communication. These might be between departmental managers who meet and discuss business issues outside the organised meetings.
- Informal structures can be beneficial if a useful exchange of information takes places. However, sometimes the informal communication can be a disruptive influence and can be seen as subversive and as undermining the official structure or hierarchy of the business.

> **Now test yourself**
>
> 13 Distinguish between a formal and an informal structure.
> 14 Briefly explain what is meant by channels of communication.
>
> **Answers on p.214**
>
> Tested

Span of control

The span of control can be narrow or wide (see Figures 5 and 6). The skill level of employees or the nature of the work being done can determine which is most appropriate.

Advantages of a narrow span of control
- A narrow span of control allows employees to be closely supervised.
- There are fewer people for each manager to communicate with.
- Each manager has fewer employees to be responsible for.

Disadvantages of a narrow span of control
- A narrow span of control is frequently used in a bureaucratic organisation and gives little opportunity for lower levels to contribute to decisions.
- Communication is frequently only one way.

Advantages of a wide span of control
- Employees often have some involvement in decision making, which makes them feel more satisfied and valued.
- Some management costs might be saved as fewer managers/supervisors are required.

Disadvantages of a wide span of control
- Large numbers of workers might be difficult to monitor and control and can lead to mistakes being overlooked.
- It can be time consuming to communicate with every individual employee so more frequent meetings might be required, which might be unpopular.

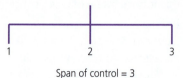

Figure 5 Example of a narrow span of control

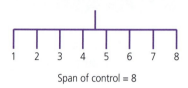

Figure 6 Example of a wide span of control

Matrix structure

A matrix structure overrides the normal chain of command. It functions within an overall formal hierarchical business structure. Matrix structures are used to carry out a specific project and will bring together expertise from a range of departments. The project leader is not always the most senior person in the team, but for the purpose of that project they will direct the team regardless of their 'normal' position in the business hierarchy.

Table 2 Illustration of a matrix structure — functional areas involved in a project

	Research & development	Production	Marketing	Finance	Human resources
Project Linus	✓	✓	✓	✓	✓
Project Relay	✗	✓	✓	✓	✓

Advantages of a matrix structure
- The best team will be chosen for a project.
- It might improve cooperation and communication between departments.
- The most effective use is made of the skills within the business as employees move from one project to another.
- This structure may improve the flexibility of a business, making it more responsive to changes in the business environment.

Disadvantages of a matrix structure
- Employees will temporarily have more than one boss — their usual line manager and the project manager.
- Employees might find it difficult to prioritise their work if they are working on more than one project at a time.

> **Now test yourself**
>
> 15 Explain one advantage and one disadvantage of using a matrix structure in a business.
>
> **Answer on p.214**

Delegation and accountability

The relationship between delegation and accountability

Delegation is when a task is passed to an employee on a lower level of the hierarchy of a business. It can spread the workload of a business and lead to more effective and efficient use of resources.

The authority to complete a task can be delegated, but the ultimate responsibility for its successful completion remains that of the manager who delegated the task. The person undertaking the delegated task will be accountable to the manager but they do not bear the final responsibility. If the employee was not capable of completing the task, then the fault lies with the manager for delegating a task to complete that was beyond the employee's skill level. The chief executive of a business will be held accountable by the shareholders if the business does not meet its targets, regardless of who was given various tasks to complete.

Advantages of delegation
- Employees can feel more valued if they are asked to undertake a job usually done by their manager, therefore increasing their level of motivation.
- Delegation can increase the confidence and skills of workers and prepare them for promotion in the future.
- The manager has time to spend on more complex issues.
- Delegation can highlight those employees who are ready for a more responsible role.
- The tasks might be completed quicker, so increasing the efficiency of the business.

Disadvantages of delegation
- Managers might fear some loss of control.
- The manager might keep checking that the task is being done correctly, so wasting time.
- Employees might be jealous if they are not chosen.
- Some managers are afraid that their employees will complete tasks more efficiently and can feel threatened.
- When a delegated task involves an employee supervising colleagues, some tension can be caused that can negatively affect the group of workers and their output.
- Time and resources can be wasted if the chosen employee does not have the necessary skills to complete the task to the required standard.

The impact of delegation on motivation
Delegation is one of the non-financial motivators that a business can use.

Why delegation can be motivating
- Delegation can be part of job enrichment and exposes employees to a wider range of more complex tasks.
- Employees feel trusted and might begin to believe that they could be promoted. This increases their self-esteem.
- Delegated tasks can also lead to an employee gaining the respect of their colleagues, therefore meeting their need for the esteem of co-workers.

> **Revision activity**
>
> Using the headings 'Retail' and 'Manufacturing', list the advantages and disadvantages of a wide and a narrow span of control, making sure that you relate each point to the particular context. This will help you to retain focus on the context in an examination question. Make a list of the type of tasks you expect might be delegated in a retail and a manufacturing situation. Make notes of the potential benefits and drawbacks of using delegation in each situation.

> **Now test yourself**
>
> 16 Outline one advantage and one disadvantage of delegation.
> 17 Explain how delegation might motivate employees.
>
> **Answers on p.214**

Control, authority and trust

The relationship between span of control and levels of hierarchy

Many people in any business will be responsible for others in the organisation. Direct control is exerted over those immediately beneath a manager and indirect control is exerted over those employees in the levels below that.

The higher levels in a hierarchy usually have a narrower span of control than those closer to the bottom of the structure. This is because the higher levels generally have more complex and responsible jobs to complete. Less complicated tasks that are completed lower down the hierarchy might not need regular discussion or supervision to take place.

The difference between authority and responsibility

A manager can have the authority to require employees to perform tasks. By delegating, a manager might give an employee the authority to carry out a particular task but the final responsibility for the task being completed correctly remains with the manager.

Conflicts between control and trust in delegation

Trust is a two-way process when delegation takes place. The manager must trust the employee to complete the task satisfactorily. The worker must feel free to get on with the task without interference from the manager. It is not always easy for a manager to give up part of their work but, once the decision has been made, frequent checking on the employee is wasting time that the manager could spend on more important matters.

Centralisation

Revised

Centralisation means that decision making is kept at the top of the organisation. The amount of decision making lower down the hierarchy is very limited.

Advantages of centralisation
- Faster decisions can be made without a need for discussion at lower levels.
- Clear goals will be given by those in charge, removing the possibility of departments digressing from the stated aims of the business.
- Decisions will be consistent across all departments or divisions.
- The desired image can be maintained due to the consistency of decisions.

Disadvantages of centralisation
- There is a larger decision-making burden on only a few individuals at the top of the business.
- Some better ideas might have been forthcoming from lower levels of the hierarchy.
- It does not allow less senior managers to develop their decision-making skills, so making them less well prepared for a more senior role.
- Centralised decision making can prove to be a problem if managers are later promoted to more senior decision-making roles.

Line and staff management

Revised

Line management is defined by the hierarchy of a business. It is demonstrated by the chain of command and the channels of communication. A manager takes responsibility for the employees beneath them either directly or indirectly.

Staff management involves those who might offer specialist advice to any department, product group or regional division within a business. They offer advice without having any managerial responsibility for the people they are currently advising. Staff management is linked to the supporting role offered by some sections of a business, for example, the IT department or finance department.

> **Line management:** follows the chain of command as indicated on an organisation structure. Managers are responsible for employees beneath them either directly or indirectly.
>
> **Staff management:** when specialist support or advice is offered to departments without any managerial responsibility for the people being advised.

Business communication

Communication can be one or two way and is the transfer of information between two or more parties.

In order for communication to be effective it should be transmitted via an appropriate medium, and needs to be received and understood by the intended recipient. In a business situation it can be dangerous to assume that just because information has been sent, it has been received and understood.

Purposes of communication

Revised

The purposes of communication are to:
- give instructions
- gain information from customers about what they expect from a business
- inform customers about the products or services that the business offers
- inform employees about the goals of the business
- act as a means of involving employees in some decisions
- coordinate activities between departments

Methods of communication

Revised

The communications methods used in any business will depend on what information is being communicated, who is sending the information and who is receiving it.

What can affect the choice of methods of communication?
- The type of information that is being communicated. Is the information sensitive or for general circulation?
- Whether or not the information is being communicated within a business or between organisations. More formal methods of communication are likely to be used when information is being passed between organisations than if the communication is only internal.
- How many people are involved.
- If feedback is required.
- If a permanent record of the communication is required, e.g. confirmation of a meeting.

Standard methods of communication
Communication might be between individuals, or between an individual and a group of people.

Written
Letter: a formal means of communication, e.g. to confirm the success of a job application or to confirm a future meeting date with the representatives of another business.

Report: this is also a formal means of communication. Reports are used in schools and colleges to give information about the progress and attainment of students. In business they are used to report on business activities to the shareholders and other stakeholder groups or to report to managers on the progress of a project.

Advantages	Disadvantages
<ul><li>There is a permanent record of the communication.</li><li>Detailed information can be given because the reader will be able to reread if necessary. For example, detailed diagrams can be included in the annual report of a business.</li></ul>	<ul><li>The communication might take some time. Not all countries have rapid postal systems. The communication might be subject to delays.</li><li>If there is too much information, the reader might not read it all and therefore important information can be overlooked. This is particularly true of lengthy reports.</li><li>Handwritten communications are not always legible although business correspondence is usually typewritten.</li><li>It is possible that the information is misinterpreted.</li></ul>

Notice board

This method might be useful if the information is intended to reach many people within an organisation. It could be used to announce a staff meeting.

Advantages	Disadvantages
<ul><li>A large number of people have access to the information.</li><li>It is a cheap method of communication.</li></ul>	<ul><li>There is no guarantee that the intended recipients will see the information.</li><li>The way in which people react to the information cannot be gauged.</li></ul>

Spoken — meetings

Meetings can be small or large scale. They can be held to pass on information, to gain information or for appraisal purposes.

Advantages	Disadvantages
<ul><li>They allow interaction between those attending.</li><li>Instant feedback can be received.</li><li>The reactions of people can be seen and interpreted.</li></ul>	<ul><li>Can be time consuming.</li><li>Sometimes other issues are raised that divert the focus of the meeting.</li><li>Output is lost if meetings take place during normal working hours.</li></ul>

Spoken — by telephone

Telephones can be used to communicate with people within an organisation or between different organisations.

Advantages	Disadvantages
<ul><li>Immediate communication with an instant response.</li><li>Questions can be asked about the information; this can prevent future misunderstandings.</li></ul>	<ul><li>The caller cannot know if the person on the other end of the conversation is actually listening or not.</li><li>Usually a record is not kept of what was said.</li><li>The reactions of the parties involved cannot be seen. Facial movements and body language can indicate how well the information is being received.</li></ul>

E-mails

Advantages	Disadvantages
<ul><li>Fast and global communication both inside the business and between businesses.</li><li>Detailed information can be sent quickly, i.e. attached documents.</li></ul>	<ul><li>The message might be one of many others and might be overlooked.</li><li>Information overload if too many e-mails are received. Do the right ones get prioritised?</li><li>The information might be accessed by someone other than the intended recipient.</li><li>They might be seen as less formal by some businesses.</li><li>Their continual use might undermine the ability of people to hold a conversation with their colleagues.</li></ul>

Websites

Websites can be used to give information to stakeholders. They can be used to portray a certain image, e.g. to show that the business is an environmentally friendly and socially responsible organisation.

Advantages	Disadvantages
• A lot of information can be passed on. • A well-designed website can help to project the image of the business. • Once a website has been established, it is low cost. • A business can reach people that it is not even aware of.	• The business cannot control who views the website and therefore care must be taken about the information that is placed on it. • It is possible for information to be altered, which could be harmful to the reputation of the business. • Websites must be kept up to date.

Video conferencing

Advantages	Disadvantages
• Video conferencing saves time as people do not need to travel to a meeting. • The travel costs are saved. • People from different parts of the world can participate creating better coordination between geographical divisions within a business. • The equipment is relatively inexpensive. • It allows for reactions to be seen.	• Physical samples or demonstrations are not possible. • Can be difficult to arrange due to different time zones around the world.

Mobile phones

Advantages	Disadvantages
• Employees can be contactable 24 hours a day, 7 days a week. • Employees can still be in contact with their office while away from their workplace.	• Employees can feel that they are always at work.

Channels of communication

How communication works within an organisation

Channels of communication often follow the chain of command. There can be times when the usual channel of communication will not be followed, e.g. if an employee wishes to make a formal complaint about his or her line manager. Most businesses require communication to occur both vertically and horizontally.

The difference between one-way and two-way, vertical and horizontal communication

Vertical and horizontal communication can both be one or two way. One-way communication is used in the passing of orders when a response or feedback is not required. Two-way communication can also involve the passing of orders but some feedback is expected.

Horizontal communication is when information is passed between people on the same level of the hierarchy.

Vertical communication is when information is passed from one level of the hierarchy to the next level, either above or below.

Communication can be one or two way. This will depend on the culture and the leadership style in the business. Vertical downward communication might be the passing down of orders, while vertical upward communication could be giving some feedback on progress on a particular project.

Barriers to effective communication

- **Inappropriate medium** — it would not be appropriate, for example, to put a message on a notice board saying that five people in the department were to be made redundant. A face-to-face meeting would be more appropriate.

- **Information overload** — important messages might be overlooked if too much information is being received. The increased use of e-mails has been recognised as a possible cause of information overload.
- **Too many communication stages** — a tall organisation structure has many levels through which information must travel. This can cause distortion of the meaning of the original message.
- **Noise** — this can consist of noise from machinery or other conversations taking place. In meetings, too many people speaking at the same time can prevent some information from being heard and received. The 'noise' might not be a physical noise but might be a distraction such as something happening elsewhere in the office, which draws your attention away from your conversation.
- **Language** — inappropriate use of technical language or jargon can prevent some people from understanding the information given. Communication between countries must be free of any words that have a different meaning in another country. Local dialects and expressions are unlikely to be understood by people outside of a particular region.
- **Attitudes, perceptions and emotions** — our interpretation of a message can depend on how we feel emotionally when we receive the message. Anger can lead us to interpret information differently from when we are calm. Anger can also cause some people to 'stop listening'.

> **Now test yourself**
> 18 Briefly explain two barriers to communication and suggest ways in which these might be removed.
>
> **Answer on p.214**
> Tested

The role of management in facilitating communication

Revised

Management must determine what form communication will take to ensure that it is effective. Points to consider will include:
- whether communication will be one way or two way, i.e. whether or not feedback is required
- how many departments are involved
- how many people will be involved in the communication

Communication networks
The different kinds of communication networks are wheel, circle, chain and connected, as outlined below.

A wheel network
A wheel network is useful if one person is in control of the information and the recipients do not need to communicate with each other. The person in the centre of the 'wheel' is usually the leader of the group and will pass information to all other people involved.

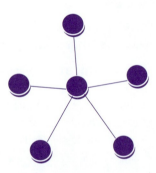

Figure 7 A wheel network

A circle network
In a circle network information is not freely exchanged between the members of the circle. Each person within the circle maintains contact with two others. Information has to be passed on to those who are not in direct contact with each other.

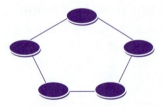

Figure 8 A circle network

A chain network
The chain network follows the hierarchical structure within an organisation. Communication can be either one or two way.

A connected network
In a connected network, everyone involved has the opportunity to communicate with each other. Information passes freely between all those involved without any set pattern or official channels of communication. All ideas can be voiced and will be heard, although agreement can sometimes be difficult to reach.

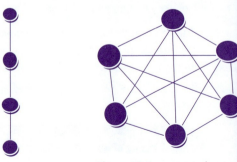

Figure 9 A chain network

Figure 10 A connected network

> **Revision activity**
>
> Make sure that you know the difference between each of the communication networks mentioned above and practise relating them to different work situations.

The role of informal communications within a business

The standard methods of communication outlined above are formal means of communication. Most businesses will also experience some **informal communication**. Employees meet in various situations inside or outside of the workplace and their conversations will often involve the place of work.

Discussion can be factual or based on unsupported rumour. Informal communication can be positive or negative for a business. Sometimes managers can gain important information about the morale of the workforce by using informal communication. There may be times when management needs to act to stop incorrect and damaging rumours being communicated throughout the business.

Ways in which communication can influence the efficiency of a business

- By managers making sure that the people who need information have the correct information.
- Effective communication can minimise the time wasted in decision making.
- Time and money can be saved by ensuring that the most appropriate means of communication are used.
- Interdepartmental communication can prevent the duplication of effort and increase the level of coordination.
- Giving relevant information to employees can raise their level of motivation because they feel involved in the business.

Ways of improving communication in a given situation

Communication can be improved by carefully assessing the information to be conveyed and the people who need to receive it so that an appropriate medium can be used. Care should be taken to provide information in a written format if a lot of details or facts need to be communicated.

It should not be assumed that the same method of communication will be appropriate in all circumstances. Managers should always assess each communication need as it arises and should be prepared to change their usual methods of communication if necessary.

> **Informal communication:** information being passed outside of the official communication channels.

> **Now test yourself**
>
> 19 Explain the difference between a chain network and a connected network, giving an example of a situation when each might be used.
> 20 Explain the difference between formal and informal methods of communication.
>
> **Answers on p.214**
>
> Tested

> **Revision activity**
>
> 1 Make a list of situations when informal communication might be used in a retail situation and in a manufacturing business.
> 2 Make notes on ways in which the managers of a business might communicate information. Try to include as many business situations as you can, e.g. passing down work instructions or notifying workers of redundancies.

8 Marketing

Marketing planning

Marketing planning
Revised

Marketing planning is the systematic approach to developing marketing objectives and setting out specific activities to implement the marketing strategy to meet those objectives. The result will be a marketing plan.

> **Marketing planning:** the systematic approach to developing marketing objectives and setting out specific activities to implement the marketing strategy to meet those objectives.

The marketing plan
Figure 1 shows the layout of a typical marketing plan.

```
┌─────────────────────────────┐
│ An analysis of the          │
│ organisation, the market it │
│ operates in, its            │
│ competitors and consumers   │
└─────────────────────────────┘
              ↓
┌─────────────────────────────┐
│ Marketing objectives set in │
│ line with corporate         │
│ objectives                  │
└─────────────────────────────┘
              ↓
┌─────────────────────────────┐
│ Target markets chosen after │
│ market research             │
└─────────────────────────────┘
              ↓
┌─────────────────────────────┐
│ Marketing mix strategy with │
│ a given budget              │
└─────────────────────────────┘
              ↓
┌─────────────────────────────┐
│ Review and monitoring of    │
│ progress in reaching        │
│ objectives                  │
└─────────────────────────────┘
```

Figure 1 A typical marketing plan

> **Expert tip**
> Make sure you know the difference between a marketing plan (the systematic approach to organising marketing activities) and a marketing strategy (the overall integrated approach to marketing a product, e.g. the 4Ps).

Benefits of a marketing plan
A marketing plan can be complex, take time to prepare, be difficult to understand and lead to inflexibility. However, a properly drawn up marketing plan will make sure that:
- marketing activities contribute to achieving corporate objectives
- marketing activities are integrated
- resources are used efficiently in a planned way
- employees are informed and committed to the plan
- the review and monitoring stage prepares the organisation for change

> **Now test yourself**
> 1. Identify two benefits of a marketing plan.
>
> Answer on p.214
>
> *Tested*

Elasticity and its usefulness in marketing planning
Revised

Price elasticity of demand considers the effect of a price change on demand. There are three other measures of elasticity — income elasticity of demand (YED), promotional elasticity of demand (PrED) and cross elasticity of demand (CrossED) — and these can all help a business to plan. Knowing the values can help decide what marketing decisions to make.

Income elasticity of demand (YED)
Consumer income is a huge factor in demand. A recession, unemployment or economic growth will affect how much consumers are willing to buy. A rise in

income will lead to a rise in demand for most goods (normal goods). **Income elasticity of demand** measures the degree of responsiveness of demand for a good to a change in consumers' income.

$$YED = \frac{\% \text{ change in quantity demanded}}{\% \text{ change in income}}$$

Income elastic demand
Income elastic goods are sensitive to price changes, i.e. a change in income results in a more than proportionate change in demand. The YED of price elastic goods will be greater than 1.

Income inelastic demand
Income inelastic goods are not sensitive to income changes, that is, a change in income results in a smaller proportionate change in demand. The YED of income inelastic goods will be smaller than 1.

Demand may rise with an increase in income (**normal goods**) or fall with an increase in income (**inferior goods**).

> **Income elasticity of demand (YED):** measures the degree of responsiveness of demand for a good to a change in consumers' income. Demand can be income elastic or income inelastic.

> **Normal good:** a good with a positive YED, meaning that demand changes in the same direction as an income change.
>
> **Inferior good:** a good with negative YED, meaning that demand changes in the opposite direction to an income change.

Example

A tailor sold 80 suits at $100 a month. His town suffered a rise in unemployment and income fell by 10%. His sales of suits fell to 60.

$$YED = \frac{\% \text{ change in quantity suits demanded}}{\% \text{ change in income}}$$

$$YED = \frac{-20}{80} \times 100 \text{ divided by } -10 = +2.5$$

The positive sign means that demand fell as income fell (suits are a normal good). As the value is greater than 1, the suits are income elastic, meaning revenue will also have fallen from $8,000 to $6,000.

Using income elasticity of demand
- If income levels are changing, a business can use YED to predict what will happen to its sales and alter its marketing mix appropriately. For example, if unemployment is forecast to rise, a business may consider lowering price or using lower quality resources to cut costs and prices.
- If a business is selling an inferior good at a time of rising incomes it may need to consider improving the quality.

> **Expert tip**
> Make sure you identify clearly which measure of elasticity is appropriate. All measures of elasticity assume that other factors remain constant, so make sure you check if any have changed. Check that you have noted correctly whether the elasticity is positive or negative.

Promotional elasticity of demand (PrED)
Promotional activity is a key factor in increasing sales. **Promotional elasticity of demand (PrED)** measures the degree of responsiveness of demand for a good to a change in promotion spending.

Promotion elastic demand
Promotion elastic goods are sensitive to changes in promotion, i.e. a change in promotion results in a more than proportionate change in demand. The PrED of promotion elastic goods will be greater than 1.

Promotion inelastic demand
Promotion inelastic goods are not sensitive to promotion changes, i.e. a change in promotion results in a smaller proportionate change in demand. The PrED of promotion inelastic goods will be smaller than 1.

$$PrED = \frac{\% \text{ change in quantity demanded}}{\% \text{ change in promotion spending}}$$

> **Promotional elasticity of demand (PrED):** measures the degree of responsiveness of demand for a good to a change in promotion. Demand can be promotion elastic or promotion inelastic.

> **Example**
>
> A shop sold 40 kettles a week for $10 each. The manager increased spending on local newspaper adverts from $30 to $36 and sales rose to 44.
>
> $$PrED = \frac{\% \text{ change in quantity kettles demanded}}{\% \text{ change in advertising spending}}$$
>
> $$PrED = \frac{10}{20} = +0.5$$
>
> The positive sign means that demand rose as promotion spending increased. As the value is less than 1, the kettles are promotion inelastic but revenue has still risen from $400 to $440. The adverts have been effective in raising revenue.

> **Expert tip**
>
> It is important to consider whether income, promotional and cross elasticities are positive or negative. Check carefully as this determines the effect of the changes on demand.

Cross elasticity of demand

The price of other goods may be important in determining the demand for a good. A rise in the price of margarine may cause an increase in demand for butter (substitute good). A rise in the price of fuel may cause a decrease in the demand for large engine cars (complementary good). **Cross elasticity of demand (CrossED)** measures the degree of responsiveness of demand for a good to a change in the price of another good.

A positive value indicates that the two goods are substitutes for each other. A negative value indicates that the two goods are complementary. A very low value means that the two goods are not related.

$$CrossED = \frac{\% \text{ change in quantity demanded}}{\% \text{ change in price of another good}}$$

> **Cross elasticity of demand (CrossED):** measures the degree of responsiveness of demand for a good to a change in the price of another good.

> **Example**
>
> Sales of books in a city fell from 60,000 per week to 50,000 when the price of e-readers fell from $200 to $160.
>
> $$CrossED = \frac{\% \text{ change in quantity books demanded}}{\% \text{ change in price of e-readers}}$$
>
> $$CrossED = -16.67 \text{ divided by } -20 = +0.83$$
>
> The positive sign means that demand for books is positively related to changes in the price of e-readers so these are substitute goods.

> **Now test yourself** — Tested
>
> 2 State two advantages of using demand elasticities to a marketing manager.
> 3 Calculate the value of the following elasticities:
>   (a) Income elasticity of demand when income falls by 10% and demand for good A falls by 15%.
>   (b) Promotional elasticity of demand when sponsorship costs increase by 6% and demand for good A rises by 10%.
>   (c) Cross elasticity of demand when the price of good A rises by 15% and the demand for good B falls by 10%.
>
> Answers on p.214

> **Expert tip**
>
> Make sure you know the definitions of all the measures of elasticity and what they mean. Practise calculating them and pay attention to the value of the result and whether it is positive or negative. Show all your workings.

> **Revision activity**
>
> 1 Produce a table to show the effects on revenue of each of the following:
>   (a) An income elasticity of demand of 2 when income rises.
>   (b) A promotional elasticity of demand of 1.5 when $50k is spent on advertising.
>   (c) Cross elasticity of demand of 0.5 for good A when price of good B rises by 10%.
> 2 Write notes to illustrate any marketing recommendations you would make based on the table.

Product development

Revised

Product development involves creating products that are new or different so that consumers can see new or added value. It is important because all products will eventually enter the decline stage of their life cycle and need to be replaced.

Product development: the creation of products that are new or modified so consumers will see new or additional benefits.

The product development process
The product development process is shown in Figure 2.

Figure 2 The product development process

Sources of new product ideas
Ideas can come from inside or outside a business, but many will come from research and development programmes, which generate and develop ideas from elsewhere. Other sources include:
- research and development department
- universities and government research centres
- market research and customers
- sales and production staff
- meetings to generate ideas

It is important to check that ideas will be saleable in the market. Few initial ideas become selling products.

> **Now test yourself**
> 4 Briefly explain the product development process.
> 5 State two reasons why product development is important.
>
> **Answers on p.214**
> Tested

> **Revision activity**
> Use a diagram to show how product development is linked to the following:
> - product life cycle
> - business objectives
> - product portfolio
> - market research

Promotional campaign models — AIDA and DAGMAR

Revised

These provide a framework for deciding what kind of promotional methods to use and how to measure their effectiveness.

AIDA
The **AIDA (Attention, Interest, Desire, Action) model** takes a business through the stages a customer goes through when deciding to buy by analysing the objectives of a promotional campaign and generating ideas matched to each stage so that consumers are taken along until they decide to buy.

AIDA (Attention, Interest, Desire, Action) model: a model describing the stages a customer goes through when deciding to buy a product.

Marketing planning

Table 1 The AIDA model

	Purpose	Method	Outcome
Attention	• Introduce product or brand. • Make consumer aware and interested in learning more.	• Bold words, striking graphics, bright colours, repeated words, logo. • E.g. television advert, billboard	• Awareness of product/ brand. • Remembers later when deciding to buy.
Interest	• Make consumer think about how the product might meet needs. • Possibility of buying introduced.	• Describes features. • Promises rewards/satisfaction. • Technical attributes. • Compares with competition • E.g. Clip coupons, info ads	• Consumer actively thinks of product. • Consumer makes inquiries.
Desire	• Make consumer think product meets his or her needs. • Make consumer think he or she 'must have' the product.	• Offers/demonstrations. • Information on where and how to buy. • Unique benefits shown. • E.g. instore display, selling.	• Consumer finds out how to buy. • Serious thought about buying.
Action	• Make consumer decide to buy.	• Purchase point. • Order form. • Personal selling. • E.g. sales staff, order forms.	• Consumer buys or takes action towards buying.

> **Now test yourself** — Tested
>
> 6 What do the initials AIDA stand for?
> 7 What do the initials DAGMAR stand for?
>
> **Answers on p.214**

> **Revision activity**
>
> For each of the AIDA stages, find an advert or promotional method from the press or other media that matches the purpose of that stage. Prepare a poster to illustrate this.

DAGMAR

DAGMAR (Define Advertising Goals for Measured Advertising Results) builds on AIDA, assuming consumers will move through the stages, then goes on to measure how effective a promotional campaign is. At the start, attention will be zero but should rise as the promotions take effect. Successive stages will see smaller percentages of consumers in them and this measurement can inform the way the campaign progresses.

> **DAGMAR (Define Advertising Goals for Measured Advertising Results):** a model that is used to measure how effective advertising or other promotional methods are, using AIDA as part of DAGMAR.

> **Revision activity**
>
> Prepare a presentation to explain how the AIDA model might help a business plan marketing activities for the launch of a new range of DIY tools. Include an answer to a question about the value of DAGMAR.

> **Expert tip**
>
> When using AIDA or DAGMAR, make sure you relate these models to marketing objectives, methods and ways of measuring effective marketing.

Forecasting marketing data — Revised

The need to forecast marketing data, especially sales

Forecasting may:

- enable a business to determine what changes are taking place in the market
- detect business opportunities and what marketing mix may be appropriate
- help pinpoint position on a product life cycle
- enable a business to analyse the actions of competitors

Moving average method (time series analysis)

Trend analysis or **moving average forecasting** assumes that the patterns or trends of the past will continue into the future. For products affected by regular changes, e.g. seasonal variation, time series analysis combines the moving average of past data in order to arrive at a forecast for the next few time periods.

> **Moving average forecasting:** a method that takes account of regular variations (typically seasonal) by combining the moving average value of a set of data over time.

A typical application is for sales. It does this by dealing with three components of a set of data over time.

- the underlying **trend**
- predictable **cyclical or seasonal variations** from the trend.
- random, unpredictable events

Moving average calculations

The data is inspected to see if there is a regular pattern of changes in time and then the moving average period is chosen accordingly, e.g. over a 3-year cycle (3-year moving average) or quarterly (4-quarter moving average).

> **Trend:** the average change for each time period, which shows the overall pattern of movement of a set of data.
>
> **Cyclical or seasonal variation:** the regular variation from the trend, often due to seasonal factors, which is the value for each time period minus the trend.

Example

Calculating a 3-period moving average, cyclical variation and forecasting

Year	Sales ($000)	3-period total	3-period moving average or trend	Cyclical variation	Average cyclical variation
2004	60				
2005	54	60+54+48=162	54	0	−0.65
2006	48	54+48+64=166	55.3	−7.3	−7.8
2007	64	167	55.7	+8.3	+9.5
2008	55	169	56.3	−1.3	−0.65
2009	50	175	58.3	−8.3	−7.8
2010	70	180	60	+10.7	+9.5
2011	60	182	60.7	−0.7	−0.65
2012	52				
2013					
2014					

The 3-period moving average will be the underlying trend of the data over time.

1. To calculate the 3-period totals add up each set of 3 years in turn and place the total opposite the middle year (col 3).
2. Divide each total by three to give the 3-year moving average or trend (col 4).
3. Calculate the cyclical variation by yearly sales minus trend (col 5).
4. For a graphic representation plot on a graph the 3-period moving average or trend and extrapolate this into 2012 and for each year in the 3-year cycle, add the average cyclical variation to the forecast point on the trend line for each year (see Figure 3).

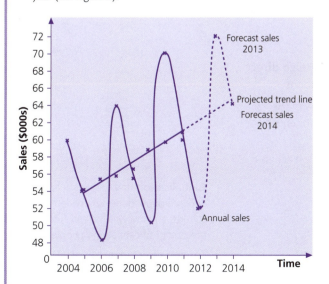

Figure 3 Moving averages: graphical forecast

Expert tip

Calculations can take a long time. Examiners are likely to present you with a partially completed table and ask you to finish it, or ask you to comment on the way the moving average method is used in forecasting.

Marketing planning

Very often quarterly figures show a seasonal variation and the same procedure is employed except the quarters have to be centred by adding the four quarter totals in pairs and dividing by two.

Evaluating moving average method of forecasting

This method produces a forecast that takes account of regular variations so is more accurate than simply projecting a trend line. Like any forecast it assumes that:

- the data used is accurate
- the future will behave in a similar way to the past

> **Revision activity**
>
> Produce a table to show the advantages and disadvantages of using time series analysis for a toy retailer.

Coordinated marketing mix

Revised

Developing a coordinated marketing mix in relation to objectives

A marketing mix is only successful if it achieves the marketing objectives set out in the marketing plan. These objectives must be clear and relate to the overall business objectives.

- The 4Ps must be integrated and reinforce each other.
- The marketing mix must take account of position in the product life cycle and market conditions.
- There should be research and development for new products to replace older ones.
- Marketing strategies should be within their set budgets.
- Flexibility to respond to change should be built in.

> **Expert tip**
>
> When discussing the marketing mix, make sure you relate the 4Ps to each other in an integrated way, showing a strategic understanding in relation to objectives and/or models such as AIDA.

Globalisation and international marketing

Globalisation

Revised

Globalisation is the growing integration and interdependence of economies and cultures and involves increased trade, movement of capital and people. It results in:

- large increases in trade between countries
- large increases in money moving between countries and in **foreign direct investment (FDI)** by governments and transnational corporations
- increasingly similar products and services being sold across the world
- a large increase in outsourcing to different countries for components or services
- large increases in international travel and instant communication across the world
- increasingly similar cultures and attitudes across the world
- converging income levels across the world

In particular, economic globalisation includes:

- decreasing barriers to trade
- increasing ease of moving capital and money across countries
- increased incentives for foreign direct investment

> **Globalisation:** the growing integration and interdependence of economies and cultures and involves increased trade, movement of capital and people.
>
> **Foreign direct investment (FDI):** when a business sets up production or distribution facilities in another country.

Increased globalisation: the implications for marketing

Globalisation is a developing phenomenon. It brings great opportunities and also more risks as businesses are increasingly able to operate in more than one country.

Opportunities
- Falling tariffs and other barriers to trade mean it is cheaper and easier to sell to other countries.
- Costs fall as more efficient, lower-cost labour and materials can be accessed, so products can be priced lower.
- Increasing incomes and access to information sources mean consumers are exposed to marketing activities and are more able to buy.
- Large markets are expanded, e.g. in Brazil, China, India and Africa.
- Internet-based marketing enables international marketing, even for smaller businesses.
- Global branding becomes possible.

Risks
- Small or nationally based businesses face increasing competition from global businesses.
- Global businesses have to fund ever more expensive marketing campaigns.
- People focus on their own culture and reject global products.

> **Expert tip**
> Globalisation means that foreign firms are increasingly entering other countries' markets for selling or production facilities. This brings increased competition but also increased opportunities at home and abroad.

> **Now test yourself**
> 8 Identify four features of globalisation.
> 9 State one implication of globalisation for marketing in:
>   (a) a business's own country
>   (b) other countries
>
> **Answers on p.214**
> Tested

Strategies for international marketing

Revised

The importance of international marketing

In today's world of interdependent economic relationships, even smaller businesses can consider expanding into selling in another country, especially as the internet enables communication to particular target groups with cheap promotion and distribution. This widens the marketing opportunities to possible customers. Many developing countries offer growing consumer bases for businesses to sell to. These emerging markets are now actively encouraging businesses to set up and sell to their populations.

Any business considering international marketing should be aware of the possible costs and resource implications, as well as making sure that this move matches their business objectives.

Factors that influence a decision to enter an international market

A business thinking of entering an international market might consider the following:
- Escaping the risks of competition at home by finding new markets abroad.
- Meeting objectives of growth and expansion by finding new markets abroad.
- Finding demand that may not exist in the home market, especially for specialist products.
- Increasing size to find economies of scale and lower costs.
- The availability of finance and business expertise.
- Risks of operating in different cultures, legal arrangements and marketing environment.

Identifying and selecting an international market

Once a business has decided to enter an **international market** it must decide where to market. Most businesses begin by looking at one or a small number of countries to export to, the choice being based on the following:

> **International marketing:** marketing products and/or services to more than one country.

- Business objectives of growth, product development, and sales.
- Business attitude to risk.
- Availability of resources including finance and personnel.
- Product type — aircraft have fewer sales possibilities than jackets.
- Market research into:
  - the size and growth of the market
  - the economic arrangements including tariffs, exchange rates, laws and regulations, incentives available
  - market competition
  - costs of marketing and distribution
  - possibility of partnership agreements
  - political and cultural arrangements

Using this information a small number of countries can be investigated in detail before a final choice is made.

A business that wishes to expand quickly, has a variety of products, is prepared to take a risk and has large amounts of finance, a skilled marketing department and other managers is likely to choose a different new market than a small business that cannot afford to take a risk and is prepared to expand slowly over time.

Methods of entering an international market

- **Merging with or taking over an existing business** — this has the advantage that there will be production and distribution networks and trained staff. The disadvantage is that two different organisation cultures and workforces have to be put together.
- **Exporting** — exporting means marketing and selling products in another country. It involves finding an importer/agent and transport and possibly dealing with the government. There may be trade tariffs or quotas to take account of but the business will retain control of the marketing process.
- **Licensing** — this is when a business licenses another business to distribute and sell a product in return for a fee. Costs are low and there is no risk to the business. However, there is also no control over the marketing process.
- **Franchising** — the business charges a fee to other businesses for the right to use trademarks, logos, promotional material and all that goes with a brand. Many services are sold internationally in this way, e.g. McDonald's and Avis. Set-up costs are small but income is limited to what has been agreed.
- **Joint ventures** — this occurs when two businesses contribute resources to a project. Knowledge, technology and marketing are shared and so are the risks and rewards. Trust is essential as there may be conflict about information or decision making.
- **Foreign direct investment (FDI)** — FDI involves building factories and/or offices. There must be an associated marketing plan. FDI can get round trade barriers, use lower labour costs, reach lower tax rates and government incentives and provide direct access to another country's market. Many large businesses now take this route despite the high initial costs and the time taken for investment.

The choice between developing pan-global or local marketing

Pan-global marketing is marketing products and/or services to global markets in many different countries. All marketing activities must be integrated across national boundaries and global branding developed using the same logos, advertisement and promotion messages so that everyone receives the same global message about the business and its products. Businesses such as Suzuki and Samsung spend large amounts of money in doing this.

> **Revision activity**
>
> Finns Furniture manufactures office furniture — chairs, desks and storage units. It produces budget low-cost pieces and a more expensive luxury range as well as offering a one-off design service. The directors are considering selling these products in other countries to enlarge the firm's international presence.
>
> Produce a report for the board of Finns Furniture that briefly:
>
> (a) Sets out the factors they might consider in choosing other countries in which to operate.
>
> (b) Considers three different methods of entering the international market.

> **Now test yourself**
>
> 10 Identify three possible methods a business might use to enter an international market.
>
> 11 State two advantages of each method.
>
> **Answers on p.214**
>
> Tested

> **Pan-global marketing:** marketing products and/or services to global markets in many different countries.

An international marketing business has to decide between:
- Pan-global marketing — little or no marketing variation across the world.
- Maintaining local differences within a pan-global approach.
- A multi-domestic strategy, which treats each country as a separate market.

Maintaining local differences in marketing might be needed because having a standard marketing approach in every country ignores variations between countries and consumers' needs may not be met. Local marketing takes account of these differences. It maintains the global approach but may adopt varying practices adapted to local markets. For example, adverts in one country may feature people who are obviously from the country in question, names may vary, recipes use local ingredients. A business engaging in local global marketing must make sure that it does not lose the overall global branding message.

Factors encouraging pan-global marketing
- Large size and global presence.
- A technical product with high development costs that can be spread.
- Experience of being involved in international marketing.
- Consumer behaviour/segment similar across world.
- Standard distribution methods.

Factors encouraging maintaining local differences in marketing
- Small size and limited international markets.
- Little experience in international marketing.
- Varying regulations and cultural attitudes in product area.
- Local distribution methods.

Choosing a strategy to develop a global market
Planning an international marketing strategy is the same process as planning a domestic marketing strategy but on a bigger scale (see Figure 4).

Figure 4 Stages in choosing an international marketing strategy

Now test yourself

12 Define pan-global marketing.

Answer on p.214

Tested

Expert tip

All applications of international marketing should be approached with the concepts outlined here but these must be applied to the individual case of the business and markets in the situation in question.

Revision activity

Former pilot Guan Lee set up Airgo, a small airline company, using a number of contacts in a range of finance companies, airlines, airports and government aviation ministries. Airgo flew passengers and freight between local airports, offering cheap flights. It was able to do this because it provided no inflight services and internet-only ticketing and checking-in plus charging for baggage. The number of inflight staff was the minimum needed for legal requirements.

Guan soon realised the domestic market was saturated. He began investigating flying to and from other countries, and research indicated that there were real possibilities to get business in an international market. He made the decision to go ahead.

(a) Explain how Airgo might set about deciding which international markets to operate in.

(b) Evaluate the most appropriate method for Airgo to use in entering the international market.

9 Operations and project management

Operations planning

Enterprise resource planning (ERP)

Revised

ERP is software that integrates management information from all business functions into a single IT-based system. It allows relevant information to be assessed and dealt with by the organisation, suppliers, customers and government so that costs and resources are minimised.

Main features of an ERP programme

An ERP system will be broken down into stand-alone or fully integrated modules, reflecting the functional areas such as marketing or finance. All the modules draw from and contribute to a central database, allowing shared information. Specialists supply off-the-shelf software or customised ERP systems. Without ERP the production department may not know details of orders or the finance department may be unaware of component costs. ERP deals with:

- supply chain management — ordering of raw materials and energy
- production — transforming inputs to output
- customer relation management — dealing with customers' enquiries, orders and delivery

Every business involved in production will be able to find out:

- what has been ordered
- how many components/raw materials of what type are needed
- whether raw material is in stock
- the progress of an order
- stocks available to meet orders
- whether payment has been requested or paid

The advantages of ERP are that it leads to lowered costs, greater communication and integration, lower inventory levels and quicker decisions. The disadvantages are that ERP systems are expensive and can take many months to become fully operational.

Now test yourself

1. What do the initials ERP stand for?
2. State three benefits from introducing ERP.
3. State one disadvantage of introducing ERP.

Answers on p.214

Tested

How ERP can improve business efficiency

Better inventory control

Inventory is the raw materials, work in progress and finished goods held. ERP allows all areas to know precisely what inventory is held, what materials are needed for planned production and levels of unsold stocks. ERP matches incoming orders to unsold stock and/or plans the required production, including using or ordering raw materials or labour. The finance for these will automatically be released and customers informed about progress and delivery times.

Inventory: made up of stocks of raw materials, work in progress and finished goods.

More accurate costing and pricing

Because ERP contains information on all the resources needed for production, the exact cost of each order and unit is known, making setting a profit-making price easier. Prices can be varied to suit individual customers.

Higher capacity utilisation
Capacity utilisation (see below) is the proportion of full capacity currently being produced. The higher it is, the more efficient the business.

ERP tells the business exactly what orders are confirmed or possible, when they might have to be delivered and what resources are needed to meet them. This information allows as full a capacity as possible to be planned for, especially as finance can be planned into the process.

Faster responses to change
Any changes in orders, stocks, prices or availability of supplies or employees will be quickly picked up and decisions can be made on this information. Decisions will link all areas together in a planned, coherent way and enable flexible fast responses.

Better use of management information
ERP is the organisation of information in all business functional areas, enabling managers to take decisions based on the whole production process rather than individual isolated parts. This enables waste to be reduced.

> **Expert tip**
> ERP is only really effective if it is fully operational across all areas of business operation. It is not a magic answer to operations problems in every business.

Capacity utilisation

Capacity is the maximum output that can be produced using currently available resources. **Capacity utilisation** is the proportion of full capacity of a business unit currently being produced. It is important because operating at under or over maximum capacity results in higher costs and less efficient use of resources.

> **Capacity utilisation:** the proportion of full capacity of a business unit currently being produced.

Measurement and significance of capacity

Revised

Maximum capacity is determined by the available resources of land, labour and capital. When these are being fully used, a business operates at full or maximum capacity. If there is spare capacity, resources will not be used but they might still incur costs, e.g. staff not working may still be paid, machines may attract interest payments. These fixed costs still have to be paid for. The lower capacity utilisation is, the higher the fixed cost per unit of output is, and it will be more difficult to make profits as the selling price will cover less of the fixed costs (lower contribution per unit to fixed costs and profit).

> **Now test yourself**
> 4 Define capacity utilisation.
> **Answer on p.214**
> Tested

How capacity utilisation can be measured
Capacity utilisation is calculated by the formula:

$$\text{capacity utilisation} = \frac{\text{current output} \times 100}{\text{maximum possible output}}$$

> **Example**
> A factory can produce 1,600 units per day and is now producing 1,200. Capacity utilisation will be $1{,}200 \times 100/1600 = 75\%$

Implications of operating under maximum capacity
Operating under maximum capacity means there are unused resources that have to be paid for but do not contribute to generating an income.

Causes of under utilisation
- Falling demand, possibly due to a new competitor, a failure to achieve marketing targets or changes in consumers' tastes or incomes.
- Seasonal variations.
- Increasing capacity in the business.
- Inefficiency in production.

Table 1 Implications of under capacity operation

Positive implications	Negative implications
• Ability to take and meet sudden large orders quickly. • Flexibility in production.	• Higher unit fixed costs leading to pressure to increase prices. • Under or unemployed resources leading to poor motivation. • Unsold output leading to higher inventory costs. • Inefficiency in production leading to higher costs.

Implications of operating over maximum capacity

If demand is greater than full capacity, a business can take steps to increase production in the short term. This may mean:

- some customers are disappointed or receive late delivery
- quality may fall
- employees and managers may become stressed
- regular machinery maintenance may be difficult
- costs increase because of steps taken to increase production

Increasing capacity utilisation

Revised

Operating at just below full capacity, e.g. 85–95%, is often seen as optimal as it lowers fixed cost per unit while retaining some flexibility to meet new orders, maintain equipment or train employees. Businesses must identify the reasons for under capacity operation. If it is market-related, a new marketing campaign to get more orders may be wise; if it is related to falling long-term sales, cutting capacity may be required.

Methods of improving capacity utilisation

Rationalisation and downsizing

Rationalisation is reorganising resources to increase efficiency and reduce capacity. It is often used when demand falls and is expected to remain lower. Three possible methods are:

- reducing labour force through redundancy, cutting working hours, stopping recruitment and/or redeploying staff to other jobs
- reducing the cost of assets by closing factories/offices and/or selling or leasing them
- selling, leasing or mothballing machinery and equipment

Increasing production

A business can start using underemployed or unemployed resources if extra orders arrive. There are other possibilities:

- adding labour by extra shifts or paying for overtime
- using zero hour contracts that only pay employees when they are actually working
- outsourcing or subcontracting work to other businesses that can deliver the right quality; this is often achieved by permanent arrangements with other businesses that can be called on when required

> **Now test yourself**
>
> 5 A business has output in May of 400 units and maximum possible output per month of 600 units.
>   (a) Calculate its capacity utilisation.
>   (b) Explain two reasons why the business might be operating at this level.
>   (c) Explain two reasons why the business might want to increase capacity utilisation to 90%.
> 6 Outline three ways a business might be able to increase capacity utilisation.
>
> **Answers on p.214**
>
> Tested

Outsourcing

Revised

Benefits of outsourcing

Outsourcing successfully requires careful checks on quality, reliability and prices. Assuming these are carried out the benefits may be:

> **Outsourcing:** when a business pays another firm to supply components or services instead of providing them as part of its production.

- Access to specialised equipment and expertise, lowering costs.
- Enabling a focus on core activities, not worrying about those outsourced.
- Sharing risks with the other business.
- Lower operational, recruitment and overhead costs.
- Flexibility to bring in additional resources when required.

> **Now test yourself**
> 7 Explain why many businesses outsource some of their production.
>
> **Answer on p.214**
>
> Tested

Lean production and quality management

Lean production is an approach to production that stresses efficiency through the systematic examination of all processes to try and achieve quality with minimum waste. Quality management is how a business tries to achieve the quality that the customer wants.

These concepts apply to whatever production method a business uses.

Lean production

Revised

Lean production uses resources as efficiently as possible to achieve desired **quality** with minimum waste. It employs a range of techniques including kaizen, cell production, just-in-time, flexible specialisms and simultaneous engineering. Using these will produce:

- higher quality
- more employee involvement and motivation
- lower costs and lower waste
- greater efficiency
- improved cash flow

> **Lean production:** a way of operating that uses resources as efficiently as possible to achieve desired quality with minimum waste.
>
> **Quality:** the fitness for purpose as required by the customer in terms of design, reliability, level of faults and durability.

> **Expert tip**
>
> Lean production is not a method like batch or flow production. It is a set of techniques and attitudes that are applied in a business to make it more efficient.

Lean production requires an effective supply chain, trained and motivated employees and can reduce the opportunities for economies of scale and flexibility to meet sudden changes in demand.

Table 2 Lean production and links with production processes

Inventory control	Low inventory levels using just-in-time
Quality	Continuous quality assurance using total quality management
Employees' roles	Highly skilled, teamwork, flexible in roles, responsible for quality using cell production.
Capacity management	Flexible production when required to meet orders using flexible specialism and time-based management.
Efficiency	Lower costs, lower waste, planned movements of materials.

Methods of meeting customer demand more efficiently

- **Cell production** — Cell production is using teams (cells) of employees who make their own decisions about the task they have to perform. The cell is responsible for dealing with material/component orders, work rotas, quality

> **Cell production:** a production technique that uses teams (cells) of employees who make their own decisions about the task they have to perform.

and use of equipment. This motivates employees, gives them control and enables better quality.
- **Time-based management (simultaneous engineering)** — Products are produced in response to consumer wants. New products have to be developed over time. This method arranges for development processes to occur at the same time whenever possible, rather than in a sequence. This enables a business to bring a new product to the market to meet consumers' demands to the market much more quickly.
- **Flexible specialism** — Flexibility in equipment and employees enables a basic product to be produced with a range of options. Cars can have different colours, engine sizes, internal features and wheels. Flexible specialism allows this to happen on a single minimum cost production line to the exact specification ordered by each customer.

> **Time-based management (simultaneous engineering):** a system for enabling development processes to happen at the same time whenever possible, saving time in bringing a product to the market.
>
> **Flexible specialism:** producing a basic product with a limited number of variations.

> **Revision activity**
>
> Use a spider diagram to show how lean production might achieve these aims:
> - meeting customer needs more exactly
> - lowering the level of waste
> - reducing business costs

Kaizen in the context of lean production

Revised

Kaizen (continuous improvement) involves all workers being responsible for making improvements in production processes. It relies on workers taking on this responsibility and managers being prepared to allow them to do so. The changes are often on-going, regular and small but add up to significant large scale improvement. Kaizen is simple and cheap to implement. The regular small changes and the constant seeking for improvement lead to:
- improvements in productivity
- less waste
- a lower breakeven level of output
- more responsiveness to customer needs
- greater employee motivation and involvement

Costs of kaizen
- Training employees and managers in new attitudes.
- Setting up teams and empowering employees.
- Dealing with employees who do not want greater involvement.
- Making sure that all staff are involved.

> **Kaizen:** continuous, regular, small improvements suggested by all employees as part of a culture of improvement.

> **Now test yourself**
>
> 8 Define kaizen.
> 9 Identify two reasons why many businesses have implemented kaizen.
> 10 Give two requirements for a successful introduction of kaizen.
>
> **Answers on p.214**
>
> Tested

Just-in-time (JIT) and its implications for lean production

Revised

Just-in-time (JIT) systems use as little inventory as possible. Raw materials are ordered as required for production, work in progress is minimised by only producing for firm orders and finished good are despatched immediately. Production is 'pulled' through from the customer, not 'pushed' by the business producing goods that then have to be sold. The result is:
- low inventory holding costs and no overproduction
- time saved in moving supplies about
- less waste
- immediate delivery to customers
- improved quality and lower costs

Successful JIT depends on:
- reliable raw material suppliers on quick delivery time, quantity and quality
- accurate forecasts of customer demand
- a flexible workforce and reliable machinery
- enterprise resource planning (ERP) to integrate demand, production and suppliers

> **Just-in-time (JIT):** JIT systems minimise inventory holding by producing goods to order using raw materials obtained for that purpose.

> **Expert tip**
>
> Remember that quality is about meeting customers' needs, not about the expensiveness or cost of a product.

Quality control and quality assurance

Revised

Quality in terms of customer demands

There is no absolute quality measurement. A quality product is one that meets the requirement of the customer. This may be defined in terms of either a set of standards or specifications or in the sense of being 'fit for use' as a minimum standard. A cheap, throw-away razor will be less well made and durable than a more expensive, metal razor but each may be acceptable to the customer in terms of quality in relation to the price. This means it is vital to know what the customer is demanding and to produce this at minimum cost to the business. Any relevant legal requirements must also be met.

The importance of quality assurance

Quality assurance is a system for assuring customers that processes exist to maintain quality at every stage in production, including raw material supplies. It is often based on the idea that each production process acts as a supplier to an internal customer — the next stage. This means that faults are picked up during production and **quality control** is built into production. Waste is minimised as faults can be corrected at each stage, instead of having to throw away a finished product. Quality assurance is closely linked to kaizen and is essential for lean production. If quality assurance is not in place, businesses face waste, dissatisfied customers, lost orders and inefficient production.

> **Quality assurance:** a system for assuring customers that processes exist to maintain quality at every stage in production.
>
> **Quality control:** the methods used to check quality is assured, including inspection, testing random samples and involving the workforce.

Advantages of quality assurance
- Greater employee involvement and motivation.
- Lower costs as defects can be corrected as they occur (right first time).
- Employees are in the best position to detect and correct faults.

Disadvantages of quality assurance
- Greater demands on employees may reduce motivation.
- Conflicts with focus on levels of output.
- Cost of training and time for checking at each stage.
- Not all products need high standard of quality so time wasted.

ISO 9000 guarantees a documented quality assurance system and there are other government or industry awards for businesses that demonstrate quality assurance procedures.

> **Now test yourself**
>
> 11 Explain the difference between quality assurance and quality control.
>
> **Answer on p.214**
>
> Tested

Methods of quality control

Revised

Quality control is the methods used to check that quality is assured. These include inspection, testing random samples and involving the workforce.

Traditional quality control has focused on quality inspectors testing examples of the finished products to check they meet the quality standards. The examples are chosen at random and if faults are found more checks are carried out on the rest of the products.

Advantages of traditional end result quality control
- Experts check quality.
- Regular production problems can be highlighted and corrected.
- Faulty products are removed.

Disadvantages of traditional end result quality control
- Not every product is checked — method relies on statistical techniques.
- Negative for employees as the focus is on detecting faults.

> **Revision activity**
>
> Use a table to compare the advantages and disadvantages of quality assurance and quality control.

Lean production and quality management

- No responsibility on employees for quality so they are less likely to monitor their production.
- Waste results as faulty products are only found when finished.

Involving the workforce in quality control

Quality control need not be carried out at the end of production. It can be done at each stage by employees checking that they have met the quality standards involved in their task. This requires employees to be trained in quality standards and how to apply them. This kind of quality control is found in quality assurance or total quality management

> **Expert tip**
>
> Remember that: quality control is used to check quality, quality assurance involves setting up procedures to assure quality and TQM involves setting up a corporate culture of quality improvement.

Total quality management (TQM) — Revised

Aims and effectiveness of TQM

Deming set out **TQM** in the 1980s as a formal plan for quality assurance requiring commitment from the whole organisation and its employees to quality control in every task. This applies throughout the production process, from quality of raw materials to finished product. Its main points are:

- Get it right first time consistently.
- All staff must be committed to continuous improvement in quality.
- Build partnerships with suppliers.
- All staff are educated and trained in responsibility for quality.
- Supervisors should encourage, not find fault.
- Problem solving to be shared.
- Clear achievable goals for each employee and task.
- Workers to take pride in their work.
- An organisation structure and culture to support the above.

> **Total quality management (TQM):** involves changing corporate culture so that all employees are involved in continuous quality improvement.

The potential of kaizen in TQM

TQM incorporates kaizen as a key part of its plan. TQM demands that all employees:

- are committed to continuous improvement
- share problem solving
- are educated and trained to take responsibility for quality

These are vital components of the kaizen approach to continuous improvement. Methods used to enact this include quality chains of internal supplier/customer relationships and quality circles where groups of employees meet to discuss quality improvement ideas.

> **Now test yourself**
>
> 12 Define TQM.
> 13 Briefly explain the link between kaizen and TQM.
>
> **Answers on p.214**
>
> Tested

Benchmarking — Revised

Benchmarking is comparing a firm's procedures or products with the best practice in other businesses. The firm can then change its procedures or products to be at least as good as the best practice.

> **Benchmarking:** comparing a firm's procedures or products with best practice in similar firms in order to identify and carry out possible improvements.

The importance of benchmarking in quality control

Successful benchmarking results in an improvement in quality. Being at least equal to the best will mean a business can present its products as market leaders and gain a reputation for reliability and quality.

Advantages of benchmarking

- By using information gained from observing other firms a business can improve quality.

- Best practice standards can lead to setting clear targets.
- Costs and waste can be reduced.

Disadvantages of benchmarking
- It is difficult to gain accurate information from other businesses.
- The temptation is to copy rather than build on best practice.
- The cost of collecting information may be more than any gains.

Project management

A **project** is a particular business scheme with a specific objective, time scale and budget. It usually contains a number of activities and tasks that must be completed, some in a particular order. **Project management** deals with how resources are planned, organised and managed to complete the project successfully from start to finish in the set time allowed. Examples of projects include the building of a stadium or installing a new IT network. A-level project management focuses on managing time.

> **Now test yourself**
> 14 Define benchmarking.
> 15 Identify two advantages and two disadvantages of benchmarking.
>
> **Answers on p.215**
> Tested

> **Project:** a series of activities with a defined beginning and end that are designed to achieve a particular objective.
>
> **Project management:** planning, organising and managing resources to complete a project within a set time scale and budget.

The need for projects and project management

Revised

Businesses operate at two levels. One is the day-to-day activities involved in finance, production, marketing and dealing with employees. The other is the way in which new activities for change are thought of, planned for and implemented. Many of these changes take the form of projects and need planning. Business environments are always changing, and projects are often a result of the need to react to change, e.g. prices change so a business decides it is worthwhile opening a factory in another country. This becomes a project.

Project failure
Project failure includes one or more of the following:
- The project is not completed at all.
- The project is not completed in the time allowed.
- The project costs more than the amount budgeted.
- Quality is not what was planned for.

Reasons for project failure
- Changes in the business environment, e.g. a ferry terminal baggage handling system has to be redesigned halfway through the project because two major new ferry routes are opened.
- Poor project management or interference by other managers.
- Weaknesses in the project management team.
- Cost overruns because prices rise unexpectedly.
- Loss of focus on the business benefits, e.g. a new building is designed well but not all its facilities are used.
- Warning signs on lateness or cost overruns are ignored.

> **Now test yourself**
> 16 Define project management.
> 17 State three reasons why a project may fail and give an example for each.
>
> **Answers on p.215**
> Tested

Network diagrams

Revised

Network or critical path analysis (CPA) uses a **network diagram** of the activities needed to complete a project. The diagram shows the time taken for each activity and the order in which they must be completed.

> **Network diagram:** a diagram that identifies all the activities in a project, the time they take and the order in which they must be completed. The diagram is a key tool in network analysis or critical path analysis (CPA).

Constructing a network diagram

To construct a network diagram, you need to:
- identify all the project activities and the time taken for each
- identify which activities must follow another and which can be done at the same time
- use this information to draw the network

Example

Building a studio art gallery

Activity		Length in days	Must follow
A	Lay foundations and floor	10	
B	Build walls	8	A
C	Add roof	5	B
D	Plaster walls and ceiling	1	C
E	Install electrics	4	B
F	Fit wooden doorframes	2	D
G	Fit windows, door and paint	4	D
H	Install hanging technology	6	D, E
I	Fit outside fixtures	4	C

Some activities need to follow another, e.g. C must follow B. Some can be done at the same time as others, e.g. F, G, H and I can all be done at the same time.

Main elements of the network diagram

- **Activities:** are the tasks to be completed. Shown as a line with their duration and an arrow to show direction.
- **Nodes** identify the start and end of an activity. Nodes are shown as circles with **earliest start time (EST)** possible for the next activity and **latest finish time (LFT)** possible for the previous activity. The LFT shows the latest time an activity can be started without delaying the whole project.
- **Dummy activities** occur when an activity cannot start until two other activities have finished and these have the same starting and ending nodes. To avoid ambiguity, the dummy has a duration of zero and is shown as a dotted line.
- **Minimum project duration** is the shortest possible time in which a project can be completed.

Critical path analysis: drawing the network diagram

To draw up a network diagram you need to work from left to right:
- draw a start node
- draw activities as lines, each one starting and ending at a node.
- make sure that activities that require a completed previous one follow from the correct node
- check for any dummy activities and show as a dotted line
- show a finishing node to draw all activities to the conclusion

Using critical path analysis

- Work from left to right and enter the ESTs, taking the highest EST where there are two routes to a node.
- This will give the minimum project duration. Note that this is usually less than the total time for all the individual activities as some can be carried out simultaneously.

> **Activity:** one of the specific tasks involved in completing a project.
>
> **Node:** identifies the start and finish of an activity. Each is given an identifying number.
>
> **Earliest start time:** the earliest possible time an activity can start after the beginning of the project.
>
> **Latest finishing time:** the latest possible time an activity can finish without delaying the whole project.
>
> **Dummy activity:** an activity that has a duration of zero and indicates when an activity cannot start until two other activities with the same starting and ending nodes have finished.
>
> **Minimum project duration:** the shortest possible time in which a project can be completed.

Now test yourself

18 On a network diagram explain what is shown by the following:
   (a) a line
   (b) a circle
   (c) two parallel lines
   (d) an arrow

Answers on p.215

Tested

- Work from right to left and enter the latest finishing times, starting with the EST in the finishing node as the LFT at that point. Use the lowest LFT at each node.
- The **critical path** is the sequence of activities that cannot be delayed without delaying the whole project. The activities on this path are **critical activities** shown with two parallel lines on each critical activity.
- Critical path nodes and activities will have EST = LFT.

> **Critical path:** the sequence of activities that cannot be delayed without delaying the whole project.
>
> **Critical activities:** activities that cannot be delayed without delaying the whole project.

Example

Building a studio art gallery

Figure 1 shows the network, ESTs, LFTs, a dummy activity and the critical path.

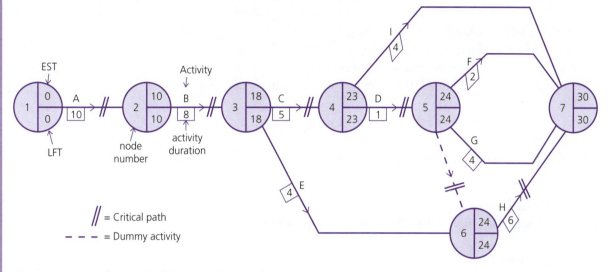

Figure 1 Network diagram: building a studio art gallery

Finding minimum project duration and critical path
- Minimum project duration is 30 days.
- Activities A, B, C, D, and H are critical activities.
- Activities E, F, G, and I are non-critical and can be delayed without delaying the whole project.
- Note that the critical path goes via the dummy activity.

Calculation of total and free float
- **Total float** and **free float** enable the calculation of how long an activity can be delayed before the next activity or the whole project is delayed.
- Total float is the maximum length of time an activity can be delayed without delaying the whole project = LFT − duration − EST.
- For activity E total float = 24 − 4 − 18 = 2, meaning that E can be delayed for 2 days and the project will still finish in 30 days.
- Free float is the maximum length of time an activity can be delayed without delaying the next activity = EST next activity − duration − EST.
- For activity E free float = 24 − 4 − 18 = 2, meaning that activity E can be delayed for 2 days until day 20 because H must start on day 24.

> **Total float:** the maximum length of time an activity can be delayed without delaying the whole project.
>
> **Free float:** the maximum length of time an activity can be delayed without delaying the next activity.

Revision activity

Produce a brief guide to critical path analysis for a student on work experience. Include brief explanations of the following:
- nodes
- minimum project duration
- earliest start and finish times
- free and total float
- the critical path
- the value of critical path analysis in carrying out a project

Expert tip

Using critical path analysis can be time consuming. You must be able to draw and interpret network diagrams, complete them if there are missing elements and understand how critical path analysis is useful when carrying out a project.

Project management

CPA as a management tool

CPA enables planning of complex projects with an indication of the times by which activities must be completed and how important meeting those times is. This enables efficiency and minimising costs. CPA can do the following:

- Calculate project duration, enabling deliveries for supplies and other resources to be planned.
- Show when activities are scheduled to happen, enabling resources to be available at exactly those times, prioritising the critical activities.
- Use EST and LFT to monitor progress and transfer resources from non-critical to critical activities if necessary to prevent lateness.
- Use total and free float to help decide which activities might need to be focused on. Those with high floats can spare resources for more critical activities.
- Decide which tasks can be carried out simultaneously.
- Indicate when there might be resource constraints, especially labour. It may be possible to carry out a number of activities at the same time but will there be enough resources to do this? CPA can show how to use a minimum of resources for the project.
- Be easily programmed into software packages to enable lean production and good supplier and customer relations.
- Use 'what if' analysis to judge the effect of different possible scenarios, e.g. the effect of taking more time for one activity.

Problems with CPA

- Relies on accurate data; this may not be available, especially as many projects are new.
- Encourages rigid thinking and does not guarantee success.
- Needs constant review, monitoring and management to be effective.
- Encourages focus on timing and speed rather than quality or flexibility.

Revision activity

An earthquake happens at 6.45 p.m. and a television company plans to feature the results on the 10 p.m. news. The producer draws up a list of the tasks that need to be done in order to make this possible.

Production tasks for earthquake report

Activity		Time taken minutes	Must follow
A	Communicate with local broadcasters	15	
B	Interview earthquake expert	20	
C	Film and interview in earthquake area	60	A, B
D	Emergency planning officer interviewed	20	C
E	Studio review	30	C
F	Prepare film	25	C
G	Edit film	30	A, B, C, D, E, F

1 Draw a network diagram.
2 Identify the following:
   (a) minimum project duration
   (b) critical path
3 Calculate free float and total float for Activity D.
4 Will the television company be able to show its programme on the 10 p.m. news?
5 The emergency planning officer cannot be located at once, and his interview takes 45 minutes. How might the company still be able to show the programme on the 10 p.m. news?
6 Evaluate the usefulness of CPA to the television company.

10 Finance and accounting

Costs

Approaches to costing

Revised

- Businesses take differing approaches to how they calculate the cost of a particular product. A business might be divided up into sections, with each of them being required to monitor and control their own costs as well as to function profitably, i.e. cost and profit centres.
- When calculating costs, it is essential that all costs are included. As well as the identifiable variable costs, businesses will also need to cover their fixed costs (overheads).
- There are two main methods that businesses use to calculate the cost information required for decision making.

Differences between absorption and contribution costing

Absorption costing

- **Absorption costing** requires all of the costs of a business to be 'absorbed' into the costs of the products made by the business. The variable costs identifiable with a particular product or service together with identifiable indirect costs must both be covered. Indirect costs that cannot be directly linked to one product or another also need to be covered. Some means of sharing out (apportioning) those costs between the various products or departments must be found.
- Absorption costing is used when a business produces a range of products or services and needs to calculate the price it should charge for a specific product or service. The business needs to know the full cost of each product that must be covered.
- The apportioning of indirect costs can vary depending on which indirect cost is involved. The cost of rent of a business might be apportioned according to how much space each of the products uses. The cost of the human resources department is more likely to be apportioned according to how many people are employed in each cost centre.
- A business might also decide to allocate all indirect costs based on the number of employees in each department.
- The business can use the full cost of a product to decide what price can be charged that would cover all of the costs involved. Some businesses will also include a desired level of profit into their calculation of full costs.

> **Absorption costing:** requires that all costs (fixed and variable) are included in the cost of production of a product.

Contribution costing (marginal costing)

- **Contribution costing** is the calculation of the cost of producing one extra product. Any revenue gained above the marginal cost is a contribution to fixed costs and will be profit after all fixed costs have been covered.
- In contribution costing the business is only concerned with the total variable costs for a product or service. Fixed costs or overheads are not included so

> **Contribution costing:** when only the variable costs of a product are considered.

the 'full cost' of making a product is not covered. The role of contribution costing is to consider whether the product makes a positive contribution to fixed costs or not. If a positive contribution is made, it is worth the business manufacturing the product or providing the service.
- Contribution costing is only used in exceptional circumstances because ultimately all costs have to be covered.

> **Now test yourself**
>
> 1 What is meant by the term 'absorption costing'?
> 2 Define 'contribution costing'.
>
> **Answers on p.215**
>
> Tested

Appropriate circumstances for using contribution costing

'One-off' special orders

A business has been asked to supply a batch of products at a price much lower than they would normally sell for. If the business were to use the absorption costing method, the order would be rejected because the total costs (FC + VC) of producing the order would not be covered by the price that the customer is willing to pay.

> **Example**
>
> Compot Ltd makes ready meals that sell to retailers for $2 each. A major supermarket has approached Compot Ltd to supply 10,000 ready meals but it is only willing to pay $1.50 per meal. The planned output per year is 150,000 units. Fixed costs per annum are $80,000.
>
> Based on the planned level of output, the costs of production are as follows:
> - direct labour cost is $0.25 per unit
> - materials cost $0.95 per unit
> - fixed costs are $0.50 per unit
>
> Should Compot Ltd accept the order from the supermarket?
>
> The full cost of production is $1.70 (0.25 + 0.95 + 0.50) meaning that it would make a loss of $0.20 per meal sold. However, the fixed costs are already covered by the planned output.
>
> Using contribution costing it is only the marginal cost of the order that needs to be considered. Therefore, the costs of the extra order for 10,000 ready meals would be $1.20 (0.25 + 0.95) meaning that a **contribution** towards fixed costs and profits of $0.30 would be made per meal.
>
> This type of costing for an additional order can only work if the business has some spare capacity and if its current regular customers do not hear that it has been selling ready meals at this lower price.
>
> **Contribution:** the difference between selling price and variable costs.

'Make or buy' decisions

A business might need to make a decision whether it should continue to manufacture all its products or whether it would be more profitable to buy them in from another business.

The business will be getting a contribution to fixed costs if the price that it receives for the product is higher than the variable cost of its manufacture. If it decided to stop production and buy the products in from another manufacturer, the contribution to fixed costs would be lost. The remaining products manufactured by the business would have to cover more of the fixed costs than previously.

> **Now test yourself**
>
> 3 State two situations in which a business might use contribution costing.
>
> **Answer on p.215**
>
> Tested

> **Example**
>
> Creative Arts manufactures large wooden ornaments that it sells to retailers at a price of $25 per item. Its planned output for the year is 6,000 ornaments. Fixed costs are $24,000. The variable costs per ornament are:
> - direct labour $8
> - direct materials $10
>
> Creative Arts has recently been approached by a local artist who has offered to supply it with identical ornaments but at a price of only $21. Should Creative Arts stop manufacturing ornaments and buy them from the local artist?
>
> Using absorption costing, the ornaments cost Creative Arts $22 to manufacture, giving it a profit of $3 dollars per ornament.

If it orders from the local artist it would pay $21 per ornament. If it continues to sell the ornaments at $25 it now has a profit of $4 — or does it? It still has to cover its fixed costs. Therefore, it has achieved a contribution to fixed costs of $4 per ornament not a $4 profit.

Fixed costs are $24,000, which is $4 per ornament, and still need to be covered whether or not Creative Arts manufactures the ornaments. This means that the actual cost of each ornament bought in would be $25 ($21 + $4).

Creative Arts might still consider buying in the ornaments rather than make them if the production capacity could be used to produce another product that could make a greater contribution to fixed costs.

To decide whether to stop production of a product

The revenue from the sale of a product might not cover the full cost of production but should a business stop production of that item? Contribution costing can be used to make the decision.

Example

Jamelee Ltd manufactures coordinating leisure wear. It makes trousers, shirts and jumpers in matching colours.

The fixed costs for Jamelee are $60,000, which are apportioned to the three items 50%, 30% and 20% respectively.

The business produces 18,000 shirts, 10,000 pairs of trousers, and 4,000 jumpers per year.

The costs and revenues are as follows:

	Trousers ($)	Shirts ($)	Jumpers ($)
Fixed costs	30,000	18,000	12,000
Fixed cost per unit	3	1	3
Direct materials per unit	10	8	8
Direct labour per unit	16	12	6
Total cost per unit	29	21	17
Selling price	34	24	16
Profit/loss per unit	5	3	(1)

Trousers provide a total profit of $150,000 and the shirts produce a profit of $54,000. The jumpers produce a loss of ($12,000). Should Jamelee Ltd cease production of jumpers?

The answer is no. The jumpers are not providing a profit but they provide a positive contribution to fixed costs of $3 each, meaning that jumpers give a contribution for the year of $12,000. If the production of jumpers ceased, the $12,000 of fixed costs would need to be covered by the remaining two products.

The shirts would need to cover extra fixed costs of $7,500 (12,000 × 50/80) and the trousers an extra $4,500 ($12,000 × 30/80). The $12,000 fixed costs would be apportioned between trousers and shirts by calculating, 50% of 80% and 30% of the 80%.

The profit per unit for trousers would be $4.25 rather than $5, and the profit per unit for shirts would then be $2.75 rather than $3. The profitability of the two remaining products has decreased as a result of having to cover more fixed costs.

Revision activity

Draw up a table as in the example above to show the new figures per unit for trousers and shirts if jumpers were no longer produced. Calculate the total profit for the business after stopping production of jumpers.

A business might have other possible reasons, besides profitability, to continue the production of a loss-making product. In the case of the jumpers, it might be because customers buying a shirt and trousers prefer to buy the matching jumper from the same producer. In this case, if production of jumpers ceased, the business could find that demand for its shirts and trousers would fall.

The business would also be maximising the use of its production capacity in terms of both labour and equipment.

To decide between the production of two competing options

Sometimes there is insufficient production capacity to produce the whole range of products that has been made by a business. A decision must be made about which product to stop producing.

In such a case the business could calculate the contribution to fixed costs and profits made by each product by multiplying the predicted production/sales by the contribution per unit. The product with the lowest **total contribution** would no longer be produced.

When entering a new market

Contribution costing can be used when a penetration price is to be charged on products when entering a new market. In the longer term, the fixed costs must also be covered but in the shorter term, the business might only focus on covering all of the variable costs, such as direct labour and materials. Once the product has become established in the new market, the price can be raised so that all costs will be covered in the long term.

Difference between contribution and profit

Contribution should perhaps be more accurately known as 'contribution to fixed costs and profit'. Contribution per unit is a contribution towards covering the fixed costs of production. Once the fixed costs have been fully covered, the remaining contributions are profit. Contribution only becomes profit after all fixed costs have been covered.

For example, a business producing 10,000 units of a product has fixed costs of $5,000 and a contribution per unit of $2. It will take 2,500 contributions of $2 to cover all the fixed costs. The 2501st unit and subsequent units produced will make a $2 contribution to profit because the fixed costs have now been fully covered by the first 2,500 contributions per unit.

> **Total contribution:** contribution per unit multiplied by the number of items produced/sold.

> **Now test yourself**
> 4 Distinguish between contribution and profit.
>
> **Answer on p.215**
> Tested

Budgets

The purposes of budgets

Revised

Budgets are future financial plans drawn up with the aim of giving some focus and parameters for business activity. They can encompass financial budgets and non-financial activities.

Performance

Budgets are frequently set for:
- cash
- sales
- marketing
- production
- administration

The use of budgets can improve the performance of a business because they can:
- help with overall business planning
- provide targets and/or limitations for the business and/or its departments
- aid the effective allocation of resources to the various business functions
- add an element of control as actual figures can be compared to the budgeted ones
- act as a motivational tool as departmental managers will aim to work within their budgets
- help departmental managers to understand their role in the achievement of overall business objectives

> **Now test yourself**
> 5 Identify two reasons why a business might set departmental budgets.
>
> **Answer on p.215**
> Tested

Benefits and drawbacks of the use of budgets

Benefits
- They introduce an element of financial control.
- They allow senior managers to identify parts of the business that are underperforming and to take corrective action.
- Targets can be motivating if they are realistic.
- They can allow managers to see the impact of their budget and those of other managers on the overall aims of the business.

Drawbacks
- Unrealistic budgets can be demotivating.
- Managers might argue a case for a higher budget than is necessary.
- A manager who has under-spent might buy unnecessary items to avoid having the budget reduced the following year.
- Inflexible budgets might prevent a business from reacting to a sudden change in the market.
- Lack of information can make it difficult to draw up a realistic budget for a new business or for a one-off project.

> **Now test yourself**
> 6 Explain one benefit and one drawback of using budgets.
> **Answer on p.215**
> Tested

How budgets might be produced
- Budgets can take the overall business objective(s) as a starting point.
- They can break down the business objective(s) into departmental or divisional budgets.
- They are frequently based on what has happened in previous years together with what the business realistically expects to happen in the future.
- Discussion often takes place with the **budget holder(s)** to agree the budget based on the business objective(s) and other available relevant information, e.g. current material costs.
- Budgeted figures often use last year's figures as a starting point. This often results in the current year's budget being last year's figure plus a small increase.
- They are set perhaps monthly or quarterly.

> **Budget holder:** person responsible for the implementation of a given budget. He or she might be involved in the setting of the budget or it might be handed down to him or her.

Use of flexible budgets and zero budgeting

Flexible budgets
It is usual to flex budgets when differences appear between the budgeted and the actual figures, e.g. if actual output or sales are higher or lower than expected. The costs associated with the output or sales would be flexed to match the actual level of output or sales achieved. If output were lower than the budgeted level, it would be unrealistic for the production department to budget for the same amount of materials. If 1,000 metres of fabric was budgeted for to make 800 shirts and only 600 shirts were actually produced, the amount of fabric required and budgeted for should also be lower. The budget would be flexed to reflect the lower level of output. The budget would include only 750 metres of fabric if only 600 shirts were being produced.

Zero budgeting
Zero budgeting ignores any previous budgets and requires that each budget holder puts forward a case for the next period's budget. They need to produce a plan for what they expect to achieve and what they need to achieve it. They must be able to justify all of their figures.

This method prevents 'budget creep' when departmental budgets are increased slightly each year without any detailed analysis taking place into whether or not an increase is necessary. This can be wasteful and might not reflect the changing needs of the different departments in a business.

> **Now test yourself**
> 7 Briefly explain the difference between flexible and zero budgeting.
> 8 Identify one situation when flexible budgeting might be more appropriate.
> **Answers on p.215**
> Tested

Budgets

Purposes of budgets for allocating resources and controlling and monitoring a business

Resource allocation

The setting of budgets is likely to encourage a detailed plan of what resources will be needed and how resources are to be allocated in order to achieve the best outcome for the business.

For example, budgeting can cause a business to identify that if a market becomes more competitive, it might be sensible to allocate more resources to the marketing department. The marketing department might see its budget increased to allow it to react to the market situation.

Controlling and monitoring

- Inefficient use of resources can be identified and corrected.
- Progress towards achieving corporate or department objectives can be measured.
- Over-spending budget holders can be identified and the cause of any over-spend can be investigated (not all over-spending is unnecessary; circumstances might have changed since the budget was set).
- The performance and progress of a department or division can be measured against the budget.
- Departments requiring additional funding can be identified.

Role of budgets in appraising a business

The success of a business can be measured by how well it meets the targets contained in its budgets. These budgets may be closely related to business objectives. A business that exceeds the expectations in the budgets would be judged to be successful, while one that continually fails to meet the expectations outlined in its budgets would need to investigate the reasons for the underperformance. It might be that the budgets were set at an unrealistic level.

> **Now test yourself**
>
> 9 Briefly explain one way in which a budget might be used to control the business activity
>
> **Answer on p.215**
>
> Tested

Variances: adverse, favourable

Revised

The meaning of variances

When an actual outcome is different from the budgeted outcome it is said to vary. The difference between the budgeted outcome and the actual outcome is known as the **variance**.

An actual figure achieved can be better or worse than the budgeted figure. When the actual figure is worse, the variance is said to be '**adverse**' and when the actual figure is better than the budgeted figure, the variance is said to be '**favourable**'.

Variance analysis is the when the causes of any differences are investigated.

Calculation and interpretation of variances

A restaurant has the following information regarding its budgeted figures and the actual figures for the month.

> **Variance:** the difference between the budgeted figure and the actual figure achieved.
>
> **Variance analysis:** the process of determining the cause of any difference between budgeted and actual figures and whether the variance is favourable or adverse.
>
> **Adverse variance:** when the actual figure is a poorer outcome for the business than the budgeted figure.
>
> **Favourable variance:** when the actual figure achieved is a better outcome for the business than the budgeted figure.

Table 1 Calculation and interpretation of variances

Item	Budget ($)	Actual ($)	Difference ($)	Favourable (F) or Adverse (A)
Rent	1,850	1,850	0	Neutral
Ingredients	2,450	2,800	350	A
Heat and light	320	300	20	F
Wages	600	630	30	A

Often a higher actual figure indicates an adverse variance but not always. In the case of output, a higher actual figure than the budgeted one is a favourable variance because this indicates that the business achieved a higher than expected level of output.

In the case of the restaurant above, if the budgeted number of meals had been 1,000 but actually 1,150 meals were prepared and served, this would be a favourable variance on the budgeted meals. An increase in the number of meals served could also account for the higher cost of the ingredients and wages. Such variances in costs should also be assessed in terms of the output that they contributed towards.

> **Now test yourself**
>
> 10 Explain what is meant by a 'favourable variance'.
> 11 Explain what is meant by an 'adverse variance'.
>
> **Answers on p.215**
>
> Tested

> **Revision activity**
>
> Investigate and make a list of the various types of budgets that might be produced in a business. Using that list, write down as many reasons as you can for why the actual figures for each of the budgets might vary from the budgeted ones.

Contents of published accounts

The income statement

Revised

Construction or amendment of an income statement

AS Accounting fundamentals looked at the contents of an income statement but for A level you are required to be able to make changes based on information given. For example, if a business had to pay a higher price to purchase goods for sale, the cost of goods sold would increase. If the selling price of the goods was left unchanged, the gross profit for the business would decrease.

This would be recorded in the trading section of the income statement. For example, the price of goods to the business is increased by 10%. The effect on the trading section would be as follows:

	Before the change		After the 10% increase	
	$000	$000	$000	$000
Sales revenue		300		300
Opening inventory	80		80	
Purchases	100		110	
	180		190	
Less closing inventory	40		40	
Cost of goods sold		140		150
Gross profit		160		150

> **Now test yourself**
>
> 12 Calculate the new gross profit if the cost of purchases had increased by 15% and the selling price had been increased by 10%.
>
> **Answer on p.215**
>
> Tested

Some changes will impact on the profit and loss section of the income statement rather than the trading section. For example, if the cost of electricity to the business or the wages of its workers increased, this would increase the value of the expenses borne by the business and as a result would reduce the profit for the year (net profit). So, if wages and electricity increased by 10%, the profit and loss section would be affected as follows:

	Before change		After price increases	
	$000	$000	$000	$000
Gross profit		160		160
Rent	10		10	
Wages	80		88	
Electricity	10		11	
Office supplies	8		8	
Sundry expenses	2	110	2	119
Net profit (profit for the year)		50		41

> **Now test yourself**
>
> **13** Based on the 'before change' figures, calculate the new profit for the year if the cost of office supplies was to increase by 25% and wages increased by 20%.
>
> **Answer on p.215**
>
> Tested

Any changes affecting the income statement will affect the statement of financial position (balance sheet). An increase in the recorded expenses will decrease the retained earnings to be carried forward to the statement of financial position.

The balance sheet (statement of financial position)

Revised

The balance sheet (statement of financial position) records the value of assets and liabilities on a particular day. The values recorded in the statement of financial position (balance sheet) will change, e.g. if an asset is sold or if a new asset is purchased.

The sale of a non-current asset would reduce the value of non-current assets (fixed assets) and increase the value of cash and cash equivalents. If the asset had been purchased using a long-term loan, the loan would be repaid, therefore reducing the value of non-current liabilities.

The purchase of a non-current asset would have the reverse effect. The value of non-current assets would increase and the value of cash and cash equivalents would fall if the asset was purchased using money from cash or bank accounts. If a loan were used to purchase the asset, there would be an increase in the liabilities of the business.

> **Now test yourself**
>
> Tested
>
> **14** A business purchases a new machine for $40,000 using a long-term bank loan. Explain the changes that would take place on the statement of financial position (balance sheet).
>
> **15** A business sells some of its production equipment for $20,000. There was an outstanding loan of $5,000 from the purchase of the equipment. Explain what changes would take place on the statement of financial position (balance sheet).
>
> **Answers on p.215**

Intangible assets

Revised

How intangible assets are treated in the balance sheet (statement of financial position)

Examples of **intangible assets** include a trade mark, **goodwill**, patents and copyright. Intangible assets have a perceived value to the business, but it can be difficult to put an accurate value on them.

The price paid to acquire a business is usually much higher than the value of the assets being obtained; the difference is goodwill. This might be to take into account the value of the reputation of the business being purchased but there is no guarantee that the reputation will be maintained by the new owners.

> **Intangible asset:** an asset that can be assigned a monetary value but which does not have a physical presence, e.g. goodwill, patents and copyright.
>
> **Goodwill:** the difference between the purchase price paid for acquiring a business and the actual value of the net assets purchased in the acquisition.

Intangible assets appear on the statement of financial affairs (balance sheet) as an asset. Potential investors are likely to ignore the value of any intangible assets when analysing the financial statements of a business because their stated value cannot be verified or guaranteed in future and, if the business was to become insolvent, the intangible assets might have little or no value.

Inventory valuation

Revised

The value of inventory is recorded in the statement of financial position (balance sheet). This is done at the end of a financial period, which is usually 1 year.

It is important that the inventory valuation is as accurate as possible. It should be valued at cost or its **net realisable value**, whichever is the lower value.

> **Net realisable value:** the actual or estimated selling price of an item less all the costs incurred in bringing that item to the market.

The difficulties of valuing inventory

1 The price paid for inventory (historical cost) would give a factually correct value but that was in the past. The current value might be higher or lower. Items that are no longer fashionable are likely to fall in value, whereas items that are sought after and now in short supply might have risen in value.
2 Damaged stock is unlikely to sell unless repairs are undertaken. This adds to the cost of the inventory. Therefore, the cost of repair must be added to the price paid for the items.
3 Inventory is valued on one day. The value might be different on every other day due to issues mentioned in (1) and (2) or because purchases or sales of inventory had taken place.
4 Some items might never be sold and so their value is of little or no benefit to the business.
5 If the inventory valuation is not completed on the day stated on the statement of financial position, the actual value of inventory might differ from that on the financial statement.

Now test yourself

Tested

16 A sportswear retailer buys in trainers at a cost of $20. They are usually sold at $35 per pair. Due to poor storage conditions the trainers have discoloured. They can now only be sold at a reduced price of $15. What figure should be used to value the trainers?
17 Some jackets were purchased at a cost of $30 but, after a fire and smoke damage, some specialist cleaning at a cost of $3 per jacket was required to bring them back to a saleable condition. The expected selling price of the jackets after cleaning is $50 each. What figure should be used in a valuation of inventory?

Answers on p.215

Depreciation

Revised

The role of depreciation in the accounts

Depreciation is a method that spreads the cost of a non-current asset over its estimated economic life. Depreciation is recorded as an expense and can be seen to reduce the profit for the year. However, the taxation department of most countries will dictate how much depreciation can be applied to a specific asset. For example, if a government wants to encourage investment, higher rates of depreciation might be allowed. This will reduce the profit for the year (net profit) further and therefore reduce the tax to be paid by the business. Depreciation allowances are set so that businesses cannot overstate the amount of depreciation simply to reduce their tax liability.

> **Depreciation:** the apportioning of the cost of an asset over its anticipated useful economic life.

The straight line method assumes that the cost of an asset is spread evenly over its expected lifetime. It also assumes that the equipment is likely to have a residual value (resale value) at the end of that time.

The formula is:

$$\text{depreciation} = \frac{\text{cost of equipment} - \text{residual value}}{\text{estimated life of the asset}}$$

> **Expert tip**
>
> You are only required to know the straight line method of depreciation for this CIE syllabus.

Example

An asset is purchased at a cost of $40,000 and is expected to have a useful life of 8 years when it is believed that the machine will have a residual value of $8,000.

The depreciation would be: $\dfrac{40{,}000 - 8{,}000}{8}$ = $4,000 per annum

$4,000 depreciation would be recorded as an expense on the income statement each year. On the statement of financial position, the original costs, the accumulated depreciation and the carrying amount (net book value), would be recorded, which after the first year would be:

	$	$	$
Equipment	40,000	4,000	36,000 (carrying amount)

There are other methods of calculating the depreciation of assets. It can be difficult to compare the financial statements of different businesses if they use different methods. It is important that businesses are consistent with the method used so that comparisons made between the financial documents of different years can be useful and more accurate. If not, it is not possible to compare like with like.

The estimated useful life of an asset is the basis for the depreciation calculation, but this can be difficult to estimate due to varying rates of obsolescence. For example, computers and other high technology equipment are likely to have a short useful life due to the rapid pace of change in such assets.

> **Expert tip**
>
> Remember that depreciation is a non-cash expense in the income statement. It is NOT money put aside to replace an asset.

Revision activity

1. Draw up a list of the possible users of financial information and the type of information that they would be most interested in.
2. From any sets of published accounts, practise identifying the various elements, e.g. the value of non-current assets, the value of trade receivables, trade payables, current and non-current liabilities. The more often you look at financial statements the more familiar you will become with the terms used.

> **Now test yourself**
>
> 18 A business buys a machine for $60,000 with an estimated useful life of 5 years. After 5 years the machine is expected to have a resale value of $5,000. Using the straight line method, calculate the annual depreciation for the machine.
>
> **Answer on p.215**
>
> Tested

Analysis of published accounts

Interested parties often use ratio analysis to gain more information about the performance of a business from the limited data contained in published accounts.

Profitability ratio

Revised

Return on capital employed (ROCE)

ROCE measures the rate at which the assets of a business generate profit. It shows how efficient the assets of a business are at generating profit and can be an indicator to potential shareholders of the return they might expect from any money invested in the business.

> **Return on capital employed (ROCE):** measures the rate at which assets generate profit.

The calculation of ROCE uses net profit (operating profit), i.e. the business profit after all overhead expenses have been deducted. The capital employed is the shareholders' equity plus long term loans, reserves and debentures.

$$\text{return on capital employed} = \frac{\text{profit before tax and interest (net profit)}}{\text{capital employed}} \times 100$$

> **Expert tip**
> Net profit might also be referred to as 'profit for the year' or 'operating profit'.

For example, the ROCE of a business with a profit for the year (net profit) of $500,000 with capital employed of $7,150,000 would be calculated as follows:

$$\text{ROCE} = \frac{500,000}{7,150,000} \times 100$$
$$= 6.99\% \ (6.9930069)$$

To judge whether or not 6.99% is a good return, this figure would need to be considered in terms of the:

- return that could have been gained from placing the money in a bank account or by investing it in an alternative venture
- return from previous years
- return enjoyed by other businesses in the same industry
- prevailing economic climate

> **Now test yourself**
> **19** Briefly explain why shareholders might be interested in the ROCE calculation for a business.
>
> **Answer on p.215**
> Tested

Financial efficiency ratios

Revised

Inventory turnover

Inventory turnover is a measure of the rate at which inventory enters and leaves the business. It can be calculated as follows:

$$\text{inventory turnover} = \frac{\text{cost of goods sold}}{\text{inventory}}$$

It is usual to use the average inventory figure for the year, i.e. the average of the opening and closing inventory.

> **Inventory turnover:** measures the rate at which inventory enters and leaves a business.

The calculation reveals how many times the amount of average inventory is sold each year or, on average, in how many days inventory sold.

Example

A business has the following inventory information:

	$
Opening inventory	40,000
Purchases	200,000
	240,000
Closing inventory	30,000
Cost of goods sold	210,000

$$\text{inventory turnover} = \frac{210,000}{35,000} \quad (\$40,000 + \$30,000 \text{ divided by 2, i.e. averaged})$$
$$= 6 \text{ times per year or every 61 days } (365 \div 6 = 60.83)$$

Is this inventory turnover efficient? This can depend on the type of inventory involved, e.g. bread sold after 61 days would not be acceptable but a television might be acceptable.

This ratio must also be compared to rates from previous years and also with those of other businesses in the industry.

Trade receivables turnover (days' sales in trade receivables)

This is the average number of days that trade receivables (debtors) take to settle their debts with a business. It is calculated by:

> **Trade receivables turnover (debtor days):** measures the average number of days taken by debtors to settle their debts with a business.

$$\frac{\text{trade receivables (debtors)}}{\text{credit sales}} \times 365$$

For example, a business has $325,000 of credit sales in a year and trade receivables of $48,000 at the end of the year.

$$\text{trade receivables turnover} = \frac{48{,}000}{325{,}000} \times 365 = 53.9076 = 54 \text{ days rounded up}$$

Can the business be happy that its trade receivables are settling its debts after an average of 54 days? This can depend on:
- The credit that is extended to the business by its suppliers; if it has to pay for its supplies within 30 days then the 54 day period could cause liquidity problems.
- If the business does most of its business on a cash basis and the $325,000 of credit sales is a small proportion of the total sales revenue, it might not be a problem to the business.
- One or two large customers who might take a long time to pay and who distort the overall picture.

> **Now test yourself**
>
> 20 Explain why an inventory turnover as low as 18 days might not be acceptable for a shop selling fresh cakes.
>
> 21 Explain why it is important for a business to control the length of time trade receivables take to settle their debt with the business.
>
> **Answers on p.215**
>
> Tested

Gearing

Revised

The **gearing** ratio shows the relationship between the amount of capital that has been supplied by people or businesses external to the business that requires interest payments to be made and the capital provided by the owners of a business.

It shows how dependent a business is on money borrowed from an external source:

$$\text{gearing} = \frac{\text{non-current liabilities (long-term loans)}}{\text{shareholders' equity + long-term loans}} \times 100$$

> **Gearing:** measures the relationship between the amount of capital supplied from outside a business that requires interest to be paid and the capital supplied by the owners of a business.

A gearing ratio above 50% is usually considered to be high; one lower than 50% is usually considered to be low. A high gearing ratio can put a business at risk if interest rates are high because the business might find it difficult to repay the loan and the interest.
- high gearing + high interest = high risk
- low gearing + low interest = low risk
- the lower the ratio, the lower the risk to the business

The gearing ratio can determine the sources of finance that are available to a business. A business with a high ratio is likely to experience difficulty obtaining a loan from a bank. Shareholders might hesitate to buy more shares if they fear the business will be unable pay reasonable dividends on the money invested because high interest payments must be made.

If a business is yielding high profits, the interest payments might not pose a problem. When profitability is lower, the business might find itself unable to service its debt. Interest payments must be made regardless of how profitable a business is and can threaten the liquidity of a business.

The trend for interest rates might be a factor in any decision made by a potential lender.

> **Now test yourself**
>
> 22 Calculate the gearing ratio for a business that has long term loans of $75,000 and shareholders' equity of $125,000.
>
> 23 State whether the same business would be considered for a bank loan and briefly explain why.
>
> **Answers on p.215**
>
> Tested

Investor ratios

Revised

Investor ratios are used by existing and potential shareholders to determine the financial benefits of retaining or buying shares in a particular business. They can assess the level of dividends received and compare them to other investment opportunities.

Dividend yield

The return on an ordinary share based on the current market value is known as the **dividend yield**.

$$\text{dividend yield} = \frac{\text{dividend per share}}{\text{market price per share}} \times 100$$

$$\text{dividend per share} = \frac{\text{total amount of dividends}}{\text{number of issued ordinary shares}}$$

The dividend yield might be considered in terms of:
- the return that could be obtained by placing the money in an interest yielding bank account
- the dividend yield of other companies
- the level of risk involved — a higher yield might be required to encourage investment in a high risk company

> **Dividend yield:** shows the return on an ordinary share in relation to the current market value of the share.

Now test yourself — Tested

24 Calculate the dividend yield for a company that has a dividend per share of $0.4 and a current market price per share of $3.65.

25 Calculate the dividend yield for a company that has a total dividend of $320,000, 400,000 issued ordinary shares and the current market price of its ordinary shares is $5.80.

Answers on p.215

Dividend cover

The **dividend cover** is a calculation of how many times the total dividend could be paid out of the company's profit after tax and interest. This can give an indication of the 'quality' of the dividend cover and how likely it is that the level of dividends being paid can be maintained in future years.

$$\text{dividend cover} = \frac{\text{profit after tax and interest}}{\text{dividend paid}}$$

For example, a company pays out a total of $184,000 in dividends to the holders of ordinary shares. The profit for the year after tax and interest was $568,000.

$$\text{dividend cover} = \frac{568,000}{184,000} = 3.1 \text{ times (3.086 rounded up)}$$

In this example the profit earned by the business can cover the dividend to be paid to shareholders 3.1 times.

> **Dividend cover:** shows how many times the total dividend could be paid out of the company's profit after tax and interest.

Price/earnings ratio

The **price/earnings ratio** illustrates the relationship between the earnings per share and the current market price of an ordinary share. Shareholders tend to have more confidence in shares that have a higher ratio.

$$\text{price/earnings ratio} = \frac{\text{current market price per share}}{\text{earnings per share}}$$

In an examination you might be given the value of the earnings per share but if not, you will need to calculate it as follows:

$$\text{earnings per share} = \frac{\text{profit after tax}}{\text{number of ordinary shares}}$$

For example, a company has a profit after tax of $370,000 and 400,000 issued ordinary shares with a current market price of $5.50.

$$\text{earnings per share} = \frac{370,000}{400,000} = \$0.925$$

> **Price/earnings ratio:** the relationship between the earnings per share the current market price of an ordinary share.

Analysis of published accounts

price/earnings ratio = $\frac{5.50}{0.925}$ = 5.95 (rounded up from 5.9459)

This shows that the current market price of the ordinary share is 5.95 times larger than the earnings per share.

Practical uses of ratio analysis

Practical uses of ratio analysis include:
- To identify any trends over time.
- To allow comparisons to be made either of the ratios from the financial statements of previous years or with those of other businesses.
- To help with the investment decisions of the current and potential shareholders of the company.
- To judge how efficiently resources are being used in a business.
- To allow potential lenders, such as banks, to assess the risk involved in offering a loan to a business.

Strategies to improve ratio results

A business trying to improve liquidity ratios might:
- arrange for extra funds into the business, e.g. from the owner(s) or a bank loan
- decide to sell some unused equipment to bring more cash into the business
- sell or lease unused premises to another business — leasing would bring a regular flow of cash into the business
- sell inventory, perhaps offering a discount to encourage purchases — this would only improve the acid test ratio and not the current ratio

A business seeking to improve profitability ratios might:
- try to increase labour productivity to decrease costs per unit produced, or perhaps reduce labour costs through the introduction of more machinery and the use of fewer employees
- increase the selling price of the product/service
- cut or reduce spending through cutting budgets to departments, e.g. reduce expenditure on research and development

> **Expert tip**
> When discussing the strategies to improve ratio results, analysis could be to discuss the implications of the actions taken. For example, if a business reduces spending on R&D and is in a fast-moving, high-technology industry, it is likely that it will fall behind the competition in terms of product development and lose market share as a result.

Comparison of ratio results between businesses

Stakeholders frequently compare the results of the ratios for different companies. They hope that comparisons show that their business is performing at least as well as others in the industry. If not, they will analyse the possible reasons for the under-performance of their company. This allows them to make some judgement about how efficiently the business is being managed.

Internal factors could be the inefficient use of resources or an increase in the cost of resources such an increase in wage rates or an increase in the rate of inflation that has caused the cost of purchases to increase.

Some disappointing comparisons are due to internal factors. Although poor results can be explained by internal inefficiencies, sometimes they are due to external factors outside the control of any individual business. For example, poor ratios might result from a global or national recession.

Any cause for a worsening of a company's ratios should be analysed to determine if it indicates a trend, perhaps reflecting the overall performance of the economy, or is the result of a one-off event, such as a natural disaster.

> **Expert tip**
> When comparing the ratios of different businesses, it is important to be aware of any key differences between the businesses, e.g. in size or whether they operate in different markets.

Limitations of accounting ratios

Ratios are used to assess the performance of a company and any changes in performance that has occurred over time. Although they can be used to compare the performance of one company with another, there are some recognised limitations of their use.

Difficulties with using ratios

- The accuracy and usefulness of all of the ratios can be influenced by the way in which the profit for the business has been calculated. Different accounting techniques might have been applied when producing the financial statements for earlier years.
- Different companies might be using different methods of calculation of items such as depreciation.
- Comparisons with companies in a different industry are unlikely to be of value.
- Comparing the ratios of businesses of differing sizes can be misleading.
- Ratios are calculated based on published financial information and a company might have adjusted its financial statements to present a particular financial condition to any stakeholders.
- Economic conditions might have had an impact on the ratios for a particular year and could produce unfair and/or unrealistic comparisons with other years.
- Ratios are quantitative and ignore the qualitative aspects of business activity, e.g. whether the business is ethical in its activities and whether it uses renewable resources for its materials.

> **Now test yourself**
>
> 26 Identify two limitations of using ratio analysis.
> 27 Briefly explain two reasons why shareholders might compare the ratios of different businesses.
>
> **Answers on p.215**
>
> Tested

> **Revision activity**
>
> Using the financial statements of several business accounts, practise the various ratio calculations. Make notes about why your results might be good or not. This will help you to develop analytical skills based on calculations.

Investment appraisal

The concept of investment appraisal

Revised

Most businesses exist to make a profit. Investment appraisal involves a business in trying to assess the likely profitability of undertaking a particular course of action usually involving the purchasing of premises and/or equipment. Businesses need to know that if they undertake a specific project it will be financially safe and will allow them to reap some reward from the venture.

The need for investment appraisal

- To compare the expected outcomes of competing options.
- To estimate the costs, e.g. the cost of new premises, equipment or training. For example, if a business had to choose between installing two different types of production equipment, the business would compare the initial cost of the equipment together with any running and maintenance costs.
- To estimate the revenue in terms of timescale and size of any return on the investment.
- To assess the possible risk involved in a venture or to compare the relative risks of two or more possible investment opportunities.

Different projects can have very different outcomes in terms of the profit received after all costs have been covered.

The future value of any costs and revenue must also be considered as far as is possible. It is accepted that $500 today will be worth more to us than if we have to wait 5 years to receive the same amount. The $500 could have been put in an interest-bearing bank account and received interest.

The significance of risk in investment decisions
- All investment decisions carry an element of risk but the potential risk can be minimised or avoided if businesses fully explore the possible implications of their decisions before embarking on any one course of action.
- When investment decisions are being made, the business is only able to estimate the costs and revenues associated with the project. Investment appraisal is an attempt to formalise those estimations and to compare alternatives.
- A sudden economic downturn can change everything that has been predicted — anticipated sales might not occur and costs might prove to be much higher than expected if a period of higher inflation occurs. Businesses use as much information as they can to assess the possible risk of any particular investment.
- Investment decisions will be based on past information and what can reasonably be expected to happen in the future. However, even consistent and stable past trends cannot guarantee that the same trend will continue in the future. For example, the financial crash of 2008 caused a lot of changes in the financial trends in many businesses.

> **Now test yourself**
>
> 28 Identify two reasons why a business would undertake investment appraisal before beginning a new project.
> 29 Identify one risk that a project might encounter.
>
> **Answers on p.215**
>
> Tested

Forecasting cash flows

Revised

An important part of investment appraisal is the prediction of future cash inflows and outflows.

Interpretation of cash-flow forecasts
- Cash-flow forecasts are drawn up to show the predicted costs of an investment project and the anticipated revenue.
- The costs will include the cost of purchasing premises and equipment, and any maintenance costs (this might be annual servicing and repairs).
- Wage costs and utility costs, e.g. electricity and water, will be estimated.
- Market research should be used as a basis for the predicted revenues.

Uncertainty in cash-flow forecasts
The further into the future predictions are made, the more possibility there is that the estimations will be wrong.

What can change?
- Customer tastes and preferences might change, making a previously popular product undesirable.
- Competitors' actions or technological change might alter revenues or costs.
- The rate of inflation may go up or down, making cost predictions unreliable.
- Particular costs of materials or labour might change.
- The general economic environment — a national or worldwide recession or boom period could change spending patterns.
- Trade union action might result in wage rates being increased above the previously anticipated rate of increase.

For these reasons, once a project has begun, it is important that constant reviews are undertaken to assess whether any corrective action is needed.

There might be times when, even though a lot of money has been invested into a project, the project should be abandoned and all monies invested should be written off. It is sometimes more expensive to continue with an unprofitable project than to stop and to bear the loss of any money already invested.

Some changes are unpredictable and would make it impossible for some investment projects to be profitable. The financial crisis of 2008 caused many businesses to fail — the extent of this crisis could not have been predicted.

Once something happens to change the environment in which the business operates, the business must react to the new situation rather than continue with the planned activities that might no longer be viable.

When using cash flows for investment appraisal purposes, the cash flows are at today's values and have not taken the effects of inflation into account.

Basic methods: payback and average rate of return

Revised

Payback method

This method calculates the time it will take for the revenues (cash inflows) to fully cover the cost of the investment (cash outflows).

The time of the initial investment is usually termed year 0. In year 1 the cash outflows and the revenues are added together to give a net cash inflow (this could be a negative figure in early years and would therefore increase the money to be eventually recouped from future sales and profit). The net cash flow is deducted from the cost of the initial investment to give a 'cumulative cash flow' for year 1.

> **Now test yourself**
>
> **30** Define the term 'payback' when referring to investment appraisal.
>
> **Answer on p.215**
>
> Tested

Example

The table below indicates that in the first year production must have still been very low. Perhaps a lot of training on using new equipment was required or perhaps there were some early difficulties and possibly modification needed. The revenue from the product gradually increased and the cost of the initial investment and running costs was recovered in the 5th year of this project.

Year	Cash outflows ($)	Cash inflows ($)	Net cash flow ($)	Cumulative cash flow ($)
0	(450,000)	0	(450,000)	(450,000)
1	(40,000)	45,000	5,000	(445,000)
2	(40,000)	80,000	40,000	(405,000)
3	(40,000)	160,000	120,000	(285,000)
4	(40,000)	240,000	200,000	(85,000)
5	(40,000)	270,000	230,000	145,000
6	(40,000)	310,000	270,000	415,000

The calculation of the precise payback period is achieved by using the amount still required at the end of the year before payback is achieved as follows:

$$\text{payback period} = \frac{\text{amount still to be recovered}}{\text{net cash flow in following year}}$$

$$= \frac{85,000}{230,000} \times 12 \text{ (months) or 52 (weeks)}$$

$$= 4.4 \text{ months}$$

The investment pays back in 4 years and 4.4 months.

This is acceptable if the business has an objective of payback occurring within 5 years. However, if the objective is to undertake a project that needs to pay back within 3 years, this particular project should not be undertaken.

Investment appraisal

Average rate of return (ARR)

This method calculates the expected return as a percentage of the cost of the original investment over the anticipated lifetime of the project.

> **Example**
>
> Using the example above, the investment costing $450,000 yields a cumulative cash flow over 5 years less the cost of the initial investment (which we take as profit at this level of study), i.e. $595,000 − $450,000 = $145,000.
>
> The formula for average rate of return is:
>
> $$\text{average rate of return} = \frac{\text{average annual profit}}{\text{initial cost of investment}}$$
>
> Therefore:
>
> $$\frac{145,000}{5} = 29,000$$
>
> $$\frac{29,000}{450,000} \times 100 = 6.44\%$$

You are unlikely to be asked to calculate ARR without being required to make some comment about whether the return is acceptable or not. The business might have a minimum return that it requires on all investments — if that is 5% then this investment meets that criterion. However, if the required return is 7%, this investment would not be pursued.

The ARR would also be compared to the return that could be gained if the money was used in a different way. For example, if placing the money in an interest-bearing bank account could yield 7%, or even 6.44%, the bank account would be the better option, assuming that this return lasts the length of the project. Placing the money in a bank account would avoid all the time and effort of a business project and would probably carry a lower risk.

> **Expert tip**
>
> A level accounting students might know the ARR as the 'accounting rate of return' and will have been taught a slightly different formula. For the purpose of your A level business studies examination, use the method outlined above.

Discounted cash flow methods

The investment appraisal methods above assume that money received in 5 years' time has the same value as money today. That is not true. $145,000 will be worth more to us today than the same amount in 5 years' time. Inflation in an economy reduces the purchasing power of money over time. The money in our possession today could be placed in a bank account where it could earn interest over the 5 years.

In investment appraisal, we use a discounting factor to allow us to judge the value of money that will be received in the future compared to its value to us if we had the money today. It is commonly believed that the discounting factor used is to reflect the rate of inflation. Whilst it is accepted that inflation does reduce the future value of money, the discounting tables are based on the cost of capital or the prevailing rate of interest for that business.

Discounted payback and net present value (NPV)

Discounted payback recognises that money received in 3 or 4 years will not have the same value as if the money was in our possession today. If we had the $145,000 today we could place it in a bank account and, if the rate of interest was 5% at the end of 1 year, we would have $145,000 + $7,250 = $152,250. In the second year, the interest would result in us having $152,250 + 5% = $159,862.50.

> **Expert tip**
>
> Although there are formulae for working out the various discounting factors, there is no need for you to learn them. Any discounting factors required to answer a question will be given to you in the examination paper.

Discounted payback

Taking the net cash flows from the example above, you need to multiply each one by the discounting factor relevant to each year.

Using an interest rate of 10%, the calculation would be:

Year	Discount factor at 10% rate of interest	Net cash flow ($)	Discounted net cash flow (net cash flow × discount factor) ($)	Present value Cumulative discounted net cash flow
0	1.00	(450,000)	(450,000)	(450,000)
1	0.91	5,000	4,550	(445,450)
2	0.83	40,000	33,200	(412,250)
3	0.75	120,000	90,000	(322,250)
4	0.68	200,000	136,000	(186,250)
5	0.62	230,000	142,600	(43,650)
6	0.56	270,000	151,200	107,550

Discounting the net cash flows shows that, in this example, the cost of the investment would not be recovered until part way through the 6th year, whereas without the discounting the payback period occurred during the 5th year of the project.

Net present value (NPV)
Net present value refers to the discounted value of net cash flows at the end of the investment period after discounting has been applied. In this case the investment project has a net present value of $107,550 after 6 years. This means that it would be appropriate to go ahead with the project if its life span is anticipated to be 6 years. If it is only 5 years, the NPV will be negative, indicating that the project is not worthwhile.

Internal rate of return (IRR)
IRR is the point at which the NPV (using discounted cash flows) is equal to zero. If the IRR is 14% and the prevailing interest rate is 7%, the project would be profitable. The bigger the difference between the prevailing rate of interest and the IRR, the more profitable a project is likely to be. Alternatively, the higher the IRR, the higher the profitability of a proposed investment.

Now test yourself

31 Briefly explain what is meant by a discounted cash flow.

32 What is meant by the term 'net present value'?

Answers on p.215

Tested

Qualitative factors in investment appraisal

Revised

Qualitative factors that might influence investment decisions
The investment appraisal methods outlined above are all quantitative methods. However, there are qualitative factors that should also be taken into account. Some qualitative factors might even override the financial aspects:
- Pollution. For example, if a project will pollute the environment, it would hopefully not be pursued even though it might be highly profitable.
- Employment levels. Social considerations are sometimes judged to be important, e.g. the negative impact on employment levels if workers are replaced with machinery.
- Is the quality of the product likely to be the same?
- Will staff training be required?

Now test yourself

33 Identify one qualitative factor that a business might consider as part of investment appraisal.

Answer on p.215

Tested

Comparison of investment appraisal methods and their limitations
Payback method does not take into account any profit achieved after the payback period, nor does it consider the time value of money. This method is also considered to be very simplistic and at best only a basic guide to assessing the potential viability of an investment.

Discounted cash flows attempt to take account of the time value of money but they can only be based on what is realistically expected to happen. Sudden or unexpected changes can mean that all assessments of potential investments are now inaccurate.

Investment appraisal methods that are based on profit can have different results depending on the method of depreciation used because this would influence the amount of profit.

Calculations based purely on projected returns do not consider the amount of risk involved in a project. Some businesses are more inclined to undertake risky projects than others. A high-risk project might be required to give a higher return than a low-risk one. This would be seen as a reward for the amount of risk taken.

Modern businesses need to consider the qualitative aspects of an investment as well as the quantitative factors due to increased media and pressure group activity. The increased use of the internet means that customers are quickly informed if a business is acting in an undesirable way, and customers might boycott the business.

Revision activity

1 Using as many past papers as you can and any cash-flow information given, use each of the methods of investment appraisal to calculate the potential return for a business. You need to practise your arithmetic accuracy as much as possible.
2 Practise explaining why a business should or should not undertake a particular project. You will always be expected to discuss the result of any calculation and the possible implications for a business.

11 Strategic management

What is strategic management?

Understanding what strategic management is

Strategic management is the analysis, decisions and actions an organisation takes in order to create and sustain competitive advantage.

Corporate strategy, tactics and strategic management
Strategic management sets out a framework that businesses can use to achieve success. It deals with the answers to these questions:
- Where are we now? An analysis of the market and the economic environment in relation to available resources and the competition.
- Where do we want to be? Choosing between the options that the analysis highlights as possibilities.
- How do we get there? Implementing actions that will lead to the chosen position.

Strategic management begins by setting out a vision and objectives for the business. This will help determine the route taken through the strategic decision-making framework. This is shown in Figure 1.

Levels of strategic management
Strategic thinking takes place at three different levels — corporate, business and functional. These have to be integrated and work together to reach the overall corporate objective. Communication between the different parts of the business is essential for success.

Corporate strategy
Corporate strategy sets out the overall objective and questions for the business in working through the strategic framework. All parts of the business then have to plan their actions in the light of this overall strategic thinking. Examples of corporate strategy issues are:
- Should we grow by integration or by increasing sales?
- Does our future lie in domestic or export markets?

Business strategy
Business strategy applies to a part of the whole business, for instance, the domestic building department of a construction business. Each part of the business must make decisions that will lead to the overall corporate objective being reached.

Functional strategy
Functional strategy applies to each functional area, i.e. marketing, finance or production. Decisions in these areas must take account of the corporate objective and work towards achieving it.

> **Strategic management:** the analysis, decisions and actions an organisation takes in order to create and sustain competitive advantage.

Figure 1 Strategic management framework

> **Now test yourself**
> 1. Give one reason why setting an appropriate objective is important for strategic management.
> 2. Outline the stages of strategic management.
>
> **Answers on p.216**

Strategic management and tactics

Strategic management gives the framework for the way a business will develop. **Tactics** are the methods used to achieve each objective in the framework. They provide the means by which the strategy is implemented and are usually carried out by divisions or functional areas. Tactics can be altered within a strategy framework when needed. For example:

- Objective: to become the third largest retail store in the world by 2017.
- Strategy: open branches in ten new countries.
- Tactic: position new stores in the five largest cities in each country.

> **Tactics:** the methods a business uses to carry out a strategy.

The need for strategic management

Strategic management enables a business to decide essential information about the:

- reasons it exists
- market environment it operates in
- opportunities and threats facing it
- possibilities for achieving objectives

It then enables a business to:

- plan and carry out methods to achieve objectives
- coordinate activities of departments and functional areas
- detect and respond flexibly to changes
- evaluate and review progress towards objectives

Strategic management enables a business to have clarity and certainty about what it is doing. It enables a clear, planned response to change and effective use of resources. Each stage of the framework is key to this process.

> **Now test yourself**
>
> 3. Using an example, outline the difference between strategy and tactics.
> 4. Outline three areas about which strategic management can provide information.
> 5. Outline three changes strategic management might achieve.
>
> **Answers on p.216**
>
> Tested

Table 1 How strategic management is important

Stage	Content			Result
Vision, mission, objectives	Sets out purpose.	Gives a measure to check progress.	Gives purpose to employees.	Defines clear goals.
Analysis of external environment	Sets out legal, political and economic framework and changes.	Sets out competitors' actions.	Sets out customer information.	Informed decisions.
Analysis of internal resources	Defines business strengths and weaknesses.	Defines resources available.	Enables understanding of factors within control.	Informed decisions.
Strategic choice	Sets out possible actions.	Considers advantages and disadvantages.	Ensures resources match actions.	Informed decisions.
Strategic implementation	Planned actions taken.	Matches plans to market conditions.	Tactics carry out strategy.	Planned actions.
Evaluation	Measures degree of success.	Gives flexibility in change.	Continuous feedback.	Better decisions.

> **Revision activity**
>
> You have just been appointed as the first strategic executive manager in a medium-sized furniture making company. Prepare a brief presentation to the board that sets out what strategic management is and why it is important.

Chandler's assertion that strategy should determine organisational structure

According to Chandler strategic management is 'the determination of the basic long-term goals and objectives of an enterprise, and the adoption of courses of action and the allocation of resources necessary for carrying out the goals' and organisation structure is 'the design of organisation through which the enterprise is administered'.

> **Expert tip**
>
> Remember that strategic management deals with the whole business. Make sure, even with a brief comment, that you show how functional area and business unit strategy contribute to the corporate strategic objectives and framework.

Chandler's study of large businesses made him believe that once strategic management was in place, the organisation structure was changed to reflect how the strategy would be conducted. His key findings were:
- Strategic management should be decided at the top or centre of an organisation.
- Individual business units then decide tactics to carry out the strategy.
- Structure follows strategy.

He studied US conglomerates and found every one had grown by diversification, i.e. by entering successive new different product markets. All adopted a similar structure that Chandler called the 'M form' where:
- Corporate strategy was set by top management.
- Product or geographic business units adopted their own tactics.
- Central management coordinated.

Chandler's model (Figure 2) relates structure to strategy.

> **Now test yourself**
>
> 6 What is Chandler's conclusion about the relation between strategy and structure?
> 7 Explain the 'M form' structure of large conglomerates.
>
> **Answers on p.216**
>
> Tested

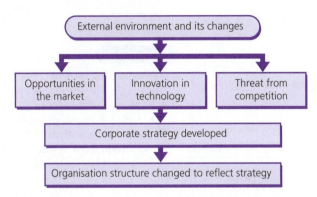

Figure 2 Chandler's model

How business strategy determines competitive advantage

On the world scale, globalisation is making markets more competitive with improved communications, freer trade and businesses entering international markets. Domestic markets are becoming more consumer driven, with existing firms facing new competitors, more widespread and sophisticated marketing methods and wider consumer choice. Being successful involves meeting consumer needs with a competitive advantage.

This advantage is what strategic management can give a business by providing planned methods linked to a full understanding of market conditions, internal resources and possible actions. If there is no strategic management, a business will not know its strengths and weaknesses, be able to detect opportunities or threats or be effective in its choice of methods.

> **Revision activity**
>
> Yousef produces leather shoes, wallets and purses to selling to tourists as souvenirs. Because they are good-quality, handmade items, he has expanded by adding a small factory for his outworkers. He uses the low level of wages and government grants to keep costs down. He thinks he might be able to sell directly abroad at significantly higher prices and has a relative in Germany who has offered to help him. He is aware of the costs and risks in exporting, including the effect of exchange rates and competition, and he thinks he might have to move to a more efficient production system.
>
> Discuss how Yousef might use strategic management at this stage in his business.

Strategic analysis

Strategic management analysis is what comes after deciding a mission statement and objectives. It analyses the resources available and the external environment the business is operating in. Finally, it considers factors resulting from these influences that will act on a business. This is done by using a variety of methods that answer the question 'where are we now?'

SWOT analysis

Revised

Undertaking SWOT analysis

SWOT analysis examines the controllable internal strengths and weaknesses of a business and the non-controllable external threats and opportunities facing

> **SWOT analysis:** examines the internal strengths and weaknesses of a business and the external threats and opportunities facing a business.

a business. It should be undertaken as part of a strategic planning process. Once carried out, a business can use it to build on the strengths, minimise the weaknesses, take advantage of opportunities and avoid or minimise threats.

SWOT analysis is presented in a grid as shown in Figure 3.

Strengths (internal)	**Weaknesses (internal)**
Finance available	High labour turnover
Customer loyalty	Unsuitable location
Skilled motivated employees	No strategic planning

Opportunities (external)	**Threats (external)**
New government subsidies	Rising unemployment
Growing market segment	New competitor
Integration with a competitor	New health and safety laws

Figure 3 SWOT analysis

The SWOT factors must be drawn from the actual situation facing a business.

Advantages of SWOT analysis
- It is relatively quick, cheap and easy to understand.
- It can generate specific objectives and actions as part of strategic planning.

Disadvantages of SWOT analysis
- It may become out-dated quickly.
- Simple conclusions may be misleading — the situation may be more complex.

Developing a SWOT analysis into strategic objectives

Once all the relevant SWOT factors have been set out, they must be ranked in terms of importance. This can be used to develop plans for action, starting with setting objectives that relate to the most important factors. If poor motivation and high labour turnover have been identified as major weaknesses, objectives such as lower labour turnover, fewer complaints and higher employee satisfaction might be set.

PEST or external environment analysis

PEST analysis examines the external environment consisting of political and legal, economic, social and technological factors facing a business. It should be undertaken as part of a strategic planning process. Environmental factors may be included in social factors. Once carried out, a business can use it to see how these non-controllable factors might be important, especially if changes are being considered.

PEST analysis is often presented in a grid as shown in Figure 4.

Political and legal (government actions)	**Economic**
Health and safety laws	Taxes
Competition policy	Changes in household income
Change of government	Tariffs

Social	**Technological**
Ageing population	Cell phone/tablet developments
Changing attitudes to drugs or car use	3D printers
Family size	More efficient machinery

Figure 4 PEST analysis

Advantages of PEST analysis
- Relatively quick and cheap to carry out and present.
- Encourages strategic thinking.
- Can develop strategic responses to change.

> **Now test yourself**
>
> 8 List an additional possible factor for each of the SWOT factors in the grid.
> 9 State one advantage and one disadvantage of using SWOT analysis.
> 10 Choose one strength and one threat from the grid. Identify an appropriate objective a business might set in response.
>
> Answers on p.216

> **Expert tip**
> When dealing with SWOT or PEST analysis, make sure that you apply the analysis to the specific situation, i.e. explain the concept, set out the reasons for the analysis and then use information given to you.

> **PEST analysis:** examines the external environment consisting of political and legal, economic, social and technological factors facing a business.

> **Expert tip**
> SWOT or PEST analysis provide ideas to add to other factors when decisions are made. They do not provide answers to problems or set out actions to take.

Disadvantages of PEST analysis
- Might date quickly.
- Too simple analysis or conclusions may lead to poor decisions.
- Relies on assumptions that may be incorrect or change.

> **Now test yourself** — Tested
>
> 11 List an additional possible factor for each of the PEST factors in the grid.
> 12 Choose one factor from each of the PEST categories and explain how a business might respond to that factor.
> 13 State one advantage and one disadvantage of using PEST analysis.
>
> **Answers on p.216**

The role of business vision/mission statement and objectives — Revised

Vision and mission statements explain the central purpose of a business. **Vision statements** set out in broad terms where a business would ideally like to be; **mission statements** give an indication of how a business will try and achieve its vision in general terms. Not all businesses use these terms and some do not have these statements, preferring to set out goals or aims.

For example, a shoe manufacturing business might have:
- a vision statement 'to become the leading provider of footwear'
- a mission statement 'to produce high quality shoes at an affordable price'

From these statements it is possible to develop specific objectives that reflect the statements. The shoe manufacturer might go on to consider objectives in relation to cost, skilled workers, distribution channels and marketing methods.

> **Vision statement:** sets out a broad, aspirational view of where the business would like to be in the future.
>
> **Mission statement:** sets out its purpose, identity, values and main business aims.

Advantages of vision/mission statements
- Define the real purpose of the business.
- Enable specific objectives to be set to achieve the vision/mission.
- Provide motivation and clarity for employees.
- Enable strategic planning framework to follow.

Disadvantages of vision/mission statements
- Can be very general — difficult to develop objectives from.
- Can limit strategic planning, e.g. the shoe manufacturer has been limited to 'footwear'.
- Can take up time and resources for little benefit if not used in planning.

> **Now test yourself**
>
> 14 Outline the difference between a vision statement and an objective.
> 15 Explain the difference between a vision statement and a mission statement.
> 16 State one advantage and one disadvantage of using vision or mission statements.
>
> **Answers on p.216**
>
> Tested

Boston matrix — product portfolio analysis — Revised

The Boston matrix (Figure 5) is useful for a business with a number of products to assess its position. The matrix uses a comparison of market share and rate of market growth for each product. It provides pointers for marketing decisions for products, and considers what might happen if there are too many products in one element leading to possible problems in the future.

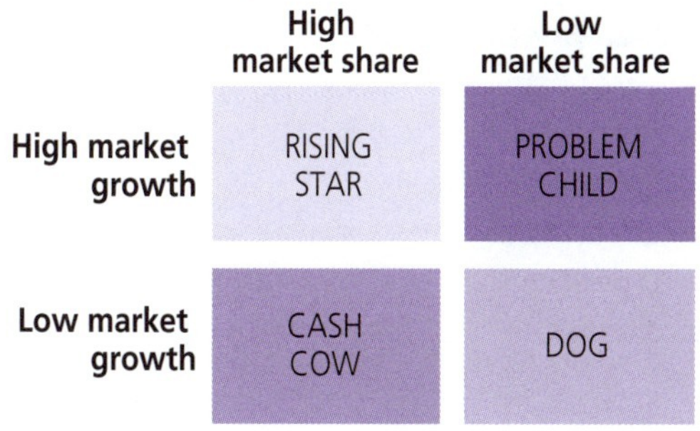

	High market share	Low market share
High market growth	RISING STAR	PROBLEM CHILD
Low market growth	CASH COW	DOG

Figure 5 The Boston matrix

Strategic analysis

Undertaking and interpreting Boston matrix analysis

Rising star: high market share in a fast growing market
- Often new products in a new market.
- Likely to have high marketing costs and face strong competition.
- Likely to face falling unit costs of production.
- Possibility of large revenues and profits if all goes well.

Cash cow: high market share in slow growing market
- Generates large revenues and profits in mature saturated market.
- High share might reflect past marketing and R and D spending.
- Customer loyalty so reminder advertising often used to maintain this.
- Might need extension strategies if there is a possibility of competition or consumer tiredness.

Problem child: low market share in fast growing market
- Often new products or ones with inadequate marketing.
- Potential for revenue and profits given investment in marketing.
- Might succeed with little extra marketing as growth occurs with the market.

Dog: low market share in low growth or declining market
- Often outdated products or high competition.
- Profit may still be generated as effective production, distribution and customer satisfaction may all exist — in this case continue as long as profitable with little marketing costs.
- May discontinue to free up resources for products with a future.

Many businesses try to have products in all sectors of the matrix to provide a balanced portfolio of cash-producing products and possible high growth products to replace those in maturity. However, care must be taken, e.g. a high market share might not mean high profits as high marketing costs are necessary.

Advantages of Boston matrix
- It is simple and easy to use and pinpoints the position of products.
- It indicates possible appropriate actions to maintain cash flows and decide on portfolio composition.

Disadvantages of Boston matrix
- Using it might lead to simplistic thinking — the model indicates possibilities. It does not lay down set answers to situations.
- Market situations might change quickly.

> **Expert tip**
>
> When applying the Boston matrix, do not just refer to products as problem children or dogs. Explain what these terms mean when you analyse the situation, and link them to market conditions. Make sure you include possible alternative actions.

> **Revision activity**
>
> The majority of Business A's products are cash cows and dogs. Business B has an equal number of cash cows, dogs and problem children, but no rising stars.
>
> 1. Draw a Boston matrix for each business to illustrate its position.
> 2. Use these to develop a suitable strategy for each firm.
> 3. Explain why a business should take care when using Boston matrix analysis.

Porter's 5 forces analysis — a framework for strategy

Revised

Porter's 5 forces model (Figure 6) analyses five external influences that help determine the strength of competition. It helps a business to judge how likely a market is to be profitable, and identifies factors to focus on changing in order to weaken competition. It may also be used by a possible new entrant to a market to assess existing competition and then produce ideas on how to weaken this. A low level of competition makes a market attractive to stay in or enter.

The 5 forces

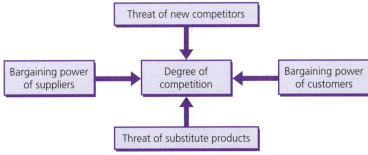

Figure 6 Porter's 5 forces model

The four forces or factors outlined below influence how competitive a market is likely to be:

- **Threat of new competitors** — new competitors arriving in a market will increase the competition and reduce possible profits for existing businesses by increasing marketing costs and/or price reductions. Threat of increased competition makes the market less attractive. Barriers to entry, including high start-up costs, patents and copyrights and customer/brand loyalty, will reduce the threat of competition.
- **Threat of substitute products** — substitute products will reduce prices and increase the price elasticity of demand for existing products. It is likely that sales and profits for existing businesses will fall. An example may be artificial fibre fleeces entering the garment market.
- **Bargaining power of customers** — many customers will mean a more attractive market than if there are a few customers who have high potential buying power. This is particularly true if the few customers are large powerful organisations such as governments or major supermarkets.
- **Bargaining power of suppliers** — if suppliers of materials, components, communication or distribution systems have power, their prices will be high and so will business costs. This makes competition much less likely.

Using Porter's 5 forces analysis

Competition may exist however many businesses there are in the market. It is shown by price competition, high marketing activity and differentiated products. If there is little competition, the market will be attractive to stay in or enter. If competition is high, an interested business might think of producing for a particular market segment, selling a differentiated product or marketing to build a brand image.

The four factors influencing the degree of competition in a market are shown in Table 2 along with the possible decisions a business might take in response.

> **Now test yourself**
>
> **17** Identify Porter's 5 forces
> **18** Suggest one possible use of Porter's 5 forces model in decision making
>
> **Answers on p.216**
>
> Tested

Table 2 Possible business responses to 5 forces analysis

	High	Low
Threat of new competition	• Increase brand loyalty. • Develop new products. • Develop dedicated distribution.	Continue existing strategy.
Threat of substitute products	• Develop new products. • Re-market existing products.	Continue existing strategy.
Bargaining power of customers	• Produce products with no substitutes. • Forward vertical integration.	Continue existing strategy.
Bargaining power of suppliers	• Backward vertical integration. • Cooperation with others to bulk buy.	Continue existing strategy.

> **Revision activity**
>
> Eatup produces ready meals, selling its products in one country. As many of its customers also buy sauces for cooking, Eatup is considering manufacturing a range of sauces. It carries out a Porter's 5 forces analysis on the sauce market.
>
> | | High | Low |
> |---|---|---|
> | Threat of new competition | Several large producers compete heavily on price and marketing. | No barriers to entry. Less competition in high-price, quality end of market. |
> | Threat of substitute products | Several similar mass-produced sauces. | High-price sauces differentiated. |
> | Bargaining power of customers | Supermarket customers have high power. | Small shops have less power. |
> | Bargaining power of suppliers | Quality raw material suppliers are few. | Can use existing suppliers. |
>
> Use the analysis to prepare a report for the board setting out:
> 1. How competitive the sauce market is likely to be.
> 2. A recommendation on whether Eatup should enter the sauce market.

Advantages of 5 forces analysis
- It enables assessment of market position or potential for market entry.
- It enables assessment of competitive strengths and weaknesses.
- It can show possible actions to reduce threat from competition or use opportunities.

Disadvantages of 5 forces analysis
- It is simplistic so it is difficult to apply to complex markets.
- Analysis may quickly become out of date.

> **Expert tip**
>
> The models in this unit are designed to give indications for analysis and action. They should all be used along with other factors to make fully informed decisions.

Prahaled and Hamel's core competencies analysis

Core competencies are the unique capabilities a business needs to be competitive. They illustrate the key concepts that make a business, product or brand valuable to a customer and may be found in any functional area. Core competencies make one business stand out against the rest. Examples include Apple, which makes IT devices that are distinctively designed and easy to use, and Walmart which sells groceries and consumer goods at low prices. These core competencies have been used in marketing to build up a distinct brand image and identity.

> **Core competencies:** the unique capabilities a business needs to be competitive.

Checklist for deciding core competencies in an organisation
- Gives customers a positive view and benefit.
- Provides access to a wide range of products and/or markets.
- Difficult for competitors to imitate.

Developing unique core competencies will enable a business to focus on what it needs to do to make customers buy its products. There are resource costs in determining the core competencies and simpler models, such as SWOT analysis, may possibly perform the same function.

> **Now test yourself**
>
> 19 Explain core competencies.
> 20 How might a core competency be identified?
>
> **Answers on p.216**

Core competencies and products

Core competencies may also be used in developing a product range strategy. They can lead to the production of a core product that is not sold directly but is embedded in all the products in the range. Black & Decker has core competencies in design and technical performance at low cost. It has focused on the production of electric motors. These are found in drills, garden equipment and machine tools.

Strategic choice

Once a business has analysed its position, it can act. Strategic choice deals with three tools that can be used to choose a strategy that answers the question 'how do we get to where we want to go?' It is important to remember that these methods have limitations. They only apply for a short time-scale and are only as good as the accuracy of the information they use. Other factors should also be taken into account in making a strategic choice.

Ansoff's matrix — choice of strategy and risk

Revised

Ansoff's matrix (Figure 7) is useful for a business seeking to expand. It analyses choices in terms of types of markets and products and gives four possible choices, with an indication of their risk. Any expansion will carry some risk because consumer behaviour and competitors' actions are not fully predictable.

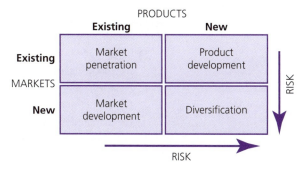

Figure 7 Ansoff's matrix

Market penetration — existing products and markets

The fact that the business already has products in the market means there is low risk. Methods for market penetration in an existing market may include:

- increasing frequency of purchase
- finding different new customers
- gaining more brand loyalty and repeat purchases
- taking sales from competitors

One or more of these will be selected as an objective, and a strategy developed using appropriate methods, such as increasing advertising and promotion, extending distribution channels, making special offers and increasing the sales force.

Factors making for success
- An unsaturated market.
- Low competition.
- Growing size of market.

Market development — existing product and new market

The fact that the business knows its products but is introducing them to a new market means there is medium risk. Methods for market development may include:

- a new use for the product
- a new area for sales
- targeting a different type of consumer

One or more of these will be selected as an objective, and a strategy developed using appropriate methods.

> **Expert tips**
> - Do not confuse market penetration as a strategy in Ansoff's matrix with the tactic of penetration pricing.
> - Do not think that the level of risk shown is a set level determined purely by the elements of Ansoff's matrix.

Factors making for success
- Thorough market research.
- Core competencies are linked to the product.

Product development — new product in existing market
The fact that the business already has customers in the market means there is medium risk. Methods for product development may include:
- altering existing products to appear new
- producing new products

One or more of these will be selected as an objective, and a strategy developed using appropriate methods.

Factors making for success
- Thorough market research.
- Strong brand identity and customer loyalty.

Diversification
The fact that the business has no experience of the product or market means there is high risk. Methods for diversification may include:
- use of R&D linked to market research
- integration with another business

One or more of these will be selected as an objective, and a strategy developed using appropriate methods.

Factors making for success
- A real driving force for diversification exists, e.g. failing existing market, management growth objectives.
- Thorough market research and advice from product/market experts.
- Flexible organisation culture and high resource availability.

Ansoff's matrix — strategy and risk
Ansoff's matrix indicates levels of risk associated with each of the four strategic choices. These levels are only indications as it may be difficult to define a market, and there may be factors other than the product and the market affecting success. A business can use the matrix to lower the risk of whatever strategy is chosen. For example, a business thinking of market development will make sure that market research is thorough and accurate, and a business thinking of product development will make sure that the product matches the brand image in the existing market. Using Ansoff's matrix is not a guarantee of success.

Advantages of Ansoff's matrix
- It is simple and easy to draw up.
- Clear choices and associated levels of risk are shown.
- It enables strategic choice within a strategic planning framework.

Disadvantages of Ansoff's matrix
- It is simplistic and ignores many relevant factors.
- Indications of risk are general guidance only.

> **Expert tip**
> Make sure that you apply Ansoff's matrix to the information given about a business and its market, relating this to the factors making for success in each choice and its advantages and disadvantages.

> **Now test yourself**
> 21 Explain what is meant by each of the following and state the level of risk associated with each:
>   (a) market penetration
>   (b) market development
>   (c) product development
>   (d) diversification
>
> Answers on p.216
> Tested

> **Revision activity**
> Draw a table to show the advantages and disadvantages of using Ansoff's matrix to a business manufacturing bicycles that is considering growth.

> **Now test yourself**
> 22 Identify one advantage and one disadvantage of using Ansoff's matrix.
>
> Answer on p.216
> Tested

Force field analysis
Revised

Force field analysis is used when deciding on a particular change. It identifies and compares the forces acting against the change with those acting in favour of it. Unfavourable forces can then be reduced and favourable ones made stronger.

> **Force field analysis:** analysis that compares forces acting to make a change with forces acting against a change.

Using force field analysis
1 Set out two columns.
2 Use the left column to list all the forces in favour of the change (**drivers**).
3 Use the right column to list all the forces against the change (**restrainers**).
4 Show the strength of each force with a score from 1 (weak) to 5 (strong).
5 Add all the scores for each column.
6 Make a decision based on the total scores.
7 Identify ways to strengthen the drivers and reduce the restrainers.
8 Repeat the analysis.

> **Drivers:** factors acting in favour of a change.
>
> **Restrainers:** factors acting against a change.

Advantages of force field analysis
- It is simple to carry out, easy to understand.
- It identifies clearly forces acting on a decision.
- It enables drivers to be strengthened and restrainers to be reduced.

Disadvantages of force field analysis
- Some forces may be omitted.
- Scores are subjective and could be inaccurate.
- Simplistic addition of scores ignores other factors.

Revision activity
A college is considering giving students access to all their records. The table below sets out the results of a force field analysis undertaken by the senior managers.

Drivers (+)	Score (+)	Restrainers (–)	Score (–)
Technology makes it possible	3	Additional cost of IT software	2
College's need for transparency	3	Cost of change to record system	4
Student expectations	4	Confidentiality fears	4
Lecturers in favour	2	Lecturers not in favour	3
Total	+12		+13

1 Using the analysis, should student access to records go ahead?
2 How confident are you that this decision is correct?
3 Suggest how the drivers might be strengthened and the restrainers weakened.

Expert tip
These techniques cannot make a decision. They are used together with other information to produce good decision making.

Decision trees

Decision trees enable a choice between possible actions to be made especially when there are:
- clear alternative choices
- numerical costs and benefits of the choices
- probabilities of success or failure for each choice

This enables calculations to determine the action giving the greatest monetary return.

Construction of a simple decision tree
Working from left to right, a decision tree is drawn by setting out:
- A square decision node showing the decision to be taken.
- Option choices indicated by lines ending in a decision node or outcome.
- Outcomes indicated by a circle (chance node) followed by probabilities of possible outcomes.
- The **expected money value (EMV)** of the outcome.

> **Expected money value (EMV):** value of a possible outcome in money terms, based on forecasts.

Strategic choice

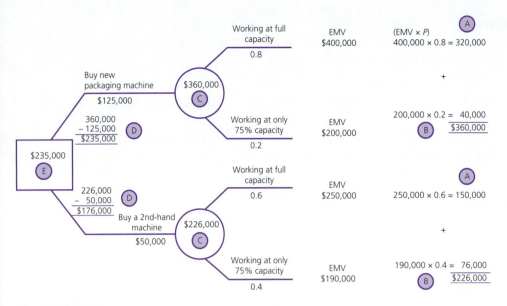

Figure 8 Decision tree

This decision tree shown in Figure 8 deals with whether to buy a new or a second hand packaging machine.

- Calculations are made from right to left.
- **Expected value** for each option possibility = EMV × probability (A).
- Add the expected values for each option (calculation shown at (B)).
- Added expected values for each outcome (chance node) (C).
- Expected value minus cost of each option (D).
- Highest possible return (E).

The new machine has a higher return ($235,000) than a second hand one ($176,000) so the analysis recommends this option. There may be other qualitative factors involved that also affect the decision. In this case, these may be the condition of the second hand machine, maintenance levels and relative life spans.

Other possible factors may include:

- availability of finance
- how the options relate to business objectives
- accuracy of the monetary information and probabilities
- external economic environment

Advantages of decision trees

- They demand clear thinking and analysis.
- They set out choices and their value in money terms clearly.
- They take account of risk and probability of an outcome.
- They demand detailed and thorough research into costs and benefits.

Disadvantages of decision trees

- The use of data may disguise poor or faulty research.
- They require reliance on accurate data and forecasts.
- They may become out of date.
- They may not take into account all relevant factors.

What-if analysis

The disadvantages of decision trees can be reduced by using sensitivity or what-if analysis. Asking the question 'what if'? of each of the outcomes can produce more information that takes account of different possibilities by having different assumptions. For example, sales are forecast to rise by 20% with a probability of

> **Expected value:** the value of a possible outcome, taking into account the probability of it occurring — equals EMV × probability.

> **Expert tip**
> Decision trees show decision points as a square, points with differing possible outcomes as a circle, probability of an outcome and expected money value of an outcome, and should include no change options where appropriate. Work left to right to set out probabilities and right to left to calculate expected values.

> **Now test yourself**
> 23 Identify three advantages of using decision trees.
> 24 Identify three disadvantages of using decision trees.
> **Answers on p.216**
> Tested

> **Expert tip**
> Decision trees take a long time to draw up. You need to be familiar with the process and be able to extract key information from a decision tree as well as show understanding about how decision trees are used.

this happening of 60%. What if an unexpected change in government reduced the probability to 40%? Carrying out this exercise for a range of scenarios will increase the accuracy of the decision tree analysis.

> **Revision activity**
>
> Regal Ltd specialises in making metal forming machines. The R&D department has designed an easy-to-programme, computer-controlled machine (Cammill) costing $6m, which would be attractive to manufacturers. Market research information is set out in a decision tree (in Figure 9). The operations department would like to move production from the town centre to a cheaper purpose-built, modern factory on a greenfield site, even if this means risking the loss of the skilled staff in the town. Maybe managers would not want to move and planning permission would be needed. The more expensive new machine would mean selling to larger businesses at a higher price, but export markets look promising. A new strategy would be needed
>
>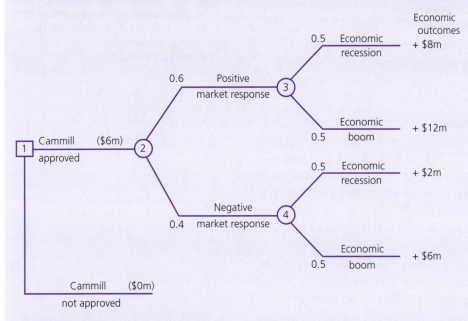
>
> **Figure 9** Cammill investment decision tree
>
> 1 Explain how either Ansoff's matrix or force field analysis might be useful in deciding whether to go ahead with the Cammill product.
> 2 (a) Calculate the expected return from manufacturing Cammill. Show all of your workings.
>   (b) Discuss how useful decision tree analysis is to Regal when taking the decision to commit to Cammill.

Strategic implementation

Once a strategy has been decided upon it is implemented through a business plan. The strategy must take account of corporate culture and the organisation should be prepared for managing necessary change, including planning for a crisis.

Business plans

Business plans are designed for an external audience — banks, venture capital suppliers, potential buyers or partners. A business plan sets out corporate objectives, functional area strategic and tactical plans, financial forecasts and market analysis.

> **Business plan:** sets out objectives and how an organisation intends to achieve them by strategic and tactical plans, market information and financial forecasts.

Key elements of a business plan

- **Summary of basic information** — a brief overview of organisation name, history, legal structure, product description, sources of resources and objectives.
- **Product or service** — more detail on what is being produced and how it meets the needs of the market. Differences from competitors' products are included, especially patents or copyright.

- **Market analysis** — a description of the market including the size, competition, market trends, target customers and possible future changes, based on documented market research.
- **Marketing plan** — this sets out the planned marketing mix and how this will meet customers' needs.
- **Production plan** — this contains details about how the product or service will be produced. It includes buildings, machinery, production methods, supply arrangements and quality assurance methods.
- **Organisational plan** — this often contains an organisational structure chart and describes how the workforce will be organised and structured, with management and training arrangements.
- **Financial forecasts** — future monthly cash flows and income statement forecasts demonstrate how finance is to be raised and managed.
- **Conclusion** — this is an overall summary of the whole plan looking forward.

> **Expert tips**
> These elements are suggestions: there is no set layout. A business plan should answer the questions:
> - What is the purpose of the business? (values/mission statement)
> - Where does it plan to go? (objectives)
> - How will it get there? (functional area strategies)
> - What is the cost? (financial)

The value of a business plan

Any size of business will find a business plan valuable, especially for obtaining finance, as it sets out exactly why a lender or partner should be interested. It also provides a detailed framework to act as a focus. This is why small businesses starting up usually find the planning process invaluable. Larger organisations proposing expansion or change may also prepare a business plan and many regularly maintain and update their business plans. This is because a business plan enables:

- close checking that an idea will be successful in reality, indicating how to overcome possible problems
- successful applications for a loan, grant, subsidy or other finance
- detailed examination of the financial and organisational implications of a proposal based on thorough research
- detailed assessment of the internal resources needed for success and exactly what external resources will be needed
- a focus and sense of direction
- constant review of progress

Possible disadvantages of a business plan

- The cost of producing it and the possibility of inaccurate forecasts.
- It may become inflexible if it is followed slavishly without being adapted to changing conditions.

> **Now test yourself**
> 25 Briefly explain what a business plan is.
> 26 Identify three advantages of drawing up a business plan.
>
> **Answers on p.216**

Corporate culture and strategic implementation

Types of corporate culture

Corporate culture is the values and behaviours shown by employees as they work. It appears in dress codes, attitudes to work, organisation structure, leadership styles, ways of communicating, and how employees relate to each other, suppliers and customers. Any type of culture may be appropriate to a successful business. The organisation must match its culture to its objectives and markets.

The types of corporate culture include power, task and entrepreneurial cultures.

> **Corporate culture:** the values and behaviours shown by employees as they work to get tasks done. These can also be determined by the attitude of managers and owners.

Power culture
The power is located in the centre or at the top, with small numbers of people responsible for decisions. Typically:
- leadership is autocratic
- decision making is centralised
- organisation structure is narrow and tall
- communication channels are defined in a hierarchy

Advantages	Disadvantages
• Decisions are made quickly and clearly. • Decisions are put into practice exactly.	• Creativity is limited, little group or team work. • Some employees are unmotivated as they have little control.

Task culture
Focused on team working, and power is located in what people contribute, not their formal position. Typically:
- leadership is democratic and empowering
- decision making is delegated
- organisation structure is flat, wide or a matrix
- communication channels are informal

Advantages	Disadvantages
• Creativity is high. • Many employees are motivated by responsibility and team working.	• Slow decision making and team rivalry. • Changing teams is costly and disruptive.

Entrepreneurial culture
Entrepreneurial cultures are focused on generating ideas from all levels. Change and risk taking are encouraged. Typically:
- leadership is democratic or laissez-faire and empowering
- decision making is delegated
- organisation structure is flat, wide or a matrix, able to change
- communication channels are informal and fast

Advantages	Disadvantages
• Many ideas, quick to react to change. • Many employees are highly motivated.	• Time and resources are wasted in unworkable ideas. • Little control over employees.

Strong and weak cultures
Whatever the culture type it may be strong or weak.

Strong cultures are ones in which employees all:
- understand the culture and conform to it
- agree on the values and behaviours

Weak cultures are ones in which employees:
- do not fully understand the culture and need detailed procedures and rules
- may have different ideas about the culture and this may lead to conflict and different ideas

> **Expert tip**
> Other corporate cultures are possible, e.g. person and role. These are not named in the examination syllabus but any discussion of them will be rewarded in examinations. Research them and produce notes on their advantages and disadvantages.

The importance of corporate culture
Businesses have their own objectives and market environments. Corporate culture should maximise the chances of reaching the objectives, so it is important to choose the most appropriate type, including the possibility of changing it as the business develops.

Power corporate culture may be very appropriate for markets that have:
- products with a long life
- prospects for expanding internationally
- a great deal of competition

and may be less suitable for markets with an emphasis on high and new technology for new products.

Task corporate culture may be very appropriate for markets that have an emphasis on high and new technology for new products, and less suitable for markets that are growing, or face a lot of competition, where products are long lived or where there is the chance of international expansion.

Entrepreneurial corporate culture may very appropriate for markets that have:
- an emphasis on high and new technology for new products
- high growth
- a great deal of competition

and may be less suitable for products that have a long life.

> **Now test yourself**
>
> 27 Explain three different types of corporate culture.
> 28 Suggest two reasons why an appropriate corporate culture might be important for a business to achieve its objectives.
>
> **Answers on p.216**
>
> Tested

Revision activity

Facebook offers an online social media site that is always developing new services and facilities to keep ahead of the competition in a high technology, growing international market. Facebook has deliberately encouraged a particular corporate culture that includes:
- shared desk spaces and team working on short-term projects
- games rooms, free food and child care
- time and resources for employees to work on their own ideas
- flexible working hours and the possibility of working from home
- induction programmes, mentors and access for all to senior staff

Some employees were critical because working hours were long, pay was low, the perks offered tied employees to the company and it was possible to waste a lot of time.

1 Giving reasons, explain the type of corporate culture Facebook has.
2 Explain whether you consider this culture to be strong or weak.
3 In what way is this type of culture appropriate to the business Facebook operates?
4 Discuss the advantages and disadvantages for Facebook changing its corporate culture.

Developing a change culture — its importance

Revised

Businesses can never be static. Their employees, markets, suppliers, competitors and the economic environment are always changing. It is vital that a business also changes to adapt with this process, whether seen or unpredicted change. Flexibility must be built into the corporate culture, whatever this is. Processes for making change happen when necessary are crucial, i.e. a culture of change should be built into the corporate culture.

Basic methods for successful change

- Create a positive working environment by focusing on what is going well.
- Identify committed change leaders in important management positions.
- Make sure that every employee knows and works to new values and beliefs by writing and communicating objectives and mission statements that really apply.
- Involve every employee in problem analysis and solving, building change into every role.
- Give every employee the chance to comment on the implications of change.
- Train all employees in change management at an appropriate level.

Managing and controlling strategic change

Revised ☐

Techniques to implement and manage change successfully

Overcome resistance to change
Resistance to change is natural. People fear loss of security, power or the unknown. The first step to successful change is to overcome resistance. Managers can minimise resistance by:
- helping employees to talk about their fears
- giving reasons for change
- giving employees full information about the change
- providing support and training
- inviting comment on the proposals

Techniques to implement change
Any corporate culture can manage change successfully. Those with structures that focus on people will already have open communication channels and involvement of employees in decision making. Organisations more focused on central decision making can use this to communicate change processes clearly and successfully. Techniques that apply to any organisation include:
- Give good advance notice of change coming.
- Make resources available for change processes.
- Give a very clear vision using mission statements that are explained in a way that shows a need to change and a new direction.
- Get key leaders at the top committed to the change — project champions are a possible way to do this.
- Communicate reasons and proposals for change clearly to every employee.
- Give every employee the chance to comment on the proposals — this involves everyone, giving ownership, and may generate positive suggestions.
- Provide appropriate training and support for all.
- Change management and organisation structures to reflect the new position.

Development of a strategy to manage change
The techniques of managing change can be used within each step of a strategic approach for managing change.

Kotter's eight-step strategy
Some of these steps may take place at the same time.
1. **Create urgency.** All employees need to know there is need for change and expect it to come.
2. **Create a change team.** Prepare committed and respected manager/leaders at all levels.
3. **Create a vision.** Decide on new values and beliefs contained in value/mission statements and objectives.
4. **Communicate the vision.** Use all the communication channels in all functional areas.
5. **Empower people and remove obstacles.** Identify reasons for resistance to change, and minimise these using leaders or project champions. Restructure and reward those working for change.
6. **Create short-term gains.** Small steps for change mean all employees can see benefits and progress.
7. **Build on the change.** Continue the process of change after each small step.
8. **Anchor change into corporate culture.** Build change into whatever culture there is by getting leaders to support change, telling success stories, inducting staff into change and rewarding change.

> **Revision activity**
>
> A manufacturing company faced the prospect of going out of business due to intense new competition from low cost businesses. Only the directors were aware of this as the factories were running 24 hours and the workforce was happy. The directors held meetings with senior managers and supervisors, and convinced them of the very real threat. Research showed that the rest of the workforce still did not realise this. Foreman supervisors were seen as key employees, in charge of translating management requirements to the workforce. Meetings with head foremen were held in which they had the chance to make contributions in debate. Following these meetings, most of them were in favour of change and were willing to promote change to their teams. Team meetings for all employees were held in company time. Major changes in working practices that reduced costs followed.
>
> 1 Outline two techniques for achieving change used by this business.
> 2 Analyse the strategic change management approach taken by the business.
> 3 What role did having a strategic approach play in this successful change management?

Contingency planning and crisis management

Events that threaten a business may occur suddenly. Most of these are foreseeable, even if they are unlikely. A well-prepared business will take steps to be ready for these events. **Crisis management** is the process by which a business deals with a major event that threatens its operation. Examples include floods, a fire, equipment failure or mass resignations. **Contingency planning** is the process of planning for foreseeable but unlikely events (crises) that will threaten a business. Correct planning will make the negative effects of a crisis as small as possible.

> **Crisis management:** the process by which a business deals with a major event that threatens its operation.
>
> **Contingency planning:** the process of planning for foreseeable but unlikely events (crises) that will threaten a business.

Contingency planning stages

1 The first essential stage is to recognise the need for planning for crisis.
2 Identify foreseeable events that may threaten the business.
3 Give each event a probability to identify which of them is the most likely.
4 Decide which events will have the biggest negative effect.
5 Prepare a contingency plan to deal with these events. The plan must include specific actions for immediate problems and actions to return the business to normal working.
6 Test the contingency plan and how well it functions.
7 Review and update the plan.

Advantages of contingency planning

- Quick response.
- Reassures stakeholders.
- Helps senior managers generate favourable public relations.
- Maintains confidence.

Disadvantages of contingency planning

- Uses valuable time and resources in preparing and training.
- Cost of reviewing procedures.
- May lead to less planning to avoid disasters.
- Likely never to be used so could be a waste of resources.

> **Now test yourself**
>
> 29 Define contingency planning.
> 30 Outline the process for successful contingency planning.
> 31 State three advantages and three disadvantages to contingency planning.
>
> **Answers on p.216**

A level questions and answers

This section contains exam-style questions for each A level topic followed by example answers. The answers are followed by expert comments (shown by the icon e) that indicate where credit is due and areas for improvement.

6 Business and its environment

Question 1

Bright Hair and Nails (BHN) plc

BHN produces a range of chemicals and other products for hair and nail care. It sells mainly to 18–40-year-old, middle-income women. Sales are rapidly rising as this group's disposable income increases. Last year BHN introduced a new organic sustainable range called Care, aimed at teenagers. BHN closed a factory so that Care and some other products could be manufactured in another country, where prices of land and labour are much lower. The bad publicity from the closure and redundancies has recently been made worse by environmental pressure-group claims that Care uses non-sustainable chemical ingredients and that adverts have been misleading. Competitors are continually developing new technologically advanced products. The directors are considering the following information.

Table A

Annual GDP growth rate in next 3 years	+4%
Annual population growth rate in next 3 years	+2%
Annual population growth 10–18 year olds in next 3 years	+4%
Forecast annual inflation	+6%
Forecast change in tax on profits	–8%
Forecast change in external exchange rate	–5%

Discuss the ways in which the information in Table A and other external factors could affect how successful BHN is in the future. [20]

Candidate answer (extract)

BHN produces consumer products. Its target group has rapidly rising incomes so sales are likely to continue to increase. Population growth at 2% p.a. also supports this conclusion, though this assumes that the target group is likewise increasing in size. The new Care range is aimed at teenagers and the number of these is forecast to rise at an even higher rate (4%), producing a larger number of potential buyers, a good indicator for higher sales. However, prices are forecast to rise at a faster level than GDP or population. This will lead to increasing costs and pressure on profit margins or prices. Both of these will tend to lead to a fall in sales and profits. The fall in profit tax is likely to more than offset these effects and lead to an increase in profits. The fall in the exchange rate will lead to import prices rising. This might increase the costs of Care, as it is manufactured elsewhere, and lead to pressure to increase prices or cut margins.

With increasing concern for environmental factors BHN has done well to introduce an organic range and is likely to increase sales. However, it will have to demonstrate that the criticisms about ingredients and advertising are not true, otherwise the pressure group actions may convince potential and existing customers not to buy. Misleading adverts may also attract legal action from government or regulatory bodies, costing BHN money and reputation, which in the personal care market is crucial. It is very difficult to assess the overall effects of these factors as they are complex and act in different directions. The actions of competitors and movement of ingredient prices will also be important in the future success of BHN.

e *In the extract, Table A information is considered, along with other external factors drawn from the case study. Understanding of the concepts and their possible effects is demonstrated in brief chains of argument (analysis) and these are related to BHN and its products (application). Understanding that the effects of one change may depend on other changes is shown (evaluation) and an attempt to weigh up the relative importance of these effects is made (evaluation). The complete answer would be expected to achieve marks in the top level, i.e. 17–20 marks.*

7 People in organisations

Question 2

People First Ltd

People First Ltd manufactures a range of kitchen equipment including cooking utensils, plates and cups and ovens. The business is American-owned but has its manufacturing base in India. The senior managers are all from the USA and many of the workers feel that they do not understand the needs of the local employees. The managers realise that they have a serious issue with the low level of

morale among the workforce and they have noticed a significant increase in the level of faulty products being produced. The managers have also been made aware that some departments have performed much better than others; some have consistently met their targets while others have not achieved as much as 75% of what was expected of them. One departmental manager has said that he has not been able to meet targets set for his department because he does not have enough suitably qualified staff to undertake the tasks required.

Discuss the extent to which a lack of workforce planning might be responsible for the high level of faulty products and the failure of some departments to meet their set targets. [15]

Candidate answer (extract)

Workforce planning involves ensuring that a business has the right number of employees with the right skills, in the right place at the right time. According to one departmental manager, targets were not met in his department due to a lack of employees with appropriate skills. If the department does not have enough staff, that could explain the failure to meet targets and more workers should be recruited. If there are sufficient employees but without relevant skills that might explain the increase in faulty products and the failure to meet targets. This could indicate that workforce planning had not taken place or if it had, then the requirements for the number and quality of employees had not been met.

The business also recognised a problem of low morale amongst employees so it is possible that it is poor motivation that has caused the increase in faulty products. Low levels of motivation might be due to the feeling that the senior managers do not understand the needs of the local workforce. It is possible that inappropriate methods of motivation are being used. The HRM department should meet with some employees to discover what could motivate them so that managers can adjust their approach to their workers.

Discussion with the employees is essential to understand which of these factors is likely to have caused the problems identified.

e *This extract identifies the two key issues from the case study that could have caused a department not to meet set targets and the increase in the production of faulty products. The candidate recognises that it might not just be a workforce planning problem and that there might be another cause, i.e. poorly motivated workers. There are other possible causes of the faulty goods that could have been discussed, e.g. poor materials or faulty equipment. These might have added some depth to the answer. However, the candidate does show a good understanding of workforce planning and motivation issues and how this can impact on the output of a business. Some evaluation is included but has limited development. For example, the idea of HRM meeting employees to discuss motivation issues could have been further discussed and would have strengthened the evaluation at the end of the answer. The complete answer would gain 13/15 marks.*

Question 3

Excelsior Ltd

Excelsior Ltd, a producer of office equipment based in the UK, has experienced rapid and substantial growth over the past 2 years. The business has had production facilities in the UK for 25 years but more recently has built factories in India and Indonesia.

A recent e-mail sent to all departmental managers in the UK factory asked them to instruct their staff to look at the notice board as soon as possible because an important message had been posted there that all employees needed to read. The notice informed employees that the business was considering closing the factory and moving production to the more modern factories in Indonesia and India.

Assess the extent to which the chosen method of communication was appropriate in this situation. [8]

Candidate answer (extract)

The managers of Excelsior Ltd wanted to convey the information quickly and a notice board can achieve that. This is information that every member of staff should have, and there is no guarantee that every employee will look at the notice board. The information means that workers in the UK factory will probably lose their jobs; the use of notice boards is too impersonal when communicating such potentially devastating news. The workers do not have an opportunity to understand the reasons behind the decision or to give feedback to the managers about how they feel about the news. It might have been more appropriate to hold a staff meeting so that senior managers could explain in more detail why this decision is being made and when it is likely to occur. They can give the employees an opportunity to ask questions. Potentially life-changing news should have been delivered in a more personal manner. Perhaps departmental meetings could have been held meaning fewer workers in each meeting giving each of them a better chance to give feedback or ask questions. Departmental meetings might each give a slightly different message causing confusion amongst workers who discuss what they have heard.

Letters could have been sent to employees giving details of the proposed closure, the reasons and timescale. This would mean they would have a permanent record of the facts but does not give the opportunity to ask questions unless a staff meeting is held after workers have received the letters.

e *In this competent answer, the extract shows the candidate is considering the content of the information and the way in which it might affect employees. The candidate also considers the amount of information that employees might want, e.g. the timescale involved. There are some evaluative comments within the answer and the complete answer would gain 8/8 marks.*

8 Marketing

Question 4

TecWear

TecWear, owned by Jameen, manufactures waterproof coats and trousers. Tecware has been in business for 3 years and has already built up a growing customer base that appreciates the distinctiveness, quality and design of the clothes. Sales to customers are made through 18 specialist clothing stores and an internet site and show a seasonal variation. Jameen uses moving averages and other methods to forecast future sales. There are several large transnational companies selling similar clothing which have much larger promotion and research budgets than TecWear. They are continually bringing out new products and fabrics. Jameen now feels that TecWear needs to develop or fail. She employs a part-time fabric scientist who is working on a new unique lightweight, washable fabric that could be used for outdoor garments. Without the waterproofing ingredient it would also be suitable for indoor clothes, including shirts and dresses. Financing further development will require borrowing. Brief market research indicates that a paper catalogue in addition to the website might be a means to attract more customers.

(a) Analyse the benefits to TecWear of product development. [10]

(b) Evaluate the importance of sales forecasting for TecWear. [14]

Candidate answer (extract)

(a) TecWear's business is built on selling to people who want something different from the large firms' products. In order to compete, TecWear has to offer something that cannot be bought elsewhere. R&D will enable it to continue to keep ahead of the big companies. Failure to develop new products means that the competition will soon copy TecWear's fabrics and their big research and promotion budgets will attract business from TecWear. The performance clothing market demands clothing that is waterproof and light and TecWear needs new designs and fabrics to keep up with market changes. The new fabric will maintain competitive advantage and enable expansion into a new market. All TecWear has to decide is whether the potential benefits are bigger than the investment needed.

This extract considers the benefits, so addressing the question. Several benefits are suggested, with reasons given for their importance, all in relation to TecWear's situation. The complete answer would be expected to achieve 8–10 marks.

(b) TecWear uses moving averages to forecast sales. This method is useful because sales vary by season and calculating a trend and adding seasonal variation will give an accurate prediction. It will not be able to determine random changes to sales, nor predict the effect of changes in the market, such as a competitor bringing out a new design or promotional campaign. But it will enable Jameen to have a clear idea of sales revenue in the future, enabling investment decisions such as developing the new fabric to be well made. Other methods might include asking outlets their views on the market and expected sales and using customer information from the website, looking at the percentage of people who visit and buy. These forecasting methods are not expensive and will give a clear idea of expected sales quantity and revenue. This will enable production plans to be accurate, costs to be minimised, and cash flows and any borrowing requirements to be forecast. However, in a rapidly changing market, sales forecasts must be constantly revised and treated with care.

This extract discusses the role of forecasting, showing knowledge of possible methods, with some reference to TecWear's situation. Benefits and drawbacks are considered, with reasons for each. Some attempt is made at a conclusion. The complete answer would be expected to achieve 12–14 marks.

9 Operations and project management

Question 5

Problems at Bikki Ltd

Jon and two associates left their jobs with a food manufacturing firm to set up their own business, Bikki Ltd, making biscuits. They took up an offer of leasing a factory with the equipment needed for mixing, baking and packaging. They hired workers, engaged in a marketing launch and achieved all their sales targets, selling to small shops and one large supermarket chain. After a year several problems appeared:

- The supermarket began returning significant numbers of packets because biscuits did not meet the quality criteria.
- Stocks of ingredients and finished packets built up and some spoilt.
- The equipment began to break down frequently.
- Labour turnover rose and many employees complained of boredom.

Jon was warned that repeat orders were in danger unless quality improved. Employees became aware of this and their motivation fell even further. The supermarket buyer had a quiet word: 'Unless quality is improved within three months you lose our order. Why not try lean production?' Jon quickly investigated this idea.

Evaluate the introduction of lean production at Bikki Ltd. [20]

Candidate answer (extract)

Lean production is using resources to produce in the most efficient way to minimise waste. It keeps costs as low as possible and enables consistent quality criteria to be achieved. It does this by focusing on four areas.

First, just-in-time production. This involves only ordering materials when they are needed for production, and sending finished goods to suppliers quickly so that inventory at all stages is kept to as near zero as possible. This is exactly what Bikki Ltd needs to introduce to stop the costs of holding too much stock as at present. However, JIT requires some setting up and there are dangers. There must be accurate forecasts for demand, otherwise it might not be possible to suddenly obtain raw materials. In Bikki's case the supermarket will be able to supply demand requirements. Suppliers must be reliable in terms of quality and delivery, there must be flexibility in the equipment and workforce and some kind of enterprise resource planning (ERP) to enable resources to be matched exactly to orders. All this will require initial costs in terms of training employees, setting up suitable suppliers and designing an ERP system. There will be ongoing costs of monitoring. In Bikki's case, where production is relatively simple and materials easily obtainable, setting up JIT should be possible and will lead to much cost savings. It will not really address the quality issues.

These can be tackled by introducing total quality management (TQM) — a plan for getting quality assurance by all employees putting quality first from start to finish. This will mean making sure suppliers are committed to giving quality and employees are trained to have a pride in achieving quality. This means changing the culture of Bikki and supporting workers in their jobs. This sounds easy but will require management of the change. This can cost time and energy. To get employees involved in TQM means changing their roles. This can be done through increasing the importance of teamwork through cell production, providing flexible roles and giving workers more responsibility. This will reduce the complaints about boredom, lower labour turnover and its costs and increase quality. There will be costs and the total commitment of the owners and managers will be needed. Work patterns have to be changed and it may be necessary to invest in different machinery that is less prone to breakdown.

Changing to lean production involves cost. In Bikki's case it is difficult to see how it can survive unless a big move towards lean production is made.

e In this extract, the candidate addresses the question. A clear understanding of lean production is shown, though there are omissions, e.g. capacity management, the role of kaizen, benchmarking and how quality assurance may

be achieved. Advantages and costs of lean production are discussed and there is some attempt to reach a conclusion, but this is not fully justified by the arguments. The answer is general in tone and could be more focused towards the issues faced specifically by Bikki Ltd, though there is some reference to particular case study points. The mark for the complete answer would be in the range of 14–18 marks.

10 Finance and accounting

Question 6

Exploration Equipment plc

Exploration Equipment plc specialises in drilling and mining equipment that is sold worldwide. It has its headquarters in Malaysia with production sites in Malaysia, China and Indonesia. The board of directors has recently decided to open another factory in Europe but is undecided about its location. The following figures have been estimated for each proposed location:

Predicted net cash flows $000s

	Year 0	Year 1	Year 2	Year 3	Year 4	Year 5
France	(800)	120	250	300	325	350
UK	(875)	100	225	350	375	425

(a) Calculate:
  (i) the average rate of return and [3]
  (ii) the net present value [3]

Discount factor for 10% rate of interest

Year 0	Year 1	Year 2	Year 3	Year 4	Year 5
1	0.91	0.83	0.75	0.68	0.62

(b) Analyse the factors, other than financial, that the board should consider when making its decision. [10]

Candidate answer

(a)(i) ARR for France = (1,345 − 800) ÷ 5 = 109 average profit per year

ARR = 109 ÷ 800 × 100 = 13.63% rounded

ARR for UK = (1,475 − 875) ÷ 5 = 120 average profit for the year

ARR = 120 ÷ 875 × 100 = 13.71% rounded

(ii) Net present value (NPV) France = $179,700

NPV UK = $183,750

e These calculations are correct and score the full 3 marks for each.

(b) The board might consider the attitude of the governments in France and the UK to overseas companies locating within their countries. Some governments encourage foreign inward investment, while others discourage it in order to protect domestic industries.

Will the company be able to locate where it wants to or will the governments dictate where the factory can be built?

Both the ARR and the NPV indicate that the UK would be the most beneficial location but legal restrictions might be stricter than in France. The business must consider the relative wage rates and the strength of the trade unions in both countries. If France has generally lower wage rates than the UK, the business should locate in France. The level of trade union activity might be an important factor in the decision. If there is a chance that production can be frequently disrupted by industrial action then EE plc might lose too many days of work and be unable to meet deadlines for delivery of equipment.

Some governments give grants and/or cheap loans to businesses that locate in their countries but often dictate where in the country the business should locate. This might not be the best location for the business.

The infrastructure is important. Is there a good road and rail network? Can the business locate close to a port because the equipment is likely to be large and heavy and will be exported to the final customer?

This answer does mention some financial factors, i.e. the ARR and NPV and the wage rates, but it also identifies several non-financial valid factors, e.g. the infrastructure and the level of trade union activity. There is some analysis of the possible impact of trade union activity. More analysis of relevant factors would be required in order for higher marks to be gained. It gains 7/10 marks.

Question 7

Heppack Ltd financial data

Year	2008 (%)	2009 (%)	2010 (%)	2011 (%)	2012 (%)
Gross profit margin	42	40	44	46	49
Net profit margin	15	12	16	14	12

Analyse the possible reasons why the net profit margin of Heppack Ltd is decreasing when the gross profit margin is increasing. [8]

Candidate answer (extract)

The most likely explanation is that Heppack Ltd has allowed costs to increase. This could be an increase in the cost of electricity or fuel for the company's vehicles. It could be due to an increase in any of the items listed in the income statement. This could have been caused by an increase in the wages paid to workers reducing profits and therefore the net profit margin. If workers had negotiated a significant wage increase this could cause such a downward trend. Over 5 years the net profit margin fell by 3% but in 2010 it increased. Heppack Ltd needs to discover how it achieved this increase and try to introduce measures to repeat this. Over the last 3 years net profit margin has steadily declined. Have increases occurred on several items or is it one particular expense that is the cause? It might be a result of inflationary pressures in the economy.

This extract focuses on the question and on the elements that determine the profit for the year. It shows an understanding of the relationship between expenses, profit for the year and the net profit margin. The impact of inflationary pressure and the question of one or several cost increases needs some explanation to make it relevant to the answer. The complete answer would achieve 6/8 marks.

11 Strategic management

Question 8

Rack Radios (RR) plc

Rack Radios (RR) plc produces a range of radios that sell at a low price. The range includes portable battery, solar power and wind-up models plus some small mains radios. It has had great success in sales through large, low-price retailers, gaining a good market share. It has achieved this by keeping the cost of materials down, using low-tech specification circuits to enable low prices but low profit margins. RR has two concerns:
1. Competitors are increasingly active and RR's sales are levelling off.
2. Disposable incomes in the country are increasing and research shows that many people are not satisfied with cheap, low-quality radios.

The directors have an idea that it is time to produce a higher-quality, more expensive radio to sell to people with greater disposable income. Components, cases and finishes would appeal to the new target market. The radios would be sold in department and specialist stores. Manufacture would be outsourced to specialists in low wage economies. There would be a new brand name — Real. This would complement the existing brand but would have to be marketed differently to ensure that there was no confusion with the cheaper model ranges. Consultants were employed and they carried out some strategic analysis for RR.
- Boston matrix analysis considered the position of the current models in the market.
- A SWOT analysis established where RR was at the moment.

- **Porter's 5 forces model was used to assess the possible competition.**
- **A PEST analysis considered the external factors related to the market for radios.**

Consider the strategic analysis the consultants carried out. Assess how important this analysis might be for RR to be successful in introducing the Real range. [20]

Candidate answer (extract)

Strategic analysis is a business setting out where it is with resources, the market and the external environment. It follows the setting of objectives and enables strategic decisions to be taken about the future using the information from the analysis. The consultants used four tools of analysis. The Boston matrix considers the range of products a business has and assigns them to a matrix with four parts, high or low market share and fast or slow growing markets. RR's products have a medium market share in a slow or declining market — a cash cow that is generating money in a consistent way. This could be used to finance the development of another product like the proposed Real. Real would be a problem child — low market share in a growing market, giving the possibility of future revenues. The Boston matrix does not make a decision but indicates possibilities — markets may change.

A SWOT analysis considers the strengths, weaknesses, opportunities and threats facing RR.

Strengths	Weaknesses	Opportunities	Threats
Solid existing market share.	Reliance on one radio sector likely to decline.	Entering new market segment.	Active competitors.
Good products.		New distribution channels.	Sales likely to fall.
Good reputation.			
Good distribution networks.			

Using this can help RR to pinpoint a possible direction that will build on its strengths, bypass the weaknesses, use opportunities and avoid the threats. SWOT analysis does not give prescriptive answers but indicates simple conclusions.

Both these tools indicate that the proposed move to Real has a definite possibility of success and that continuing as RR is at the moment is not really an option.

Porter's 5 forces can be used to assess the degree of competition in an existing market or in a market a business may wish to enter. In RR's case the existing market has a threat of competitors, customers are increasingly likely to switch to other products, there are substitute products available and there is little information on the bargaining power of suppliers, though outsourcing may put greater power to them. This means that there is likely to be some competition that will increase. In the proposed market there appears to be less competition as there will be fewer available substitute products and customers will have less bargaining power. This indicates that RR is likely to face less competition by selling more expensive upmarket radios.

PEST analysis considers the political, economic, social and technological aspects of the external environment. Relevant factors would be that disposable incomes are growing (E), people are less happy with cheap radios and want more expensive quality (S) and the technology exists to make better quality radios. Again, this indicates that the proposed move may well be a good one.

Strategic analysis enables a business to set out where it is now, with an indication of what it might face in the future. However, all of them are simplistic and the situation may change rapidly, making the analysis outdated and faulty. RR should build on the conclusions by carrying out detailed market research, investigating suppliers' costs and quality, drawing up production plans for costs and making initial approaches to department and specialist stores.

This extract shows a comprehensive answer that covers all four tools. Knowledge and understanding of these tools is good and is applied to RR's situation. The advantages and disadvantages of the tools are considered and the conclusion sets out other things that RR would need to do. The complete answer would be expected to achieve 16–20 marks.

Now test yourself answers

Topic 1

1. Added value is the additional value gained at each stage of production. It can be economic (work done on inputs) or marketing (consumers see more value).
2. Opportunity cost is the next best alternative given up when a choice is made.
3. Characteristics of a successful entrepreneur include: determination, drive and energy; passion, initiative and self-confidence; good leadership — being able to persuade and involve others.
4. Three possible changes in a business environment include a new law; a new product from a competitor; a new technology; a change in taxes.
5. A shelter for homeless people; a food growing cooperative; a Grameen lending scheme for women-led businesses.
6. Triple bottom line is used to assess business performance in all of financial, social and environmental targets/achievements.
7. Profit-making businesses aim to make profits but social enterprises aim to achieve social impact; profits belong to owners in the profit making business and to the business in a social enterprise. The assets in a profit making business that stops trading belong to the owners. The assets in a social enterprise that stops trading have to be passed to similar businesses.
8. *Primary:* marble quarry, rice farm, palm oil plantation, gold mine.
   Tertiary: accountant, clothes shop, doctor, car mechanic.
9. *Public sector:* local government car park, council refuse collection, government school.
   Private sector: market stall, Coca-Cola, clothing manufacturer.
10. Private sector businesses often have profit objectives; public sector businesses have other objectives such as providing a service at a set standard.
11. Limited liability means that the financial liability of the owners of a business is limited to the amount they have invested.
12. Owners of the business will not be personally responsible for paying the loan back so they will be willing for the company to take the loan out. Also, a bank will be willing to lend to a company, knowing the business is legally responsible and will use its resources to pay the loan back.
13. Shares in plcs may be traded in public, including a stock exchange, plc accounts and reports are open to the public and large amounts of finance can be raised by share issue. Private limited companies cannot sell shares on a stock exchange, can keep their accounts private and cannot raise very large amounts of finance by share issue.
14. Number of employees, capital employed, market share, sales revenue.
15. Large market share might be of a very small market. High capital employed might be due to capital intensive methods used by a small business.
16. *Advantages:* quick response to changes in customer tastes; personal service.
    Disadvantages: lack of finance; difficult to employ a range of specialists; sometimes small range of goods/services etc.
17. Emotional involvement or family feuds affecting the business.
18. Small businesses can be an important part of the supply chain supplying larger businesses with components and services. Small business today can be big business of tomorrow. Small businesses can create a lot of jobs.
19. To gain economies of scale; to increase potential for sales; to gain status; to increase market power through larger market share.
20. Specific; measurable; agreed/achievable; realistic; time-specific.
21. Profit maximisation; profit satisficing; increase market share; increase sales revenue; growth; survival.
22. The state of the economy; the culture of the business, i.e. risk averse or not; size of business; public or private sector; length of existence.
23. CSR means that a business considers the potential impact of its activities on society; it aims to behave in an environmentally friendly and ethical manner.
24. Customers might refuse to buy the products of a business that is judged to be behaving in an unethical manner, especially if alternatives are available from ethical businesses.
25. Shareholders; employees; suppliers; local community; lenders of finance; government. Examples include:
    - Shareholders expect the business to be profitable and give a return on their investment, i.e. dividends.
    - Employees hope that they will continue to have employment and to be paid a fair wage.
26. Employees might lose their jobs; shareholders might fear lower profits in the future; the local community might suffer a multiplier effect as those now without work cannot afford to spend in the local shops.
27. Examples include: shareholders might sell their shares if they do not receive dividends; employees might seek employment elsewhere if their needs are not met; the local community might fight any plans that the business has if they have not been treated well in the past.

Topic 2

1. *Control:* to be able to determine the activities in a business to ensure that all effort is working towards the business objectives. *Monitoring:* checking constantly that all individual and departmental objectives are being met and if not then to take corrective action. *Commanding* makes sure that clear instructions are given so that everyone knows what is expected of them. *Planning:* being responsible for deciding on the business objectives and how they might be achieved. *Coordinating:* ensuring that duplication of effort does not occur and that all departments are working at the required pace and towards the appropriate targets.

2 Characteristics could include: charisma, self-confidence, intelligence, creativity, being multi-skilled. Example explanation: charisma means that the leader will be able to get people to believe in him or her and to follow in the pursuit of business goals. Self-confidence might be essential when no one else can understand the path being taken but the leader can see the desired outcome and how it can be achieved.

3 More ideas because employees can make valuable contributions. More highly motivated workers because they feel valued and included in business decisions. Workers get feedback from managers and are able to feed back to managers on ideas put forward.

4 Consulting with employees can be very time consuming. Emergency situations and some business situations cannot afford time to consult when quick decisions must be made. Times when management do not consult employees can cause resentment. Employees might not know best how to deal with a particular situation; they do not have the experience or skills, unlike the managers.

5 Quick decisions can be made, which is essential in some situations. Employees are told what to do and time is not wasted gaining the feedback from them. Some employees do not want to be included in decision making and would be more comfortable being given instructions.

6 Highly skilled and self-motivated. This means that they do not need constant supervision as they are probably doing highly technical work, e.g. R&D. They are driven by their interest in what they do and therefore do not need supervising. They are motivated by the nature of the work.

7 Self-awareness; self-management; social awareness; social skills.

8 They are able to deal with the situation/employee in the most appropriate manner thereby gaining the best possible outcome.

9 Motivation is the desire and willingness to work towards a stated goal.

10 *Social needs:* people usually need to feel part of a group and to have interaction with other people. *Esteem needs:* people need to feel the respect of their peers; they need to feel recognised and appreciated either as a worker and/or as a person.

11 Piece work means that employees will be paid a stated amount for each unit or piece of work completed.

12 The more employees produce then the more they will earn. This will motivate those workers who are motivated by money and desire a higher income.

13 *Hygiene factors* do not motivate but their presence prevents dissatisfaction. *Motivators* are the factors that will create a desire and willingness to work among employees.

14 *Achievement:* the need to reach goals and be recognised for doing so. *Authority:* the need of employees to have some control and power over the way they work. *Affiliation:* the need to be part of a group, to be liked — the desire to work in a friendly atmosphere.

15 Without an effective appraisal system it would not be possible to determine whether targets had been achieved and who had met them and who had not. The system must be fair so that people who do achieve their targets are rewarded and those who do not reach pre-set targets will not receive rewards. Without this the expectance of workers is undermined.

16 *Commission:* sales people could receive a percentage of the total sales that they achieve. This would motivate them to sell more. *Profit-related pay:* if the retail business becomes more profitable due to the efforts of its employees it could reward its workers with a share of the profits. This ensures that all employees strive to make the business as profitable as possible.

17 *Employee of the month awards. Participation:* the workers could be involved in making production decisions.

18 *Disciplinary and grievance procedure:* in the case of disciplinary action being taken against an employee, the HRM department would arrange for the employee to be notified and would arrange any necessary meeting. Similarly with a grievance procedure. *Training:* induction training and any other required training would be organised through the HRM department. It would also identify training needs in some instances, e.g. when new equipment is acquired. *Recruitment of workers when required.*

19 To motivate existing employees; to save advertising costs; because the recruit would be familiar with the business and its systems; faster recruitment process.

20 Internal recruitment is when a vacant position is filled by someone already working in the business. External recruitment is when a vacant post is advertised outside the business and the applicants do not currently work for the business and are likely to be unknown to the business.

21 A *job specification* details the tasks and responsibilities that will be performed by the person doing the job. It might detail hours of work, place of work and holiday entitlements. A *person specification* details the qualifications and qualities that the applicants are expected to have. These can be personal qualities, such as patience and confidence, or could be the amount of experience that they should have in similar work.

22 Advertise in local or national newspapers; place details on a job search internet site; advertise in a specialist trade magazine etc.

23 Using recruitment agencies; posting the vacancy on job internet sites; through personal contacts of existing employees; by head-hunting people from other businesses.

24 *Interview:* pre-planned questions asked of each candidate and compare responses — enables body language to be seen plus follow-up questions if necessary. *Aptitude tests:* give each candidate a test on the skills that they will need in the job — can see if the candidate is physically/mentally able to do the work.

25 Details of the work; job title, working hours; length of contract; holiday entitlement; how the contract can be ended.

26 *Redundancy* occurs when the work is no longer required and so the person doing that work is also no longer required. *Dismissal* is when the contract of employment is terminated by the employer and the person is asked to leave the place of work.

27 Employees more skilled from acquiring more skills and knowledge; motivated employees because they feel valued if the business invests in them; helps to prepare employees for promotion.

28 *On-the-job training* takes place within the business and is often done by watching other workers doing their work. *Off-the-job* training takes place in a school or college away from the business premises and is usually given by external specialists.

Topic 3

1 *Business objective:* increase profits by 10% in the next year. *Marketing objectives:* increase customer recognition of the product by 20% and increase sales by 10% over the next year.

2 *To increase customer recognition:*
   – Product — produce a brighter range of colours.
   – Price — sell at a price no higher than the competition.
   – Promotion — increase advertising by 10%.
   – Place — increase the number of sales outlets by 10%.

   To increase sales by 10% over the next year:
   – Product — produce updated design.
   – Price — reduce price by 5%.
   – Promotion — increase in-store promotions.
   – Place — introduce online selling.

3 Price; costs of corn, rice and wheat; taxes on cereals.

4 (a) No effect.
  (b) Supply curve moves to right.

5 Price of boots; income of consumers; attitude of consumers to wearing boots; how fashionable boots are; advertisement campaigns for boots.

6 (a) No effect.
  (b) Demand curve moves to left.

7 (a) The supply of a good is the quantity of goods or services being made available for sale at a particular price and time.
  (b) Demand is the quantity of a good or service that customers are willing and able to buy at a particular price and time.
  (c) Market price is the price of a good resulting from the interaction between demand and supply in a market.

8 Either may be correct.

9 *Building market:* advertise in building/trade magazines and construction. *Footwear market:* advertise as an accessory to clothing and sell in high street shops or malls.

10 *Consumer products:* evening dress, bubble gum, saloon car, possibly spreadsheet
   Producer products: shrink wrapping machine, large computer system, spreadsheet

11 Answer may depend on exactly what the product is:
   – *Local market* — golf club, painter/decorator
   – *National market* — jeans, chocolate bar, sports car, cigarettes
   – *Regional market* — jeans, chocolate bar, sports car, cigarettes
   – *International market* — oil drilling equipment, jeans, chocolate bar, sports car, cigarettes

12 (a) Market share is the percentage of the total market held by a business or product.
   (b) Market growth is the absolute or percentage increase in the size of a market.
   (c) A consumer market is one in which consumers are the buyers.
   (d) A national market is the market within a particular country.

13 *Consumer markets:* cough sweets, Wellington boots, pocket radios.
   Producer markets: 30 tonne lorry, brakes for cars.

14 *Place of sale:* consumer market sold in shops, malls, market stalls, producer market sold by sales staff, in trade fairs/exhibitions.
   Promotional methods: consumer market by television advertising, producer market by targeted flyers.

15 Unique selling point (USP) is the one particular factor that makes a product different.

16 Targeted advertising; specific unique design; branding.

17 (a) Niche marketing is when a business satisfies the needs of a small segment of a larger market.
   (b) Segmentation is the process of identifying particular groups in a market that have similar needs and wants.

18 By age, household income, gender, personality type.

19 Portfolio analysis arranges replacement products for failing ones, gives flexibility.

20 Age, gender, reason for buying, place dolls are bought from, income.

21 (a) Market research is the process of gathering information about markets, customers, competitors and the effectiveness of marketing methods.
   (b) Primary or field research is gathering information for the first time, directly from sources in the market.
   (c) Desk research is using information that has been gathered already, either by the business or by other organisations.
   (d) Qualitative research is gathering information that is expressed in words, e.g. about feelings and attitudes.

22 (a) Surveys — take time to set up, carry out, and analyse results, respondents may not tell truth.
   (b) Observation — interaction between observer and observed, usefulness limited to a few research objectives.

23 (a) Focus group — allows discussion of reasons, detailed responses, consumer sees products.
   (b) Test marketing — real marketing situation, expensive mistakes can be corrected before full launch.

24 Sampling is the process of gathering information from a representative group of all those you are interested in (sample from the population).

25 A stratified sample is taken by dividing up the population into groups of shared characteristics and choosing from them. A quota sample chooses a set number of people with different characteristics.

26 It is important to obtain a random sample because it will represent the total population exactly.

27 (a) *Line graph* — advantages are it is clear, can show more than one variable and shows change over time; disadvantages are that it is limited to choice of scale and may be misleading if the axes are not checked.

  (b) *Pie chart* — advantages are that it is easy to read and shows percentages; disadvantages are that it can only show one variable and is limited to 3–7 categories for a clear display.

28 (a) *The mean* is an average calculated by adding up all the numbers in the data and dividing by the total number of the numbers in the data.

  (b) *The mode* is the most commonly occurring number in a set of data.

  (c) *The range* measures the difference between the lowest and highest values.

29 The marketing mix is the combination of product, price, promotion and place that enables customer requirements to be met.

30 Price, product, promotion, place.

31 Customer solution/value; Cost to customer; Communication with customer; Convenience for customer.

32 Website contact e-mails/phone numbers, free product trials, free gifts, clear ordering instructions.

33 (a) Electric kettle: tangible attributes — polished metal case, water level indicator; intangible attributes — design awards, brand name.

  (b) Restaurant: tangible attributes — fresh vegetables, silver cutlery; intangible attributes — noted chef, celebrity diners.

34 Product development is the creation of products with new or different characteristics that offer added value to the customer.

35 Reinforces brand image, gives USP, enables entry to new markets.

36 Product life cycle describes five stages from development to decline, showing sales over time.

37 Development, introduction, growth, maturity, decline.

38 An extension strategy is marketing activities designed to maintain or increase sales of a product in decline.

39 (a) Penetration or skimming

  (b) Full cost or competitive

  (c) Full cost or contribution

  Other answers are possible — it is important to be able to give reasons for a choice.

40 Market skimming, penetration.

41 Competitive, contribution, full cost.

42 Loss leaders, psychological, bait and hook.

43 (a) 2, elastic

  (b) Fall of $660.

  (c) Changes in costs for new level of output; planned portfolio changes; long-term reactions of competitors.

44 Promotion is a range of activities that communicate and interact with consumers in order to inform and/or persuade so that attitudes and buying behaviour changes.

45 (a) Above-the-line methods use media space that is paid for, below-the-line methods do not.

  (b) ATL (TV advertising) reaches many people but at a high cost. ATL (billboards) reach many people but in restricted locations often not noticed.
  BTL (in-store posters) are cheap but only reach people in store. BTL (BOGOF) attracts buyers but may make product seem cheap, low quality and desperate for a sale.

  (c) Objective of promotion; cost of methods; type of product.

46 (a) A wholesaler is an intermediary between a producer and a retailer.

  (b) An agent acts on behalf of the seller without taking ownership of the product.

  (c) A retailer sells products produced by other businesses direct to the public.

47 Cost of storage and distribution too high; selling to retailing can be done in bulk; product may be perishable.

Topic 4

1 Designing equipment; selecting suppliers; maintaining health and safety; setting stock levels; hitting quality criteria.

2 (a) Land includes land, buildings, minerals, oil and wood, e.g. fuel oil.

  (b) Labour is the work done by people, either manually or mentally in managing and decision making, e.g. metal machinist.

  (c) Capital is machinery and equipment, including intellectual capital such as qualifications, e.g. sewing machine.

3 (a) actors; scenery; props; the theatre

  (b) wool; knitting machine; machine operator

  (c) computer; electricity; adviser; paper

  (d) lorry; diesel; hoist

4 Labour productivity is output per worker per time period and measures labour efficiency.

$$\text{labour productivity} = \frac{\text{output in units per time period}}{\text{number of employees}}$$

5 Lowers unit costs so price can be lowered or profits raised; may enable fewer workers to be needed.

6 Capital investment in more efficient machines; training for employees; decentralised decision making to motivate employees.

7 4 accounts per person per week or 0.1 accounts per person per hour.

8 Efficiency measures the way resources are used (cost); effectiveness measures how well the product meets customers' needs.

9 (a) Produces profit; measures efficiency.

  (b) Is key decider on whether to purchase; enables product comparison.

10 Transforming inputs; branding; advertising; after-sales service; personal selling.
11 (a) Large scale; availability of efficient machinery.
   (b) Large scale; batch production; identical products.
12 (a) Personal service; small scale; individual products; customer needs.
   (b) Personal service; small scale; customer needs.
13 (a) new technology and new organisation
   (b) new organisation
   (c) new technology
   (d) new organisation
14 Quicker and more certain deals made; motivation of students increased; faster overall production times; better customer relations as decisions clear, fast and personal.
15 (a) Job production is producing unique or small-scale products one at a time by skilled workers.
   (b) Mass customisation uses mass production to meet individual customer's needs by setting workstations to produce a range of pre-set options.
16 (a) *Job*: advantages — flexibility, high customer satisfaction, high added value; disadvantages — high cost, slow.
   (b) *Batch*: advantages — low unit cost, range of products possible; disadvantages — high inventory costs per batch, less flexible, time lost resetting machines.
   (c) *Flow*: advantages — very low unit costs, easy to automate; disadvantages — high start-up costs, faults stop whole line, unmotivating work.
17 Infrastructure is the utilities, transport networks, finance, educational and health facilities in a location.
18 Laws on tax; availability of workforce; closeness to resources; political stability; nearness to market.
19 Industrial inertia is when a business stays in its current location even though the factors that led it there no longer apply.
20 Already paid for buildings; cost of finding new employees and materials; costs of setting up in new place; losing existing local contacts.
21 (a) Economies of scale result in falling unit costs; diseconomies of scale in rising unit costs.
   (b) Internal economies of scale result from conditions inside the firm, e.g. new machines; external economies of scale result from outside the firm, e.g. similar firms in the same area.
22 (a) Technical, e.g. new equipment; managerial, e.g. specialist managers; bulk buying; marketing, e.g. advertising costs the same whatever quantity is produced.
   (b) Communication difficulties; control and coordination costs; less motivation.
23 (a) Raw materials are the basic physical resources needed for production.
   (b) Work in progress is partly finished goods in the process of being transformed into final product.
   (c) Finished goods are products ready for sale.
24 Enables production to continue even if no raw materials are available for a time; enables sudden demand to be met; large orders gain discounts.
25 Reduce storage costs; reduce insurance costs; avoid inventory becoming out of date, damaged or obsolete.
26 (a) Buffer inventory is the minimum inventory that prevents variations in supply, production or demand stopping production or sales.
   (b) Reorder level is the level of inventory at which more inventory will be ordered.
   (c) Lead time is the time taken for inventory to arrive after it has been ordered.
27 Little inventory held so costs of providing buildings, insurance, inventory staff are less.
28 If suppliers do not deliver, production is stopped; may lose sudden orders; requires expensive IT systems to link suppliers, orders and inventory monitoring; accurate demand forecasts essential.

Topic 5

1 Start-up capital is the money that a business needs when first setting up. It is used to acquire premises and equipment so that the business can begin to operate.
2 The length of time the finance is required for will determine the source used; an overdraft would not be used for longer-term projects because the interest rate payable would be extremely high. If a project does not give a return for a long time a long-term source is used; if money is required for a short period, e.g. until customers settle their debts, then short-term sources could be appropriate.
3 Working capital is the money used for the day-to-day business activities. Working capital is current assets minus current liabilities.
4 Too much working capital means that the business is experiencing an opportunity cost; the extra working capital could be invested in an interest-bearing account or could be used to purchase equipment that could increase business profit.
5 One disadvantage is that the money is not earning anything for the business. One advantage is that is gives the business security that it can settle its short-term debts.
6 Revenue expenditure is on day-to-day items that will be used in the business in a short period of time (less than 1 year). Capital expenditure is spending on assets (equipment or premises) that will be used in the business for several years.
7 Short-term finance is finance that will be repaid within 1 year.
8 A return on the project for which the money was acquired might not occur for some time. The amount borrowed might be very large and so the business needs longer to repay.
9 Advantage: no interest will be payable on the money used. Disadvantage: the business might not have sufficient funds to meet short-term debts.

10 It does not require any interest to be paid. It is available instantly.

11 Overdraft: the money should be available when the customers settle their debts and so the money is only required for a short period.

12 Advantage: regular payments help with budgeting. Disadvantage: interest will have to be paid to the bank.

13 Bank overdraft; short-term bank loan.

14 Long-term bank loan; debentures.

15 Might not want to lose any ownership and control to a venture capitalist. Venture capitalists often require some ownership of the business to protect their investment.

16 When a business is undertaking a major new project that will not be very profitable for a long time, e.g. a few years.

17 Cash is notes and coins or bank accounts and is available immediately to settle debts. Profit is the difference between sales revenue and costs and might include payments from customers that have not yet been received.

18 To be able to settle their short-term debts, e.g. to pay suppliers. Cash is needed to be able to pay wages. Too little cash can cause a business to become insolvent.

19 The money could have been used in a way that could benefit the business, e.g. buy new machinery.

20 To set targets; to show to a bank when applying for a bank loan.

21 The failure of customers to settle their debts; a sudden increase in the price of materials.

22 $9,000

23 Total cash outflow = $11,000 and the opening balance was ($5,000).

24 *Short term*: debt factoring — the outstanding debts of customers are sold to a debt factor who takes a percentage of the money repaid as commission. Businesses typically receive approximately 80% of the value of the debt. *Long term*: sale of assets — unused assets can be sold if the business will not require them in the future.

25 Customers might object to their debts being sold to a third party and might not buy from the business again. In addition, the business only receives a proportion of the outstanding debt.

26 Suppliers have to pay their suppliers, and the credit period given to them could make them unable to extend the credit period to their customers.

27 *Reduce the credit period given to customers* — this does not bring in more money but speeds up the flow of money into the business. *Cut costs* — this reduces the cash outflows. This can be achieved by changing suppliers or buying cheaper materials. Need to be careful that quality does not suffer.

28 Fixed costs are costs that do not vary according to the level of output.

29 Variable costs vary directly according to the level of output, e.g. raw materials.

30 Direct costs are costs that can be specifically linked to the production of a particular item, e.g. direct labour costs.

31 When deciding on what price to charge for a product/service — the price charged would need to cover all costs incurred and possibly some profit. Businesses use cost information to monitor the performance of different parts of the business to identify inefficient areas and examples of good practice.

32 Total cost = $120,000. Average cost = $30. Profit = $24,000.

33 The breakeven level of output is the level of output where the business makes neither a profit nor a loss — total revenue = total costs.

34 Contribution method = $\dfrac{\text{fixed costs}}{\text{contribution per unit (SP – VC)}}$

35 The margin of safety is the difference between the actual level of output and the breakeven level of output when the actual level is above breakeven level of output.

36 *One use*: to calculate the level of profit at any given level of output. *One limitation*: it is assumed that all output is sold whereas some might stay as inventory.

37 Opening inventory and purchases.

38 Wages, heat and light expenses.

39 Retained earnings and shareholders' dividends is the amount left in the business after all expenses, tax and interest payments have been deducted.

40 *Current assets*: inventory; bank accounts; cash; debtors. *Non-current assets*: premises; vehicles; machinery.

41 *Current liabilities*: trade payables (creditors); bank overdraft.

42 An *income statement* is the document that shows the costs and revenues incurred by a business and the resulting profit or loss for a specified time period — usually 1 year. A *balance sheet* (statement of financial position) shows the net worth of a business listing the value of assets and liabilities on one specific day.

43 1.5:1

44 1.17:1

45 The acid test ratio shows that once inventory is ignored, the business is only just capable of meeting its short-term financial obligations. If the customers of the business do not settle their debts on time, the business might be unable to pay its suppliers or to finance the bank overdraft. It could become insolvent.

46 Gross profit margin = 37.5%.

47 Net profit margin = 20%.

48 When a business applies for a bank loan the bank might analyse the liquidity ratios to confirm that the business will be capable of making regular repayments. Ratios can be used to make comparisons between businesses. A business would hope to see that it is performing at least as well as other similar businesses in the same industry. Shareholders would make the comparison to decide which company they should purchase shares in.

49 They are based on historic data and cannot predict what can happen in the future. Comparisons between businesses might not be useful if different accounting techniques have been used. The ratios cannot reveal qualitative information, e.g. if the workforce is motivated.

50 *Shareholders*: check the financial efficiency of a business and the profit to estimate the return that they can expect on their investment. *Government*: uses the financial documents to calculate the amount of tax payable by the business.

51 They are based on past information and the economic situation might have changed significantly making future estimates based on financial documents unreliable. Window dressing means that the financial documents have been prepared so as to give a more favourable impression of the financial state of the business. This makes them less reliable for external users.

Topic 6

1 A national business operates within the geographical boundaries of one country, whereas a multinational business has a headquarters in one country but operates (produces and/or sells) in several countries.

2 *Advantage*: an increased market enables achievement of economies of scale; access to cheaper and/or better materials; reduced import duties. *Disadvantage*: increased competition for domestic producers; higher costs in producing for specific countries.

3 Increased employment levels as the multinational employs local workers, reducing the burden on government.

4 Tax concessions might be demanded; prevents the growth of infant industries.

5 *Advantage*: essential goods and services provided at an affordable price. *Disadvantage*: slow decision making.

6 Government might prefer to keep a strategic industry, such as the generation of electricity, in state ownership to protect the supply. If foreign-owned then the government loses control and cannot prevent very high prices being charged or supplies being reduced.

7 A *merger* is the joining together of the ownership of two or more businesses with the consent of all parties involved. A *takeover* is when ownership and control is acquired by another business and might be with or without the consent of all parties.

8 The business doing the taking over might want its own workers in place or might move the business to another location, causing employees to lose their jobs.

9 The new business might be too big and experience diseconomies of scale such as lack of coordination.

10 The businesses can gain access to expertise and skills that they do not have in-house; they can embark on bigger ventures than they could individually.

11 To increase the health of the population; to provide good transport systems.

12 Education; refuse disposal; the justice system; bridges.

13 *Low inflation* — a small rise in prices over time. *Stable exchange rate* — a constant value for the price of the currency. *Low interest rates* — keeping the price of borrowing money low. *Increasing employment* — a greater number of people with paid work.

14 Inflation is a persistent rise in the average level of prices.

15 (a) Price of imports falls.
 (b) Price of exports rises.

16 Economic growth is an increase in the total value of a country's output, normally measured by gross domestic product (GDP).

17 To help poorer families afford basic goods and services; to help high technology industries start and grow.

18 Poor families would have enough income to support children's education; knowledge/IT businesses get money for investment to provide work and exports.

19 (a) Raising employment; lower price rises.
 (b) *Monetary policy*, e.g. lowering interest rates to make borrowing costs lower so more equipment and thus jobs are provided; *fiscal policy*, e.g. lowering income tax to provide more incentive to work and more consumer spending.

20 Corporate social responsibility is the actions, legally required or voluntary, needed for an organisation to act responsibly to all its stakeholders.

21 Employees, shareholders, customers (external), government (external).

22 CSR can be very expensive and a large increase in costs may not be possible. This is especially true if the business gets orders from foreign firms because it is cheap.

23 To protect workers' health and safety; to encourage competition; to ensure consumers are given accurate information.

24 Employees' working conditions; advertising claims; mergers and takeovers.

Topic 7

1 Training needs can be identified; the ambitions of employees can be identified and discussed and appropriate steps taken.

2 Management by objectives is a management approach used to ensure that all employees are working towards the overall business objective. Objectives can be agreed or imposed.

3 Employees know what is expected of them; if objectives have been agreed rather than imposed, employees are likely to be more committed to achieving the business objectives.

4 To protect the workforce from exploitation by unscrupulous employers; to support employers against being exploited by their workforce; to guide businesses regarding appropriate behaviour towards their employees.

5 Anti-discrimination legislation is designed to prevent any worker being discriminated against on grounds of their gender, race, religion, disability or sexual orientation.

6 Workforce planning is planning ahead to ensure that a business has the right number of employees with appropriate skills in the right place at the right time.

7 To gain the protection of a large organisation; to have access to legal advice and support.

8 *Conciliation* is using an impartial outside body in an attempt to arrive at a mutually acceptable agreement. *Arbitration* is when an impartial outside body hears the evidence and then makes a decision that will be binding on the parties involved.

9 It would only have to negotiate with one organisation and so save time.

10 It shows the chain of command and who is responsible for and to whom.

Now test yourself answers

11 *Advantage*: usually a narrow span of control therefore easier supervision. *Disadvantage*: danger of distorted communication due to many layers.

12 *Advantage*: easier communication due to fewer layers. *Disadvantage*: fewer promotion opportunities.

13 *Formal structure* conforms to the hierarchical and established organisation structure. An *informal structure* might mean that relationships do not always conform to the agreed structure and the official chain of command might not be followed.

14 Channels of communication are the agreed paths that official communications should follow. They generally follow the chain of command.

15 *Advantage*: specialists can be brought together to contribute to a project. *Disadvantage*: employees working on more than one project find work difficult to prioritise and have more than one manager.

16 *Advantage*: senior managers have more time to dedicate to complex issues/decisions. *Disadvantage*: managers might fear a loss of control.

17 Employees are motivated by delegation because they feel trusted and valued if tasks are delegated to them.

18 *Noise*: physical noise can be avoided by taking discussions away from noisy machinery. The *use of jargon or technical language* should be avoided. Information should be given in a form that all can easily understand.

19 A *chain network* is communication in a hierarchical structure with information passing from one level to the next, e.g. communicating an architect's plan to building workers. This can be two-way. A *connected network* is where information passes between all people involved without having any set pattern. Information can be exchanged as required, e.g. discussions on an advertising campaign by employees from different functional areas.

20 *Formal methods* of communication follow the chain of command whereas *informal methods* could be employees meeting in the canteen and discussing business issues.

Topic 8

1 The marketing objectives in the plan will contribute to overall objectives; resources can be planned for and used efficiently.

2 Enables planning for predicted changes; avoids unnecessary spending on marketing activities.

3 (a) −1.5
(b) +1.67
(c) −0.67

4 Product development is the process of planning a new product, from market analysis and the first idea, through to development and testing to a market-tested product launched with a marketing strategy.

5 To ensure a business does not get left behind competitors' new products; to be able to enter new markets ahead of the competition.

6 Awareness, Interest, Desire, Action

7 Define Advertising Goals for Measured Advertising Results

8 Increased trade; more FDI; increasingly similar culture; more outsourcing; increased capital movement.

9 (a) Increased competition from global businesses makes selling more difficult.
(b) Easier to set up or sell to other countries but needs thorough market research.

10 Merging with domestic business; franchising; exporting; FDI.

11 *Merging* — existing production, supply chains and marketing in place; cost savings.

Franchising — low start-up costs; marketing strategy already in place.

Exporting — keep control of selling and distribution process; less costs to other businesses; not tied in to agreements.

FDI — possible lower tax rates; lower labour costs; more government incentives; direct marketing access.

12 Pan-global marketing is marketing products and/or services to global markets in many different countries.

Topic 9

1 Enterprise resource planning.

2 Better inventory control lowers costs, more accurate knowledge of costs, higher capacity utilisation, faster response to change, more integrated information, less waste.

3 The time taken to implement it plus the cost of design, setting up and training.

4 Capacity utilisation is the proportion of full capacity of a business unit currently being produced.

$$\text{capacity utilisation} = \frac{\text{current output} \times 100\%}{\text{maximum possible output}}$$

5 (a) 67%
(b) Demand may have fallen; may be slack season; firm may have invested in production facility for the future.
(c) Lower fixed cost per unit; motivate employees; use inventory more efficiently.

6 Extra shifts for employees, more efficient ways of organising work to use equipment more, outsourcing some production and re-organising.

7 Allow specialists to produce; lower costs; more flexibility; share risks; gain access to skills outside the firm.

8 Kaizen is continuous regular small improvements suggested by all employees as part of a culture of improvement.

9 Simple and cheap to implement; generates efficiency ideas; motivates employees.

10 Training and teamwork — all staff must be involved, overcoming resistance.

11 *Quality assurance* is a system for making sure that processes are in place to maintain quality; *quality control* is the methods used to do this.

12 TQM involves changing corporate culture so that all employees are involved in continuous quality improvement so quality assurance is guaranteed.

13 *Kaizen* means every employee is continually involved in suggesting small improvements; *TQM* involves the whole workforce in reaching quality standards so kaizen enables quality to continually improve.

14 Benchmarking is comparing a firm's procedures or products with best practice in similar firms in order to identify and carry out possible improvements.

15 *Advantages:* quality improved where a company lags behind other firms; clear targets generated; costs reduced. *Disadvantages:* difficult to get accurate information from other businesses; expensive to collect information; may just copy not improve further.

16 Project management is planning, organising and managing resources to complete a project within a set time scale and budget.

17 A weak project management team who cannot control contractors and make workers keep to time; sudden unexpected price rises in materials or scarcity of skilled labour; change in the business environment, such as a new technological development, making the project outdated.

18 (a) line = activity
   (b) circle = node
   (c) two lines = critical path
   (d) arrow = direction of activity

Topic 10

1 Absorption costing requires that all of the costs are included in the cost of producing a product (FC and VC).

2 Contribution costing is when only the variable costs of a product are considered.

3 When considering whether or not to accept a one-off order; when deciding whether to make or buy a product.

4 *Contribution* is the difference between selling price and variable costs. The difference is put towards covering the fixed costs. When all fixed costs have been covered then, and only then, is the contribution classed as *profit*.

5 To monitor the performance of a particular department; to motivate departmental managers who will aim to work within budget.

6 *Benefit:* they allow managers to identify sections of a business that are financially inefficient by monitoring expenditure compared to the budget. *Drawback:* managers might plead for a higher budget than is necessary — wasting financial resources.

7 *Flexible budgeting* allows changes to be made to a budget if circumstances change, e.g. a nationally agreed increase in wages. *Zero budgeting* ignores any previous budgets and requires budget holders to justify what finance they require for the next period.

8 During periods of unstable prices, e.g. periods of high inflation. Adjustments to the budgets can be made as appropriate.

9 Budgets guide individuals and departments. Inefficient financial management can be identified and corrective action taken. Departments will be required to stay in budget and this can restrict their activities, e.g. the marketing department might not be able to embark on a large promotion campaign if the budget does not allow it.

10 A favourable variance is when the actual outcome is better for the business than the anticipated outcome.

11 An adverse variance is when the actual outcome is worse for the business than the anticipated outcome.

12 $175,000

13 $32,000

14 The figure for non-current assets (fixed assets) would increase by $40,000 and the non-current liabilities (long-term liabilities) would increase by $40,000.

15 Non-current assets would reduce by $20,000. Cash and cash equivalents would increase by $15,000. Non-current liabilities (assuming long-term loan) reduce by $5,000.

16 $15 as this is the net realisable value of the trainers.

17 $33 — the purchase cost of the jackets plus the cost of cleaning to make them saleable.

18 $11,000

19 To compare it with the return they could have gained elsewhere.

20 The cakes would not be edible if they were sold after an average of 18 days.

21 Businesses have to settle their own debts within a specified period. They need the money from their customers to be able to pay the suppliers to the business.

22 60%

23 The business is unlikely to be considered for a bank loan because it is highly geared and might be unable to maintain the required repayments. The business is highly dependent on borrowed money.

24 10.96% (rounded)

25 13.79% (rounded)

26 Different businesses use different methods of depreciation affecting the net profit margin; there might have been a one-off event that influenced the ratios for one particular year.

27 To make sure that they are getting the best return possible on their investment. Shareholders might also judge the efficiency of financial management by comparing the ratios of different businesses.

28 To reduce or assess the risk involved and the potential for profitability; to estimate the costs involved in a proposed project to check whether or not it is affordable.

29 A sudden downturn in the economy can mean that the predicted sales do not occur due to spending cutbacks.

30 Payback method of investment appraisal calculates the time it will take for revenues from the project to cover the costs of the investment.

31 A discounted cash flow discounts the predicted cash inflows by the anticipated prevailing rate of interest to make allowance for changes to the future value of inflows.

32 Net present value is the discounted value of net cash flows at the end of the investment period after discounting has been applied to all projected cash inflows.

33 The level of pollution that might be caused by a project.

Topic 11

1. An objective gives a specific aim that enables resources to be organised to achieve it. Objectives provide a framework for a strategy to be implemented.

2. Mission, vision, objectives; strategic analysis of market, competition and economic environment and internal resources available; strategic choices considered and decided; strategic choices implemented; evaluation of strategy.

3. A *strategy* is an overall aim, e.g. 'to grow by increasing sales in export markets'. A *tactic* is a method used to implement a strategy, e.g. 'to obtain government contracts in another country'.

4. The market operated in; the threats faced; the resources available.

5. Better coordination of functional areas; faster flexible response to external change; determining appropriate methods to achieve objectives.

6. Strategy determines structure.

7. Top management sets corporate strategy and coordinates the tactics of product or geographical divisions.

8. *Strength:* good location. *Weakness:* reliance on one supplier. *Opportunity:* new technology available. *Threat:* strong trade union.

9. *Advantage:* quick and cheap. *Disadvantage:* very simplistic.

10. *Customer loyalty:* maintain or improve this. *Rising unemployment:* maintain current sales level.

11. *Political: targets* for energy efficiency. *Economic:* interest rates rise. *Social:* increased emigration. *Technological:* new power sources.

12. *Health and safety laws:* increase resources to health and safety; *rise in sales tax:* reduce profit margins; *ageing population:* research new products aimed at older people; *more efficient machinery:* investment rises.

13. *Advantage:* quick and cheap. *Disadvantage:* relies on changeable assumptions.

14. *Vision statements* deal with the overall view of where a business is aiming for; *objectives* are particular defined goals to be achieved in order to fulfil the vision.

15. A *vision statement* sets out a broad view about where a business might like to be. A *mission statement* outlines the main values and purpose of a business.

16. *Advantage:* enables specific objectives to be set. *Disadvantage:* can take up resources to little effect.

17. Threat of competition; threat of substitutes; bargaining power of customers; bargaining power of suppliers; degree of competition.

18. In deciding on whether to start selling a product aimed at a particular market segment.

19. Core competencies are the concepts that make a business, product or brand unique and valuable to customers.

20. They give customers a positive view of the business, access and application to products and markets the business is in, difficult for competitors to imitate.

21. (a) *Market penetration* is selling an existing product into an existing market: low risk.
    (b) *Market development* is selling an existing product into a new market: medium risk.
    (c) *Product development* is selling a new product into an existing market: medium risk
    (d) *Diversification* is selling a new product into a new market: high risk.

22. *Advantages:* simple, clear indication of risk. *Disadvantages:* simplistic and gives guidance not certainty.

23. Producing them requires rigorous analysis; they set out choices and money values; they take account of risk.

24. Research used may be faulty or inaccurate; may date quickly; may not take all relevant factors into account.

25. A business plan sets out objectives and how an organisation intends to achieve them by strategic and tactical plans, market information and financial forecasts.

26. Sets out possible problems so these can be anticipated and avoided or solved; obtaining finance — successful applications for a loan, grant, subsidy or other finance; sets out resources needed so these can be put in place; provides focus and direction; sets out organisation structure required for success.

27. *Power culture:* autocratic, hierarchical, centralised decision making. *Task culture:* team working, democratic delegated decision making, flat structure. *Entrepreneurial culture:* ideas focused, democratic empowered decision making, flexible flat or matrix structure.

28. Appropriate culture avoids different parts of the organisation having different objectives; enables structure to be matched to objectives.

29. Contingency planning is the process of planning for foreseeable but unlikely events (crises) that will threaten a business.

30. Recognise need for planning for crisis; identify foreseeable threatening events; give each event a probability; decide which will have the biggest negative effect; prepare a contingency plan to deal with these events; test the plan; review and update the plan.

31. *Advantages:* quick response; reassures stakeholders; helps senior managers generate favourable public relations; maintains confidence. *Disadvantages:* uses time and resources in preparing and training; cost of reviewing procedures; may lead to less planning to avoid disasters; likely never to be used so resources wasted.